SERMONS FROM
JOB

SERMONS FROM

JOB

John Calvin

SELECTED AND TRANSLATED
by
LEROY NIXON, TH. M.

With an Introductory Essay by
Harold Dekker, Th. M.

BAKER BOOK HOUSE
Grand Rapids, Michigan

PHOTOLITHOPRINTED BY CUSHING - MALLOY, INC.
ANN ARBOR, MICHIGAN, UNITED STATES OF AMERICA
1979

TRANSLATOR'S PREFACE

The translator wishes to express his appreciation to many persons who have made this work possible. I owe thanks to the publishers for suggesting this work to me about three years ago and for their patience in waiting for the work to be finished. The Rev. Edward Bishop, of New Brunswick, New Jersey, read several of the sermons and offered constructive criticism. The kindness of Mrs. Margaret Wilson and the staff at the Gardiner Sage Library at New Brunswick Theological Seminary enabled me to do most of the work in my study. I am grateful for the interest of the Rev. Harold Dekker and his deft handling of the introduction.

Of all the sermons by Calvin, the 159 on the book of Job have probably been the most famous. They express clearly his sense of the majesty of God. To work with them over a period of three years has been a rich and exciting spiritual experience.

The translator has selected twenty sermons from the 159 upon the basis of his own interests. Eight sermons were selected because the Scripture texts upon which they are built are quoted or alluded to in *The Institutes of the Christian Religion.* Job 25:1-6, the text for sermon 11 which I have entitled "The Majesty of God," is treated four times in the *Institutes.* The text for sermon 2 is treated three times in the *Institutes.* The texts for sermons 4, 5, 8, and 9 occur twice in the *Institutes.* The texts for sermons 1 and 3 are mentioned only once in the *Institutes.*

Sermons 12, 13, and 14 were preached consecutively and show the uprightness of Job's character. Sermon 6 was included so that I could compare it with a sermon by G. Campbell Morgan upon the same text. Sermon 15 on "righteous indignation" was included because of its historical interest. The personality of Calvin shines through sermons 17 and 19.

v

Sermons 10, 16, and 18 are included for their theological range and depth. Sermon 20 on "the Lord's answer" seemed an appropriate conclusion.

If the reader gets only a fraction of the benefit which came to the translator, the reader will be amply rewarded. Calvin's piety is well expressed in "the Lord gave, the Lord has taken away"; "blessed is the man whom God corrects"; "though He slay me, yet will I trust in Him"; "does not God count my steps?" and "the right use of affliction." Pervading these sermons is the prayer and the conviction that whatever comes to pass may all be for the glory of God.

LEROY NIXON

The Parsonage
Queensboro Hill Community Church
Flushing 55, New York
718.359.2681

June 5, 1952

vi

CONTENTS

INTRODUCTION

by Harold Dekker, Th. M.

It is one of the anomalies of history that John Calvin has become best known as a systematic theologian in spite of the fact that he considered himself to be first of all a preacher. He believed that his sermons, not the *Institutes,* were his most important contribution. Although he did serve as a part-time lecturer in theology, this was for him always a secondary role. He looked upon himself primarily as a pastor.

Calvin's contemporaries came closer to his self-evaluation than did later centuries. In his own day, and for several decades thereafter, his sermons rivaled the *Institutes* in popularity. They were well-known in all the countries of the Reformation and were read widely. Frequently they were used in the pulpits of churches which were without pastors. Hundreds of them were printed in the original French, as Calvin delivered them, and were systematically smuggled to the oppressed Protestants in Calvin's homeland. Large numbers were also translated into other languages, especially English and German.

A total of over seven hundred sermons became available in English, and they enjoyed a wide distribution. Although numerous translators were engaged in this task, over half of the entire output came from the pen of Arthur Golding. The first edition appeared already in 1553, and the presses continued to pour them out for over forty years. Beginning in 1574 the entire set of 159 sermons on Job went through five editions within ten years. In three years five editions of the sermons on the Ten Commandments were printed. A complete set of the two hundred sermons on Deuteronomy was published in 1581, and the demand was so heavy that a new edition was turned out less than two years later. Doubtless the wide circulation of these volumes was the largest single factor in the early development of Calvinism in England.

The *Institutes* did not appear in English until 1561 and were reprinted only six times by the end of the century.

Early in the seventeenth century, however, there was a steady decline in the use of Calvin's sermons. This is understandable since sermons are always particularly fitted to certain times and circumstances, and as oral compositions they lose much of their force and some of their clarity in writing. It is only natural that very few sermons become written classics. It could not be expected that Calvin's preachments would be popular indefinitely in Reformed churches and homes. But that they were very soon almost completely ignored seems strange. Within a short time they were overlooked not only by Reformed people generally, but even the theological schools neglected them. In fact, there was no further printing of English translations until the middle of the nineteenth century when two small collections appeared.

These sermons of the great Reformer, once in such strong demand by his followers everywhere, were held in so little esteem in 1805 that forty-four precious folio volumes containing original, unpublished stenographic manuscripts were sold by the Library of Geneva to a pair of booksellers, with the price determined according to the weight of the paper. Perhaps this was inadvertently done, but it at least indicates that these manuscripts were seldom consulted and their value not realized. Due to this unfortunate mistake most of Calvin's sermons on the Old Testament prophets are lost, and many on the Gospels and Epistles as well. Eight of the forty-four volumes were retrieved twenty years later by some theological students who found them for sale in an old clothes shop, and at the end of the century five more volumes reappeared and were restored to the library. Calvin scholars still hold a waning hope that the others will turn up somewhere.

Certainly the Calvinistic churches have been the poorer for not having easily available to their ministers and other leaders the rich and prolific expression of their mentor's teaching found in his hundreds of sermons, not to mention the inspirational encounter with his warm pastoral heart which they afford. Students of Calvin have dealt extensively with his life and reformatory work, his systematic and apologetic writings, his commentaries, tracts and letters, his social, political and economic thought, as well as his theology generally, all with surprisingly little attention to the sermonic discourses which are by far the largest single expression of his mind. Reformed theology and Calvinistic studies generally have strangely neglected one of their most significant sources.

In view of this long-continued deficiency, it is noteworthy that modern scholars have been giving increasing notice to the sermons. Emile Doumergue, easily the greatest of modern Calvin students, has done much to reopen this perspective on the great Reformer. His definitive seven volume work supplies much data regarding Calvin as a preacher.[1] In addition, he has written a small treatise on this specific subject.[2] During the latter part of the nineteenth century, partly under his tutelage and largely under his influence, a number of monographs appeared dealing with Calvin's preaching. Most of these are in French.[3] In addition to one in German,[4] there was also a contribution by Professor P. Biesterveld of Kampen Seminary in the Netherlands.[5] More recently we have had another German work on the subject, by Erwin Mülhaupt,[6] and finally, in 1947, something in English, a very thorough and readable study by T. H. L. Parker, a British clergyman, entitled *The Oracles of God*.[7] Beside these specific treatments, several modern writers on Calvin's teaching have gone thoroughly into the sermons as source material.[8] And it should be added that within the last ten years at least six volumes of

---

1. Doumergue, Emile, *Jean Calvin, les hommes et les choses de son temps*. 7 vols. Lausanne-Neuilly, 1899-1927.
2. Doumergue, Emile, *Calvin le Prédicateur de Genéve*, Geneva, 1909.
3. E.g.: Cruvellier, A., *Etude sur la Predication de Calvin*, Montauban, 1895; Viguié, A., *Calvin Prédicateur*, Paris, 1879; and Watier, A., *Calvin Prédicateur*, Geneva, 1889. Also similar works somewhat earlier, by F. Flamand, G. Goguel, and E. Pasquet.
4. Krauss, A., *Calvin als Prediger*, Frankfurt, 1884.
5. Biesterveld, P., *Calvijn als Bedienaar des Woords*, Kampen, 1897.
6. Mülhaupt, Erwin, *Die Predigt Calvins*, Berlin, 1931.
7. Parker, T. H. L., *The Oracles of God*, London: Lutterworth Press, 1947.
8. E.g.: Torrance, T. F., *Calvin's Doctrine of Man*, London: Lutterworth Press, 1949. This work is replete with references to the sermons, particularly to those on Job.

sermons have appeared, newly translated into the Dutch language.

It is therefore particularly gratifying that now also within the circle of American Calvinists there is a stirring of interest in this field. In 1950, a miscellaneous collection of sermons, the only one published in the United States before, originally translated and published in 1830 and recently unobtainable, was happily reprinted.[9] Even more encouraging, a minister of the Reformed Church in America, Leroy Nixon, has very recently produced two books. The first is a fresh and stimulating study of Calvin as an expository preacher.[10] It is both comprehensive and discerning. The second is a completely new translation, from the Latin and French, of twenty of Calvin's New Testament sermons, entitled *The Deity of Christ and other Sermons*.[11] This was done with distinct competence, and has caused pleasurable anticipation of the appearance of his second set of translations, which he now presents in this volume. Its publication is most welcome. It makes available to English readers for the first in centuries some of the riches of Calvin's thought contained in his prodigious sermonic treatment of the book of Job.

The current revival of interest in Calvin is progressing beyond many earlier studies in at least this one respect, that it is taking into more careful account than any time since 1600 the sermonic discourses which are really indispensable to his true understanding. Emile Doumergue said very fittingly at a great celebration of the four hundredth anniversary of Calvin's birth, on July 2, 1909, speaking from the very pulpit from which Calvin had preached, "That is the Calvin who seems to me to be the real and authentic Calvin, the one who explains all the others: Calvin the preacher of Geneva, moulding by his words the spirit of the Reformed of the sixteenth century."[12] American Calvinists will serve their cause well if

9. Calvin, John, *The Mystery of Godliness and other Sermons,* Grand Rapids: Wm. B. Eerdmans Publishing Co., 1950.
10. Nixon, Leroy, *John Calvin: Expository Preacher,* Grand Rapids: Wm. B. Eerdmans Publishing Co., 1950.
11. Calvin, John, *The Deity of Christ and other Sermons,* Grand Rapids: Wm. B. Eerdmans Publishing Co., 1950.
12. Nixon, Leroy, *John Calvin: Expository Preacher,* p. 38.

they follow the suggestion implied in these words. They are indebted to pastor Nixon for a notable beginning.

Pulpit Method

Calvin was truly an extemporaneous preacher. He used neither manuscript nor notes. He carried with him to the desk only the Scriptures. His preparation consisted of reading the comment of others (including the early church Fathers, and probably the Scholastics, as well as his fellow Reformers), working out a very careful exegesis of the text with his remarkable linguistic skill and his tremendous knowledge of the Bible, and finally reflecting on the application which he would make to the congregation and in what way he could best communicate it. All of these thoughts were then sorted and stored in his amazing memory. There is no evidence that he prepared an outline in writing, and the construction of his sermons would seem to indicate that he did not.

One might reasonably contend that such preparation is inadequate for preaching. It certainly is insufficient for the vast majority of ministers who have gifts so much smaller than Calvin's. Presumably Calvin would not recommend it as standard homiletical practice. The main reason that he did not make more precise preparation was the pressure of time. He sometimes preached twice on Sunday and every day during the week, in addition to his regular theological lectures, his pastoral work, his civic duties and his enormous correspondence. The preaching alone would have overtaxed the capacities of many a lesser man. And all these things Calvin did in a state of almost continuous ill health. The dimensions of his genius can scarcely be overestimated, and sermons such as those in this volume take on an even brighter lustre when seen in the light of his entire performance.

Beyond this, however, there was something in his method which Calvin would earnestly recommend even to the preacher who may enter the pulpit only once or twice per week, and have ample time for preparation. Preparation must not be too mechanical. Preaching must not be fettered to a word for word recitation of something previously composed. The sermon should never be read, but always proclaimed as the living Word of God. Calvin once complained in a letter to Lord Somerset that there was so little living preaching in England of that day, but that like Cranmer preachers wrote out their sermons word for word with artificial rhetoric and then slavishly read them. Calvin firmly believed that there must be a place in the act of preaching for the continuing inspiration of the Holy Spirit. He did not go as far as Luther, for whom the Word preached was virtually the same as the Word written, but neither did he accept the Zwinglian and Anabaptist view that the sermon was nothing more than a sign pointing to Christ. He took a mediating position in holding on the one hand that the Bible is uniquely inspired and is in its written form objectively the Word of God, and that the sermon has authority only as an explication of the Word written; but on the other hand that the sermon becomes redemptively effective only when the Holy Spirit is operative in both the preacher and the hearers. Incidentally, on this point Calvin's doctrine of preaching is of one piece with his doctrine of the sacraments, just as in the case of the Lutheran and Zwinglian doctrines. For Calvin both the sermon and the sacrament are dependent on the written Word, but are actually means of grace only when they are also implemented with the gracious presence of the Spirit. Calvin's preaching method is not only an adaptation to the press of circumstance, but also an expression of fundamental doctrine. The sermon must be delivered as the living Word. The preacher must remain a pliable instrument of the Spirit to the very moment of utterance.

It must be reiterated that Calvin would want none of this to be used as an excuse for slipshod or careless preparation. He once put it as follows, "If I should enter the pulpit without deigning to glance at a book, and frivolously imagine to myself, 'Oh well, when I preach God will give me enough to say,' and come here without troubling to read, or thinking what I ought to declare, and do not carefully consider how

I must apply Holy Scripture to the edification of the people —
then I should be an arrogant upstart."[13]

Because of this method of preparation we have no record
of the early sermons of Calvin.   Some of his hearers kept
personal notes on them, but these consist of little more than a
rough summary of leading thoughts and are virtually worthless.   Fortunately, in 1549 a group of French and Waldensian
refugees living in Geneva, strongly devoted to Calvin, recognized the permanent value of his sermons and hired a secretary to make a short-hand transcript of each one and then
write out careful copies for preservation in folio volumes.
This secretary was Denis Raguenier.   He performed his important task as a full-time occupation until his death in 1560.

Calvin preached often.   Services in Geneva were held at
first three times per week, but in 1549 the Council ordered the
introduction of daily morning preaching.   Calvin himself
usually preached once on Sunday, though frequently twice, and
delivered the daily sermon at St. Peter's Church in alternate
weeks.   The Sunday series was always different from that on
weekdays.   Nearly all of the Sunday preaching was on the
New Testament, the only notable exception being an occasional
Sunday afternoon sermon out of the Psalms.   The weekday
sermons were always from the Old Testament.

Texts were selected by Calvin neither at random nor in
keeping with the church year.   His usual method was to
preach consecutively through entire books of the Bible, often
without alteration even for church holidays.   Texts varied
in length somewhat, depending on their content.   Those from
the Old Testament historical books and from the Gospel
narratives are usually between ten and twenty verses.   Those
on the New Testament Epistles and other didactic passages
are ordinarily two or three verses.   The texts for the sermons
on Job range from one to twenty verses in length, with four
to seven verses the most common.

The books on which he preached in their entirety are as
follows: Genesis, Deuteronomy, Job, Judges, I and II Sam-

---

13. Parker, *op. cit*, p. 69.   Cited from *Corpus Reformatum*, xxv, pp. 713-
714.

uel, I and II Kings, all of the Major and Minor Prophets, the
Gospels, Acts, I and II Corinthians, Galatians, Ephesians, I
and II Thessalonians, I and II Timothy, Titus, and Hebrews.
To cite some representative totals, there are 200 sermons on
Deuteronomy, 159 on Job, 343 sermons on Isaiah, 43 on
Amos, 189 on Acts, and 48 on Titus. One of the most striking omissions is the book of Revelation. He seems never to
have dealt with it, either by way of sermon, lecture or commentary. Concerning some of the other books not listed we
can hardly be certain because of the very incomplete records
prior to 1549.

Like those of Luther, Calvin's sermons were of moderate
length. At an average speed of delivery they would run no
more than forty minutes. As a matter of fact, due to Calvin's
serious affliction with asthma they may have taken him a
little longer to deliver. In the matter of length, as well as
of style, Calvin was finely sensitive to the capacity of his
hearers. He did not overtax their comprehension either with
undue complexity or undue length. Apparently he was not
well emulated on the score of the latter, for in 1572, eight years
after his death, the Council of Geneva issued a decree that the
ministers should preach shorter sermons, not to exceed one
hour. It is also noteworthy that the length of the sermons is
so consistently the same. In the series on Job, for example,
as the reader may observe for himself, the printed copies vary
only a little in length.

Sermonic Structure

In its preaching as well as in many other respects the
Reformation meant a return to the doctrine and practice of
the ancient Church. Led by Luther the Reformers reverted
to the homily as the standard form of sermonic discourse.
Compared with standard scholastic preaching it was expository
rather than topical, free-flowing rather than structurally
bound, more analytic than synthetic, expressed in plain statement rather than logical subtlety, and more conversationally
direct than rhetorically precise.

Calvin is no exception. His sermons are simple homilies, and in that respect they are of a wholly different fabric than his systematic writings. Preaching on consecutive passages he would treat his text section by section or verse by verse, and sometimes phrase by phrase, explaining and commenting as he went. Hardly ever did he depart from the stated order of the text itself. On the other hand he did not slavishly explicate everything in the text as if its mere presence gave it sermonic weight and its size gave it sermonic proportion. Neither did he necessarily limit his interpretation of the various textual elements either to their significance within the text, or to their meaning in the immediate context. Although he always preached textually, and certainly took into full account the importance of chapter and book, the controlling principle of Biblical interpretation for him was always that Scripture must be interpreted with Scripture, and therefore in the last analysis the context for him was the whole Bible. The result of this for Calvin, however, was not what it has often been for others having the same aim. This is most important to observe. Calvin's treatment of a text was never moulded by its abstract significance in terms of systematic theology. His sermon was never patterned by an outline or scheme out of his dogmatics. The actual body of the sermon, skeleton and flesh, was fashioned by Calvin out of two things: the text itself, seen in both its immediate and ultimate contexts, and the spiritual needs of the congregation. The preaching at Geneva was the direct product of a devoted pastor dealing with an open Book and a needy people. It was always clearly relevant to life.

That the dogmatic implication of the text was not decisive for Calvin's pulpit can be easily illustrated. The reader will find many indications of it in this volume of sermons. For example, the text Job 9:1-6, "I know it is true that man shall not be justified in God's sight," etc., might easily induce a preacher to deal largely in the doctrines of justification and the imputation of Christ's merits. Not so Calvin (see Sermon No. 4). He comes to it only in the last few sentences. For the rest he stays with Job upon the dunghill and draws his

people into that needful experience. Job's classic words, "I
know that my Redeemer lives" do not lead Calvin to an ex-
tensive treatment of the resurrection of Christ and its implications. Calvin says that Job did not have this anticipation,
and that though we certainly must view this text in the light
of our knowledge, we must primarily concern ourselves in
this connection with Job's faith that the ultimate judgments
of God transcend those of men. Calvin warns that these
words, "if they were taken out of their context, would not
be to great edification, and we would not know what Job
wished to say" (Sermon No. 8, p. 118). Many readers will
be surprised in reading this sermon, both at what Calvin does
not say and what he does say. It is largely a very practical
piece dealing with such things as family relations, attitudes of
both joy and pity in the punishment of the wicked, a warning
against hypocrisy. Similarly, in treating the verses following
("in my flesh shall I see God," etc., Job 19:26-29, Sermon 9),
Calvin does not become involved in the dogmatics of eschatolo-
gy and the resurrection of the body as a detached doctrine, but
in an impressive way sets forth the meaning of this for Job and
for the believer who undergoes Job's experience. In connection with all this it is most striking that Calvin splits verses
25 and 26 of chapter 19 into two separate larger texts, and
treats them in two separate sermons. A dogmatic, eschato-
logical interest would no doubt have kept them together.

We have also observed that Calvin does not necessarily allow
the proportions of the respective elements in the text, or even
their primary meaning within the text, to be decisive for the
sermon. The reader will find several instances in this volume.
For example, Sermon 15 deals largely with two things regarding Elihu, that he was a Buzite and that he had a capacity for
indignation. Neither really represent the main thrust of the
text as such. But Calvin, the pastor, had applications to make
to his people, and they were by no means irrelevant to the
text. It was in 1554. The Servetus affair was recent history.
Calvin's doctrine of predestination with all its implications
was under fierce attack on several quarters. The struggle with
the Libertines was at its bitterest. The preacher saw a chance

to score two practical points. Elihu, like Job, was outside the
covenant line. He probably did not know the law of Moses.
Yet he had a true knowledge of God and manifested real
piety. The godliness of such men as Job and Elihu, says
Calvin, leaves the wicked and impenitent without excuse and
vindicates God against the charge of unfairness in condemning
the ungodly, even when they have not had the full light of
the Gospel. This meets one of the criticisms of predestination.
After dealing incidentally with the charge of Elihu that Job
justifies himself rather than God, Calvin proceeds to his
second main point, quite unrelated to the first, namely, the
righteous indignation of Elihu. This affords a welcome opportunity to point out that there is a distinction between
selfish anger and holy indignation, and that the latter is most
proper and even needful for the believer overagainst such
enemies of God as the Papists and the Libertines. The latter
he does not so name, but calls them "dogs and swine," "mockers of God," and "profane villains" (p. 227). Another
instance of practical, pastoral considerations diverting the
ordinary sense of the text is Sermon No. 17. Calvin uses
this text to defend his own ministry and that of his associates
against the ruthless attacks then being made by the Geneva
Libertines. The text will permit his interpretation, but it
teaches other and broader things too, some of them more
prominently than the function and authority of the minister of
the Word. The practical situation calls for the latter.

Let the reader be sensitive to the pastoral pulse which
throbs so unmistakably in these sermons. They are never
mere theological discourses or exegetical treatises. They are
the living Word, always in dynamic tension between God's
Book and God's people.

As true homilies, the sermons of Calvin have practically no
structure except the structure of the text itself. There is no
organization which falls into a neat outline or scheme. The
parts of the sermon stand in organic relation neither to one
another nor to a single thematic idea. There may be anywhere
from one to four or five distinct ideas in one sermon, without
any discernible unity of thought except an extremely general

one. It is plain that Calvin never included outlining as a distinct step in pulpit preparation. The sermon conforms to no predetermined order of thought, except as it arises from the word order of the text. Calvin used neither theme nor topic. In this connection it should be noted that the sermonic titles in this volume have been supplied by the translator. Most of them consist of a phrase or two out of the text, and they are apt. But it is usually evident that Nixon could not provide a single title which would actually cover all the various elements in the sermon.

The only kind of synthesis which one finds in these homilies is an occasional summation of what is to follow or what has been said. Such summaries, when they occur, are often in the introduction or the conclusion. Furthermore, in the call to prayer at the end of the sermon Calvin would frequently mention certain main thoughts on which he had preached, so that the people might be mindful of them as they would "bow in humble reverence." This call to prayer was usually between 100 and 150 words in length. It is found in the sixteenth century English translations, but is omitted by Nixon. Samples of it may be seen in the collection of Calvin's sermons entitled *The Mystery of Godliness,* which was described previously.

For Calvin the introduction is never calculated to serve the purposes assigned by ordinary rhetoric, that is, to gain attention or to make the listener receptive to the main thought. It is simply the beginning of the sermon, nothing more. Watier says that for Calvin the introduction is not so much a porch as it is a threshold. And although it is usually short, it is sometimes as much as one-third of the sermon — so little is its function a carefully prescribed one.

All of this does not mean, of course, that Calvin's sermons lack orderly development or logical coherence. Calvin could be nothing but systematic in his thought and presentation. He would not be himself if he did not reason cogently and argue systematically. In their own way the sermons are no less logical than the *Institutes.* Within each particular sphere of thought Calvin proceeds properly from the known to the unknown and from the lesser to the greater. The inductive basis for his exegetical judgments may not be fully revealed, but enough of it is evident to give the assurance that it is adequate. His deductions are always inexorably logical, which, together with his pastoral acumen, accounts for the extraordinary force of the application in his sermons.

It is noteworthy that such a master of learning as Calvin undoubtedly was, should have deliberately preached without the rhetorical excellence which he could so easily have supplied. His dogmatic writings show how close-knit and highly synthetic he can be in handling any subject, and how sharply analytic can be his treatment of a concept or theme. His correspondence shows him to be a master of the adroit and the subtle when the occasion warrants it. In public appearances outside of his pulpit he showed a broadness of erudition and a brilliance of style which are proper to the oration but foreign to the homily. The preachers of the early Church may have been in most cases men of such meagre gifts and training that they were unable to use anything except the homily. But Calvin had all the ample equipment of his matchless classical education, and knew as well the fine artistry of the scholastic sermon. It was not by default, but by deliberate intent that he used the homily in his pulpit. There is only one explanation for it. It is his doctrine of preaching. He had the profound conviction that the task of the preacher is nothing more than to faithfully set forth the Word of God, to make it unmistakably plain to all who hear, to sound its call to conversion, to lay down its admonishments, and to shed its light upon life's path. In the pulpit Calvin meant to be only the humble servant of the Word, and for him the simple homily suited that role best.

The successful use of the homily requires an extraordinary mastery of Scripture, for the sermon does not rely on logical or rhetorical devices for its effect. That Calvin had such a mastery of Scripture, and that he preached through most of the Bible is well known. It should be noted, however, that he was by no means alone in this. Bullinger, for instance, preached nearly through the Bible in the first ten years of his ministry, preaching an average of once per day. Ministers in the early churches of the Reformation made it their first business to study and master the Scriptures. The very manner of their preaching made it indispensable. The Bible was their primary source book, and the homily their method. Dogma and creed moulded the thought but did not actually give body to the sermon. Later centuries, however, shifted the emphasis. In the seventeenth century dogmatics and creed replaced the Bible as the preacher's main source, and though Scripture was by no means ignored, rhetoric again governed the structure of the sermon. The reform and revival movements which arose from time to time in various countries always returned to a more Biblically oriented preaching, but never quite restored the homily itself. As far as modern Protestantism is concerned, its chief homiletical sources are neither Scripture nor creed, but a host of things from the classic poets to collected anecdotes, from the daily newspaper to the latest study of the inferiority complex, from international treaties to plans for better race relations. Though this is particularly characteristic of the liberal part of Protestantism, conservatives have their own version of it and are still a long way from the preaching of the Reformation.

No doubt the homily can be improved upon. There are sound reasons for more synthesis and for making somewhat better use of the principles of rhetoric. But we shall also have to admit that there are few preachers today who could effectively use the style of Calvin's homily, even if they were to try. Synthetic structure and rhetorical device are more often a crutch than a tool, more of a substitute for the mastery of Scripture than a useful servant to it.

Considering sermonic structure, one more observation should be made in regard to Calvin's sermons. They are all of one piece. They do not classify into various types. It cannot be said that some are primarily exegetical discourses and others dogmatic essays. Calvin's congregation knew no distinction between expository and doctrinal sermons. There were no categories such as "practical messages" or "evangelistic messages." Calvin did not preach what are sometimes called "morning" and "evening" (afternoon) sermons. His weekday and Sunday sermons are indistinguishable, except that the former were from the Old Testament and the latter from the New Testament. Geneva knew no such thing as "catechism preaching." Never was the sermon deliberately creedal. But this did not mean a neglect of doctrine. Each verse was placed in the context of the whole Bible. So powerful was the principle of *analogia fidei,* and so thorough the mastery of Scripture, that Calvin and his fellow Reformers could not help but preach doctrine when they set forth the full-orbed meaning of Scripture. Furthermore, there are not two distinct sections, "expository" and "applicatory," in Calvin's sermons. Exposition is the warp and woof of application, and application is the very habilament of exposition. Perhaps the arbitrary distinctions which are often made into various kinds of sermons and various sections of the sermon are a reflection of the inability of preachers to handle the Word of God in expository discourse in such a way that each sermon is both doctrinal and practical, both Scripturally adequate suited for both believers and unbelievers, and at once both expository and applicatory. Calvin gives no comfort to his followers who find disparity and tension between these factors in preaching. He is the exemplar of preaching with every element of moral and spiritual relevance remarkably harmonious, consistent and sustained. His sons may learn much from him.

Sermonic Style

As already indicated, the style of Calvin's sermons is simple and lucid. They are delightfully plain. They are meant to be understood. The preacher of Geneva speaks to every man. In reading his sermons one can easily picture him, with the flexibility of his fully extemporaneous delivery, closely watching the intent faces of his hearers, and not forsaking a point until he is sure that it is reasonably clear to them. The written sermons indicate that he frequently developed a point, and then went back to rework it in a new way, evidently prompted to do so by the delicate rapport which he maintained with the congregation. No studiously phrased, highly polished manuscript deterred him from these sensitive reactions.

As translator Nixon has suggested in his preface to the volume, *The Deity of Christ,* the sermons of Calvin should be read aloud in order to gain their full effect. They were never meant to be anything but oral communication, and they best speak from heart to heart when they go from voice to ear. Most readers will heartily approve the method of the translator by which the oral style is faithfully preserved without any concession to the printed form.

The authenticity and accuracy of the shorthand transcript from which the written sermons are taken is evident in many ways. One sermon is more clear and fluent than another. The wording of one day's sermon may be more concise and vivid than that of the previous day's or the following day's. Furthermore, in going through the entire 159 sermons on Job, one sometimes senses that for several days at a time Calvin was not in his best form. It is not hard to imagine the reasons. In spite of his extraordinary genius, he must have been affected by the mysterious cycles of mental alertness and dullness which afflict all men. Besides, there were no doubt days when vigor of spirit and keenness of mind were impaired by weariness due to his enormous labors or lassitude due to his several illnesses. These things are less evident in the sermons of this volume because they naturally have been selected from the best. Following Calvin day after day through Job, for 159 days, there are many more signs of it. But no doubt the careful reader will notice, even in these selected sermons, passages which are repetitious or confusing, sentences which are vague or involved, and places where the preacher seems to have difficulty in finding the right words. It is then heartening to feel that one is meeting the man John Calvin, intimately and personally, in a way that is not possible encountering him in the oft-revised *Institutes* or the carefully reworked commentaries.

The outstanding quality of Calvin's style is its clarity and simplicity, together with its directness and earnestness. This quality is especially notable when compared with the fashion of his day. From a literary standpoint the other Reformers and most of the writers and speakers of the time belonged to the Medieval period with its ornateness and obscurity. As Parker says, Calvin is "essentially a member as well as a creator of the modern world. If he is compared as a preacher with Luther or Latimer, for instance, there might seem to be a century between them. His habit of mind was modern, and it shows itself in his preaching. . . . The difference between Calvin's style and that of many of his contemporaries is illustrated clearly when we compare the original French of his sermons with their Elizabethan translations, for Calvin's French reads smoothly and clearly beside the tortuous periods of the translations. A schoolboy might sometimes be more puzzled by Arthur Golding's English than by Calvin's French."[14] It is a tribute to translator Nixon that he has so faithfully reproduced the quality of Calvin's French in his translation. The English reader can now fully appreciate the comment of Parker regarding Calvin's modernity. (To illustrate one difference between the translations of Golding and Nixon, it may be observed that by actual count of several short sections Nixon uses from eight to ten percent less words.) In reading the sermons in this volume one easily forgets that they were originally delivered four hundred years ago. They are amazingly up to date in thought and presentation. Such a sermon, for instance, as the one entitled "The Inspiration of the Almighty" (Sermon No. 16), which deals largely with the place and the role of young people in the Church, could be profitably read almost as it stands to one of our present-day congregations.

Calvin avoids the use of academic and technical terms in his preaching, and when it is necessary to use them they are carefully explained. He also to a surprising extent avoids the use of abstract words. One who knows him only in his systematic writings might expect his pulpit style to be heavy and colorless. On the contrary, although it does not often soar with wings, it moves lightly. There is a liberal use of picturesque, graphic terms. Many sentences sparkle with concrete and vivid words. Calvin employs fetching illustrations, taken from life's pedestrian way. He uses simile and metaphor

14. Parker, *op. cit.*, pp. 74-75.

sufficient for effective expression, but not so much as to be wordy. In dispute of many of his critics, it must be said that he is not without imagination, and that there are word pictures in some of his sermons which reveal an artistry of great passion and beauty. Few preachers excel him in depicting the splendor and majesty of God's creation. Besides numerous instances of this in his sermons on the Psalms, there are outstanding examples in the sermons on Job from the passages where the Lord speaks out of the whirlwind (Job 37-39). If the present volume of translations is ever expanded, readers would no doubt welcome the inclusion of one of these. All those who consider Calvin a person cold and intellectualistic, his style abstract and prosaic, have certainly not known the warmth and color of his sermonic style.

Doumergue was seeking to correct this mistaken view when he spoke in Geneva on the four hundredth anniversary of Calvin's birth. He called attention to the way in which Calvin used common proverbs, sometimes several to a sermon, citing as examples: "Sicknesses come by horse and go away on foot." The greedy are those who "would drink the sea and the fishes." Calvin has Moses object to going up Mt. Sinai by saying, "It's all right for me to go and break my legs, climbing up there!" Instead of saying, "It's bad," he would say, "It makes the hair stand on one's head." Instead of "I blame" — "I spit in his face." Instead of "perverse human nature" — "Each one would scratch out his neighbor's eyes if there were not some restraints." Calvin, concluded Doumergue, used the vernacular, words heavy with the smells and tastes and sights of everyday life in city and country, and was clearly observant of the smallest things in the life of his people.[15]

This present volume offers many instances of Calvin's lively style. There are strikingly vivid and concrete passages in every sermon. Over and over again the reader will find that the preacher of Geneva knew how to express himself in terms of the common life. A few examples may be mentioned. "When the devil lights the fire he also pumps the bellows." Those living the godly life often "drag their legs and droop

---

15. Based on Nixon, *John Calvin: Expository Preacher*, pp. 39-43.

their wings." God is like a physician who finds that "no gentler means will serve than the letting of blood." Or, God gives us "many lashes with the whip that we should be compelled to consider him." We are "as astonished with this doctrine as if a man had hit us on the head with a hammer." Concerning the wicked, their sins "are so many it seems they are pickled in them." Those who worship stones and trees are "as if a man at full noonday knowingly walked off a cliff," considering that they have the law written in their hearts. The Papists "get drunk upon these devilish doctrines." Debating against God "many thus throw themselves off their hinges."

It is striking that Calvin so frequently used metaphors and similes from animal life. The following are in this volume. Reprobates "stand barking like dogs." The ungodly are "like restive horses." Intemperate young people are "like young chicks hatched only three days." The proud are those who "without wings want to take the moon in their teeth," or who "admire their feathers like peacocks." When their sins are pointed out, the wicked "throw their snouts on the ground like hogs." When we entertain opinions contrary to faith, we "chew our bits." A certain text is "calculated to make us pull in our horns." "We hop like toads, and we imagine ourselves doing like runaway horses."

Such references can easily be multiplied. These forceful figures of speech may seem crude to us. They were quite characteristic of Calvin's day. Certainly our times call for their own mode of expression. But all preaching needs the plainness and vigor of Calvin's style. And it should be noted that Calvin's language is much like that of the Bible itself. There is a danger that our modern sophistication and polish will sadly impair the effectiveness of the very Word which we preach, by softening its rigor, blunting its sharpness, and toning down its severity. Calvin chose his language not to adorn, but to teach. His style was never merely ornamentive or colloquial, but was devised for nothing more nor less than to communicate the Word of God. In simplicity, clarity and forcefulness it was uniquely fitted for this exacting purpose.

Theological Accents

Of all the great theologians of the Christian Church there is none who is more consistent with himself than Calvin. The basic structure of his theology underwent no change from the age of twenty-five when he wrote the first edition of the *Institutes* until the last revision was made at age fifty. The same consistency is to be found between his dogmatics, his letters and tracts, and his commentaries and sermons. At the same time, however, it is worthwhile to notice certain theological emphases in the sermons which are characteristic of his preaching method and suggestive of his pastoral technique.

One of the most noticeable features of Calvin's preaching is its utter theocentricity. Although anyone who is acquainted with his general thought would expect to find this quality, the actual effect of it in his sermons is most instructive. Not only is God the authority and motive for the preacher, the source and object of every preachment, and the abiding center of reference for every sermon, but very conspicuously He is that in His Triune fulness. There are many instances where Calvin preached day after day for several days or more without once mentioning separately a person of the Godhead. He consistently designates the deity by the inclusive term "God." Very significantly, most of the Old ·Testament sermons make no specific mention at all of Christ. This is in sharp contrast to the sermonizing of Luther which had as its deliberate intent a Christ-centered exposition of every passage of Scripture. Whereas preaching for Luther found its purpose in pointing to Christ, for Calvin it was realized in showing forth more comprehensively the Triune Redeemer God. Calvin seldom mentions one of the persons of the Trinity separately without setting Him in dynamic relationship to the Godhead. To treat them independently was for him to hazard idolatry. It was for this reason that He hesitated to use the term "person," preferring the term "substance" (*hypostasis*).

There are numerous indications of this in the series of Job. Of the twenty selected sermons in this volume, only about half contain an individual designation of the second person of the Trinity. A survey of the entire series of 159 sermons on Job indicates that separate mention of any of the three persons occurs in far less than half. When the individual persons are specified, the Trinitarian framework is either immediately present, or not far removed. At the end of Sermon No. 7 (p. 104) is an example of Calvin's Trinitarian touch, where Father, Son and Holy Spirit are introduced side by side and the redemptive work of each is stated. There is a similar instance at the end of Sermon No. 11 (p. 165) where we read, "Being received by God through His pure goodness, He purges and cleanses us through His Holy Spirit of all our spots, and washes us in the blood of our Lord Jesus Christ." Conversely, but illustrative of the same feature in Calvin's preaching, at the close of Sermon No. 8 (p. 119) there is an invitation to each hearer to come to the "heavenly judge . . . to ask forgiveness for his faults," without mentioning either the love of the Father, the atonement of the Son or the cleansing of the Spirit. In this case all are implied in the "grace and mercy" of God. Calvin's presentation of the Gospel is unmistakably God-centered.

The great Reformer is intent not only to dispute the church-centered system of Rome and the man-centered philosophy of the Libertines, but also the tendencies among the sects to focus on either the second or third persons of the Trinity. Polemical passages in his sermons are always explicitly rooted in the doctrine of God. Every heresy is a heresy in the first article of the creed. He seems convinced that to be Spirit-centered is the first step toward a fatal subjectivism, and that Christo-centrism may yield the first small inch to humanism God Himself, in all His glorious fulness, is both the root and the flower for every sermonic stem.

The difference between this and contemporary preaching is unmistakable. Most of our present-day preachers tend to refer to the individual members of the Trinity in a wholly detached manner. Not only sermons, but pastoral prayers as well reveal this. The pulpit has slipped into a terminological tritheism, even if not actually into the monophysite heresy. Liberalism and Evangelicalism are both at fault on this score, though the latter probably less self-consciously. A regular reading of Calvin's sermons should be a healthy corrective for many orthodox preachers who have unwittingly stumbled into this pitfall.

This utter theocentricity involves certain characteristic stresses in Calvin's effort to meet the spiritual needs of God's people. One of these is the stress on providence. The doctrine of God's all-inclusive providence is a staple in feeding the hungry of heart. It is balm for every wound. One feels that it is basic to every sermon, and it comes out in one way or another in a majority of them. Providence is understandably prominent in the sermons on Job. Job must come to rest in the ultimate goodness of the divine purpose, wrought by a strange and vexing plan. It is interesting to note how closely related in Calvin's thought are the doctrines of providence and perseverance. They are distinct, and yet they are often compounded into one salve for the bruised spirit. The assurance of salvation is rooted deeply in the counsel of God which operates through a unified process, both providential and soteriological, both natural and spiritual. The reader of the present volume will find Sermons 2 and 19 especially interesting in this connection, although he will be confronted by the teaching of divine providence in all. Calvin presents God's dealings with men in their unity. He is nothing less than a magnificent preacher of the providence which moves out of both creation and redemption, as embraced in the Triune God.

A similar stress is that on divine incomprehensibility and inscrutability. The final dimension of God's sovereignty for Calvin was not His revealed will but the unrevealed, and there was hardly a sermon in which this perspective was not present. One of the most distinctive features of Calvin's entire pastoral theology is his accent on the hidden in God, and the final mystery of all His dealings with His children. He has no better comfort to offer to troubled spirits than the unrevealed purposes of a God of sovereign grace. The present writer is of the opinion that the incomprehensibility of God, and the final inscrutability to man of all His doings, constitute the leading thought in Calvin's preaching on Job. Out of all the various doctrines which are taught, this one emerges as the most prominent. This is for Calvin the great message of Job, and it runs through all of the 159 sermons. One can easily cite instances out of this volume. "We have to pursue the statement that we began yesterday: which is, that the Scripture shows us many things which are beyond our understanding" (p. 60). "This, then, is the procedure which we ought to follow whenever the incomprehensible judgments of God come before us: namely, that we know that our mind is not capable of ascending so high, and that these are depths too profound for us" (p. 223). Comparing the arguments of Bildad and Job in Sermon No. 4, Calvin gives what is really a key statement for his interpretation of the entire book: "Let us note well, then, that these are two different manners of speaking. One says, 'God is just; for He punishes men according to what they have deserved.' The others says, 'God is just; for, irrespective of how He treats men, we must keep our mouths shut and not murmur against Him, because we can gain nothing by it'" (p. 47). "We must acknowledge the incomprehensible majesty of God" (p. 50).

In developing this teaching, Calvin carefully takes a position beyond rationalism and irrationalism. Real faith is neither. God "is not like creatures who ought to be obedient to the common rule in such manner that they be brought to account and measured by the Law which He has given to us; to us, I say, for He has squared out His Law to be our measure, and not to be subject to it Himself. So also must men understand that He is totally other than they have imagined Him to be; for they have not had an eye to the infinite glory which is in Him" (p. 66). And on the other hand Calvin asserts; "It is especially said that Job attributed to God nothing without reason, that is to say, that he did not imagine God did anything which was not just and equitable . . . If we were afflicted we must not think that it happens without reason" (pp. 29-30). God does have reasons, but ultimately they are strictly His own. The reader will find that Calvin strongly applies this principle against the essential rationalism of the Papists with their rituals of work righteousness for salvation, and of the Libertines with their bold and presumptuous autonomy overagainst God, both of whom transgress against the incomprehensible sovereignty of God wherein He deals with men according to His unsearchable good pleasure. Less obvious, but nonetheless present, is an apologetic against all irrationalism. Calvin counsels against blind despair. To consider life meaningless is for him as much a violation of the undiscernible wisdom and goodness of God as to consider its meaning fully knowable. Whether Calvin detected any seeds of irrationalism in Luther's thought we do not know. But certainly the irrationalism of futility and despair which is so common in our day can find none of the support in Calvin which it claims to find in Luther.

The fulness and the grasp of Calvin's theology is evident in the way he handles the central message of the book of Job. The man in the pulpit of Geneva stood like Job with his hand over his mouth, and bade his people do the same. Where God's purpose could be seen he triumphantly displayed it. But he did not trifle with rationalizing the perplexities of men or trying to explain away their grief. The comfort which he pastorally offered was the only one at last sufficient, that is, the hidden grace of a sovereign God. "There is nothing better than to be entirely subject to the majesty of God" (p. 28).

The divine incomprehensibility and inscrutability in Calvin's writings merit more attention than they have had, and will highly repay careful study. This certainly is a timely interest in a day when the cross-currents of rationalism and irrationalism are running so strongly. One suspects that many orthodox Calvinists by their small dealings in these doctrines betray the climatic influences of rationalism, if not the climate of Liberalism then of an Evangelicalism which, though orthodox, is nonetheless rooted in the twin heresy of an autonomous man and a searchable God. What orthodox Christianity needs more than anything else today is the full sense of the majesty of God. There is no better place to find it than in Calvin's sermons on Job. On the other hand, the systematic study of these doctrines in Calvin's theology will provide firm basis for disputing Neo-orthodoxy's claim for Calvin's support in its view that only sensory data are really knowable, that the answer of faith is not really knowledge, and that God is absolutely unknowable. This is a perversion of the doctrine of divine incomprehensibility. It is a misuse of Calvin. Calvin must speak today on this crucial doctrine to both orthodox Evangelicalism and liberal Neo-orthodoxy. His followers must cause him to be heard. The sermons on Job have this special relevance.

In addition to characteristic theocentric stresses on divine providence and incomprehensibility, we may observe a stress on the doctrine of election. Election was a broad and vital thing in Calvin's preaching. It was no theological fragment or Biblical segment. Neither was it brought in only when the text required it. There were overtones of election to be heard in every sermon, and as a distinct chord it was struck often and forcefully. This the reader will discover for himself. Sermons 3, 4 and 5 of the present volume are of particular interest in this respect. For instance, Calvin finds that those who with Bildad believe that God treats men "according to the demerits of each one," "must attribute to men free will; election by God must be ruined and annihilated . . . and (they) upset the first foundations of our faith" (p. 48). Job's position is basically a faith in God's gracious, unconditional election, and all of his counsellors make the fundamental mistake of not reckoning with this truth. Calvin tends to dispute all false doctrine in terms of predestination. Whereas for Luther the basic error of Rome was justification by works, for Calvin it was free will. All those who come under Calvin's condemnation, from Servetus to the Anabaptists, regardless of other errors, are denounced in the last analysis for espousing free will and rejecting election. Unconditional election was for Calvin the fundamental of all fundamentals, and his preaching shows it.

In the sermons of this volume there are several places in which reprobation is dealt with alongside election. This may have been due partly to the fact that at the time he was preaching on Job his doctrine of double predestination was under fierce attack by the Geneva Libertines. In any case, this is hardly representative of all of his preaching. He does not preach reprobation every time he preaches election. It seems to have had for him only occasional sermonic relevance. This should be carefully noted, because too many of his spiritual sons, taking brittle logical abstractions into the pulpit, have wrongly measured their sermonizing in election by that in reprobation, and the former has been neglected.

The way Calvin preached election it was the Gospel, and as such it was, in the terms of the Heidelberg Catechism, an "only comfort" for man's "sin and misery." As a preacher Calvin used the doctrine of divine sovereignty first of all as the balm of Gilead. Sovereignty in his sermons is not viewed in the abstract, or developed as a page in dogmatics. It is never dissociated from grace. In a real sense sovereign grace is the theme of every sermon. Grace, for which there are numerous synonyms in the sermons, is not a static idea but a living, dynamic one. It is not narrowly localized at the manger or the cross, nor is it mechanically fettered to an *ordo salutis,* but it is as comprehensive and pervasive as God's dealings with men. Neither is it limited to the processes of salvation, but comprehends also those of creation. Calvin takes up the whole of the believer's life and views it in its totality as an act of God's grace. Election in its broadest sense includes everything that happens to the Christian in his encounter with a redeeming God. Thus even the sufferings of Job are a part of the process of sovereign grace, for "God cannot procure our salvation except by showing Himself to be against us" (p. 39).

The Book of Job

The book of Job is one of the few major Bible books on which Calvin did not write a commentary. Therefore the publication of these twenty sermons is of exegetical and expository interest as well as homiletical. These who are accustomed to consulting Calvin's comment in their study of Scripture will be grateful that Nixon's careful selection of sermons for this volume provides an adequate basis for learning Calvin's general interpretation of the book of Job. Sermon No. 1, beside being a preachment, is virtually a chapter out of an Old Testament Introduction. With his usual sure-footed exegetical skill Calvin identifies Job as an actual historical figure, of the lineage of Esau, probably living in the Mosaic era. His character as "perfect and upright" is carefully explained. Job's general significance is that he is an example to believers, but in addition "the Holy Spirit has dictated this book to this use, namely, that the Jews might know that God has had people who have served Him, although they were not separated from the rest of the world, and although they had not the sign of circumcision" (p. 7). (Students of Calvin's view of the inspiration of Scripture will be interested in the use of the phrase, "the Holy Spirit has dictated.") The significance of extra-covenantal grace, and of revelation outside Israel, is further developed in Sermon No. 15 where Elihu is introduced. All of this is valuable hermeneutical material.

The exegetical riches of these sermons are great. The reader will find them on every hand. Important Old Testament concepts are carefully set forth. Many terms appear with fine shadings of meaning. Calvin's philological mastery of the Old Testament is apparent. Sermons such as Nos. 8 and 9 give a thorough exposition of well-known and important passages. Calvin's version of the Hebrew text, as rendered by Nixon, is in itself of great interest. The careful student will find that a comparison of Calvin's text with that of the accepted English versions is most fruitful. These sermons will fully repay several readings. They can be read in at least two ways, strictly as sermons and also as exegetical notes, but to try both at once is probably to do justice to neither.

Calvin repeatedly states what he considers to be the key to understanding the book as a whole. The reader is advised to have this one point firmly grasped and clearly understood. In reading the entire series of 159 sermons, this key thought becomes increasingly plain as it did to Calvin's original hearers. But it should be remembered that Sermon No. 2 in this volume is already Sermon No. 7 in the complete series,

and Sermon No. 3 is Sermon No. 21. Consequently it is
suggested that the reader give especially careful attention to
what Calvin says in Sermon 1, on pages 5 and 6, which begins: "We have also to note that in the whole dispute Job
maintains a good case, and his adversary maintains a poor
one. Now there is more, that Job maintaining a good case
pleads it poorly, and the others bringing a poor case plead
it well. When we shall have understood this, it will be to us
as it were a key to open to us the whole book." Job's good
case is that affliction is not always divine punishment, and
that therefore it is not necessarily a measure of sin. For the
reprobate affliction is indeed punishment, but for the elect
it is chastisement. He pleads it poorly by rash self-defense,
excessive self-assertion, seeming resistance to God, and un-
restrained passion. The poor case of his friends is that affliction is divine punishment, meted out according to the
measure of men's sins. They plead it well by making statements about God and man which are altogether true and
valid, and which must be accepted as being in themselves the
pure teaching of the Holy Spirit. This key thought about
a good case poorly presented and a poor case well presented
recurs several times in these twenty sermons. It may be well
for the reader to consult the representative statements of it
which may be found on pages 45-51, 116-117, 128-130, and
214-216, before going beyond the first sermon. A clear
understanding of this central principle is essential.

Calvin's treatment of Job is intensely practical. It is a
living, breathing thing. It throbs with moral and spiritual
reality. Job's pulse is there. Ethical passages are prominent,
involving the family, society, the church and the state, as well
as the individual life. The legal framework of so much of
Calvin's thought is entirely lacking. Forensic relationships
are at a minimum. Sin is pride more than disobedience.
Salvation is reconciliation more than justification. Duty is
submission more than precept. No abstract disquisition on a
dogmatic formula detaches the congregation from Job's ex-
emplary life, his struggles of soul, the wrestlings of his counsellors, and the majesty of God. This is the living Word! It

has to do with Job and his God, Job and his fellows, Job and himself. And Job is always Every Believer. That makes great preaching.

We will not have learned well of Calvin until we have distinctly heard his pulpit accent as well as that of his systematic theology. Often they are not the same. May his sermons in the course of time receive the kind of attention that his other writings have had. It should never be forgotten that in his own estimation he was first of all a preacher.

SERMON 1

The Character of Job*

There was in the region of Uz a man by the name of Job, perfect and upright, who feared God, and kept himself from evil.—Job 1:1

To REALLY profit by the contents of this book, we must first know the scope of it. The story which is here written shows us how we are in the hand of God, and that it belongs to Him to order our lives and to dispose of them according to His good pleasure, and that our duty is to submit ourselves to Him in all humility and obedience, that it is quite reasonable that we be altogether His both to live and to die; and even if it shall please Him to raise His hand against us, though we may not perceive for what cause He does it, nevertheless we should glorify Him always, confessing that He is just and equitable, that we should not murmur against Him, that we should not enter into dispute, knowing that if we struggle against Him we shall be conquered. This, then, in brief, is what we have to remember from the story, that is, that God has such dominion over His creatures that He can dispose of them at His pleasure, and when He shows a strictness that we at first find strange, yet that we should keep our mouths closed in order not to murmur; but rather, that we should confess that He is just, expecting that He may declare to us why He chastises us. Meanwhile we have to contemplate the patience of the man who is here set before our eyes, according as Saint James (5:11) exhorts us. For when God shows us that we have to suffer all the miseries that He will send us, we surely confess that it is our duty; however, we allege our frailty and it seems to us that this ought to serve us as an excuse. For this cause it is good that we have examples who show us that

---

* From *Calvini Opera, Corpus Reformatorum*, volume 33, pp. 21-33.

there are men frail like us, who nevertheless have resisted
temptations, and have persevered constantly in obeying God,
although He afflicted them to the limit. Now we have here
an excellent example of it.

Besides, it is not all that we should consider the patience of
Job, but we have to look at the result, as Saint James also mentions; for if Job had remained confounded, although there was
a virtue more than angelic in him, it would not have been a
happy ending. But when we see that he was not disappointed
in his hope, and inasmuch as he was humbled before God he
found grace, seeing such an ending, we have to conclude that
there is nothing better than to subject ourselves to God, and
to suffer peaceably all that He sends us until by His pure
goodness He delivers us. However, beyond the story we
have to regard the doctrine which is comprehended in this
book: namely, from those who come under the pretense of
comforting Job, and who torment him much more than did
his own illness, and from the answers he gives to repulse their
calumnies, by which it seems they wish to crush him. First,
we have to note with respect to our afflictions, although God
sends them and they proceed from Him, yet the devil brings
them on us, as also Saint Paul warns us that we have to fight
against spiritual powers. (Ephesians 6:12). For when the
devil thus lights the fire he also pumps the bellows, that is to
say, he finds men who are his own to continually prick us and
to lengthen and augment the illness. So then, we see how
Job, beyond the illness which he endured, was tormented,
even by his friends, and by his wife, and above all by those
who came to tempt him spiritually. Now I call it spiritual
temptation when we are not only beaten and afflicted in our
bodies; but when the devil so works in our imaginations that
God is a deadly enemy to us, and we can no longer have
recourse to Him, and we know that He never has to be merciful toward us. All the propositions put forward by the friends
of Job tended to persuade him that he was a man reproved
by God and that he was certainly mistaken in trusting that
God should be propitious toward him. Now these spiritual
struggles are much more difficult to bear than all the evils and

all the adversities that we can suffer when we are persecuted. All the same God releases the bridle to Satan that he may draw with him his servants, who make such assaults upon us as we shall see that Job endured.

So much for one item. However, we have also to note that in the whole dispute Job maintains a good case, and his adversary maintains a poor one. Now there is more, that Job maintaining a good case pleads it poorly, and the others bringing a poor case plead it well. When we shall have understood this, it will be to us as it were a key to open to us the whole book. How is it that Job maintains a case which is good? It is that he knows that God does not always afflict men according to the measure of their sins; but that He has His secret judgments, of which He does not give us an account, and yet we must wait until He may reveal to us why He does this or that. He was, then, entirely persuaded that God does not always afflict men according to the measure of their sins, and by that he has testimony in himself that he was not a man rejected by God, as they wished to make him believe. This is a case which is good and true, though it is poorly pleaded; for Job here now throws himself off balance and uses excessive and exaggerated propositions, so that he shows that he is desperate in many respects. And he is even so heated that it seems that he wishes to resist God. So here is a good case that is pleaded badly. Now on the contrary those who sustain the poor case, that God always punishes men according to the measure of their sin, speak beautiful and holy sentences; there is nothing in their propositions that we ought not to receive as if the Holy Spirit had pronounced it; for it is pure truth, these are the foundations of religion, they discuss the providence of God, they discuss His justice, they discuss the sins of men. Here, then, is a doctrine which we have to receive without contradiction, and yet the result that these people try to put Job into despair and to destroy him completely is bad. Now by this we see when we have a good foundation that we must consider how to build thereon, in such a way that all may harmonize, as Saint Paul says (I Corinthians 3:10), that he built, since he founded the

Church upon the pure doctrine of Jesus Christ; and yet that there is such a conformity that those who will come after him will use as foundation neither straw nor thatch, nor worthless material; but that there be a good foundation, firm and solid. So, in all our life we have to consider that if we are founded in good and just reason, each one must be on his guard not to bend or turn this way or that way; for there is nothing easier than to pervert a good and just case, according as our nature is vicious and we experience every bit of it. God will have exercised the grace toward us that our case will be good, and yet we shall be pricked by our enemies so that we cannot keep ourselves in bounds and we cannot simply follow what God orders for us without adding to it in any fashion whatever. Seeing, then, that we are so easily carried away, all the more ought we to pray to God that when He shall have given us a good case, He may lead us by His Holy Spirit in all simplicity, that we may not pass beyond the limits that He has established for us by His Word. However, also we are admonished not to apply the truth of God to bad use; for we profane it by this means; like these people, though they speak holy words (as we have already declared, and as we shall see more fully) yet however they are sacrilegious; for they corrupt the truth of God, and they abuse it falsely; they apply to a bad end that which is good and just in itself. So then, when God has given us knowledge of His Word, let us learn to receive it in such fear that it may not be to darken the good nor to make the bad attractive; as often those who are the most keen, and the most wise will let themselves go and will abuse the knowledge which God has given to them, in fraud, in malice, and they will upset everything, so that they only tangle themselves up in knots. Seeing that the world is addicted to such vice, all the more have we to pray to God that He may give us the grace to apply His Word to such use as He intends; namely, a pure and simple use. This is what we have to observe in summary.

Now since we understand what the book deals with we have to pursue things more at length, so that what we have mentioned briefly we may deduce according to the procedure of the narrative. It is said: *"There was a man in the land of Uz, named Job, a man perfect, and upright; and fearing God, and withdrawing himself from evil."* We cannot and we do not know how to divine at what time Job lived, except that it can be perceived that it was very ancient; some Jews have even estimated that Moses was author of the book, and that he had given this example to the people in order that the children of Abraham who were descended from his race might know that God had shown grace to others who were not of this line, and that they might be ashamed if they did not walk purely in fear of God; seeing that this man, who had not had the mark of the covenant, who had not been circumcised but was Pagan, conducted himself so well. Now because this is not at all certain, we must leave it in suspense. But let us take what is without any doubt, namely, that the Holy Spirit has dictated this book to this use, namely, that the Jews might know that God has had people who have served Him, although they were not separated from the rest of the world, and although they had not the sign of the circumcision, who nevertheless have walked in all purity of life. The Jews, knowing this, have had occasion to be all the more careful to observe the Law of God, and, since He had exercised the grace and given them the privilege of gathering them from among all the foreign nations, that they had to dedicate themselves entirely to Him. And also it is perceived through the book of Ezekiel (14:14) that the name of Job was renowned among the people of Israel; for we have seen that in the 14th chapter that it was said, "Though Noah, Job and Daniel were found among the people who were to perish, they would save only their own souls, and the rest of the people would be destroyed." Here the Prophet speaks of three men, indeed, as of those who were known and renowned among the Jews, as we have already mentioned. So we see the intention of the Holy Spirit: namely, that the Jews might have a mirror and a pattern to recognize how they had to observe the doctrine of salvation which was given them, since this man who was of a foreign nation had so preserved himself in such purity. And it is the principal thing that we have to retain from the name

which is here mentioned, when it is said that he was of the
land of Uz. It is true that this land is located by some rather
in the East; but there is in the Lamentations of Jeremiah
(4:21) the same word, used to indicate a part of Edom. We
know that the Edomites were descended from Esau. It is
true that they still had the circumcision, but inasmuch as they
had wandered from the Church of God, there was no longer
any sign of the covenant. If we take it, then, that Job was of
Uz, he was an Edomite, that is to say, of the lineage of Esau.
Now we know what is said by the Prophet (Malachi 1:2),
that although Esau and Jacob were twin brothers, indeed
from one womb, God had chosen Jacob by His pure goodness
and had rejected Esau, and had cursed him with all his lineage. That is how the Prophet speaks of it in order to magnify the mercy of God toward the Jews, showing them that He
had elected them not on account of any dignity that was in
their persons, seeing that He has rejected the elder brother of
Jacob, to whom belonged the birthright, and that He had
chosen him who was the lesser, and the inferior. So then, although this man was descended from the lineage of Esau, yet
we see in what integrity he lived, and how he served God, not
only with respect to conversing with men in uprightness and
equity; but by having a pure religion which was not polluted
with the idolatries and superstitions of unbelievers. As for
the name "Job," it is true that some translate it as "weeping"
or "crying;" but others take it as "a man of enmity," not that
he hated, but that he was as it were a target, at which one
could shoot. Yet we ought not to doubt that this man, whose
country is here noted, whose name is expressed, really was,
that he lived, and that the things which are here written have
happened to him; in order that we may not think that this is
an argument contrived by a man, as if under a pen-name there
was here proposed to us that which never happened. For we
have already alleged the testimony of Ezekiel, and that of
Saint James, who well show that Job truly was, and also when
history declares it, we cannot erase what the Holy Spirit so
notably wished to say.

Besides we have to note pertaining to that time that, although the world was alienated from the true service of God, and from the pure religion, nevertheless there was much more integrity than there is today, even in the Papacy. In fact, we see how from the time of Abraham, Melchizedek had the Church of God, and sacrifices which were without any pollution. And so, although the greater part of the world was wrapped in many errors, and false and wicked fantasies, yet God had reserved some little seed to himself, and there were always some who were retained under the pure truth, indeed, waiting for God to establish His Church; and that He should choose a people, namely, the successors of Abraham, in order that they might know that they were separated from all the rest of the world. Now it is very true that Job lived during that time, but the Church of God was not yet as trained up as it has been since; for we know that while the children of Israel lived in Egypt it seemed that everyone was to be annihilated. And we even see to what extremity they came in the end, when Pharaoh commands that the males should be killed; and in the desert it still seems that God had rejected them; when they have come into the country of Canaan, they have great battles against their enemies, and even the service of God is not yet established there, nor the tabernacle, as would be required. God then, not yet having set up a form of the Church which could be seen, wished that there might always remain some little seed among the Pagans, in order that He might be adored, and that it might also be to convict those who had turned away from the right road, as the Pagans; for He needed only Job to be judge of an entire country. Noah has also condemned the world, as Scripture speaks of it, since he always kept himself pure and walked as before God, although everyone had forgotten Him, and all had gone astray in their superstitions. So then, Noah is judge of all the world to condemn unbelievers and rebels. So it was with Job, who condemned all those of that region, because he served God purely, and others were full of idolatries, of infamies, of many errors; and this came to pass because they would not condescend to recognize Who was the true and living God, and how, and in

what manner He wished to be honored; yet God has always
had this consideration (as I have said) that the wicked and
unbelievers should be rendered inexcusable. And for this
He willed that there might always be some people who would
follow what He had declared to the ancient Fathers. Such
was Job, as the Scripture speaks to us of him, and the present
narrative shows well how he purely served God and that he
conversed among men in all uprightness. It is said, *"He was
a perfect[1] man."* Now this word[1] in Scripture is taken as a
general term when there is neither falsehood nor hypocrisy in
a man, but what is inside is shown outside, and that he does
not keep a shop in the rear to turn himself away from God,
but he displays his heart, and all his thoughts and affections,
he asks only to consecrate himself to God and to dedicate
himself entirely to Him. This word[1] has been rendered "perfect" by both the Greeks and the Latins; but because the word
"perfection" was later improperly expounded, it is much to be
preferred that we should have the word "integrity." For
many ignorant people, who do not know how this perfection
is taken, have thought, "There is a man who is called perfect,
it follows then that we can have perfection in ourselves, while
we walk in this present life." They have obscured the grace
of God, of which we always have need; for those who will
have walked the most uprightly still must have their refuge
in the mercy of God; and if their sins are not pardoned them,
and God does not support them, behold, they all perish. So
then, although those who have used the word "perfection"
have well understood it, yet since there have been those who
have turned it to a contrary sense (as I have said) let us
retain the word "integrity." Here then is Job who is called
"entire."[1] How? It is because there was no hypocrisy or
falsehood in him, for he did not have a double heart; for the
Scripture, when it wishes to state the vice opposite to this
virtue of integrity, says, "heart and heart," that is to say,
"double heart." Let us note, then, that in the first place this
title is attributed to Job to show that he had a pure and simple

---

1. Fr. *Entier.*

affection, that he did not have one eye on one side and the other on the other, that he did not serve God only half, but he tried to give himself entirely to Him. It is true that we shall never have such integrity that we would reach this goal, as would be to be desired; for those who follow the right road, still go hobbling along, they are always weak, they drag their legs and droop their wings. So, then, is it with us, as long as we shall be surrounded by this mortal body; until God may have delivered us from all these miseries, to which we are subject, there will never be in us an integrity which is perfect, as we have said. Nevertheless, we must come to this openness, and we must renounce all pretense and falsehood. Besides, let us note that true holiness begins within; even if we should have the finest appearance in the world before men, even if our life were so well ruled that everyone should applaud us, if we have not this openness and integrity before God, it will be nothing. For the fountain must be pure, and then the streams trickle down from it pure; otherwise the water could well be clear, and yet it will not cease to be bitter or to have some other evil corruption in it. We must, then, always begin by what is said, namely, "God wishes to be served in spirit and in sincerity of heart," as he says in Jeremiah (5:3).[2] We must, then, learn in the first place to conform our hearts to the obedience of God.

Now after Job has been called "entire,"[1] it is said, "He was upright"; this uprightness is referred to the life which he has led, which is as it were the fruits of this root, that the Holy Spirit had put first. Did Job, then, have his heart upright and whole? His life was simple, that is to say, he walked, and lived with his neighbors without harming anyone, without injuring or molesting anyone, without applying his study to fraud or to malice, without seeking his profit at the expense of another. This, then, is the meaning of the "uprightness," which is here added. Now by this we are admonished to have a conformity between the heart and the outward senses. It

---

2. I think Calvin means Jeremiah 3:10 and John 4:24.

is true (as I have said) that we can well abstain from doing
evil, we can well have fine appearance before men, but it will
be nothing, if before God there is hidden hypocrisy and fic-
tion, when we examine this root, which is within the heart.
What is necessary, then? that we should begin at this end, as
I have said; yet to have good integrity, the eyes, and the
hands, and the feet, and the arms, and the legs must respond,
that in all our life we may declare that we wish to serve God,
and that it is not in vain that we protest[3] that we wish to keep
the integrity within. And that is also why St. Paul exhorts
the Galatians (5:25) to walk according to the spirit if they
live according to the spirit as if he said, "It is true that it is
necessary that the Spirit of God should dwell in us, and that
He should govern us; for it would be nothing to have a beautiful life, which pleased men, and which was in great esteem,
unless we were renewed by the grace of God. But what then?
We must walk, that is to say, we must show in fact, and by
our works how the Spirit of God reigns in our souls, for if
our hands are polluted either by larcenies, or by cruelty, or
other injuries, if the eyes are infected by evil and immodest
glances, by coveting the goods of another, or by pride, and by
vanity the feet run to evil[4] (as the Scripture speaks of it), by
this we shall show well that the heart is full of malice and of
corruption; for there are neither feet, nor hands, nor eyes
which are led by themselves; the leading comes from the
Spirit and from the heart." So then, let us learn to have the
conformity that Scripture shows us in this passage, when it
is said, "Job, having this integrity and openness, also lived
uprightly," that is to say, he conversed with his neighbors
without any injury, without seeking his particular profit, but
he kept equity with all the world. And this is also wherein
God wishes to prove whether or not we serve Him faithfully;
not that He has need of our service, or of all that we can do
for Him; but when we do good to our neighbors, and we keep
loyalty to each one, as even nature teaches us, by this we

---

3. Latin, *protestamur*, we bear witness.
4. Proverbs 1:16.

render testimony that we fear God. We shall see many, whom we make great zealots, if it is only a matter of disputing and holding many conversations, to say that they study to serve God and to honor Him; but as soon as they have to do with their neighbors, it is known what is in their heart; for they seek their own advantage, and they have no conscience against drawing to themselves and cheating when they will have the power to do so by any means whatever. Those, then, who seek their advantage and profit — there is no doubt that they are hypocrites, and that their heart is corrupted; however beautiful zealots they may be, God declares that there is only filth and poison in their heart. And why? If there is openness, it is necessary that there should be uprightness, that is to say, if the affection is pure within, when we converse with men, we shall procure the good of each one, so that we shall not be addicted to ourselves, and to our particular interest, but we shall have the equity which Jesus Christ said is the rule of life, and the whole sum of the Law and the Prophets — that we should not do to anyone except what we would wish done to us.[5] So then, let us note that in this praise of Job there are many people who are condemned when the Holy Spirit declares that this man had not only an integrity before God, but also uprightness and openness among men. This openness that He pronounces will serve sentence and condemnation against all those who will be full of malice, against all those who ask only to ravish and to entrap the goods of another, who ask only to pillage the substance of others. These are condemned by this word.

Now it follows, *"He feared God, he was a God-fearing man, and he withdrew from evil."* Also when Job had the praise of having kept uprightness and equity among men, it was very necessary that he walked before God; for without this the rest would be considered nothing. It is true that we cannot live with our neighbors (as I have already said) without doing evil to anyone, procuring the good of each one, ex-

---

5. Tobit 4:15. "And what thou thyself hatest, do to no man." Cf. also Matthew 7:12 and Luke 6:31.

cept we regard God; for those who follow their nature, though they may have beautiful virtues (it will seem), yet are preoccupied with love of themselves, and compelled only by ambition, or some other consideration, so that all appearance of virtue which is in them, is corrupted by this; but although we may not be able to have this uprightness without fearing God, yet these are two distinct things: (1) serving God, and (2) honoring our neighbors, as also God has distinguished them in His Law, when He willed that it should be described in two tables. Let us note, then, that, as by putting before us the word "uprightness" the Holy Spirit wished to declare how Job conversed among men, also when He says, "He had fear of God," He wishes to bring out the religion which was in him. Now by this we are admonished that to rule[6] our life well we must regard God and then our neighbors; let us regard God, I say, in order to give ourselves to Him, in order to render Him the homage which is due Him; let us regard our neighbors in order to acquit ourselves of our duty toward them according as we are admonished to help them, to live in equity, and uprightness; and since God has joined us to one another, let each one be advised to employ all his faculties to the common good of all. That is how we have to regard both God and men to rule our life well, for he who regards himself — it is certain that there is only vanity in him; for if a man wishes to order[7] his life so that it seems to men that there is nothing to find fault with in him and meanwhile God disavows him, what will he gain when he will have taken much trouble to walk in such a way that everyone magnifies him? There is only pollution before God, and the sentence written by Saint Luke (16:15) must be fulfilled: "He who is high and excellent before men is only abomination before God." Let us note, then, that we never shall be able to order our life properly, if we have not our eyes fixed on God, and toward our neighbors. On God, and why? In order that we may

---

6. Fr. *regler,* to rule, regulate, order, settle.
7. Fr. *ordonner,* to order, enjoin, appoint, rule by settled conviction or deliberate purpose.

know that we are created to His glory, to serve and adore Him; for although He may not have to do with us as our neighbors will have to, and though this may bring Him neither hot nor cold, yet He wished to have reasonable creatures, who would recognize Him, and, having recognized Him, would render to Him what belongs to Him. Besides, when it is spoken of the fear of God, let us note that it is not a servile fear (as it is called) but it is for the honor that we owe Him, as He is our Father and our Master. Would we fear God? It is certain that we should ask only to honor Him, and to be entirely His own. Would we recognize Him? We must do it according to such attributes as He declares of Himself: namely, our Creator, and He Who sustains us, and Who shows such a fatherly goodness that we surely must be His children if we do not wish to be too ungrateful to Him. Also we must recognize the mastery and superiority which He has over us, in order that, rendering to Him the honor which is due Him, each one of us may learn to please Him in everything and by everything. That is how under the word "fear of God" all religion is comprehended, namely, all the service, and the homage that creatures owe to their God. Now it was a very excellent virtue in Job to fear God thus, seeing that all the world had turned away from the right road. When we hear this, let us learn that we shall have no excuse, though we may converse among the worst outcasts in the world, if we are not given to the service of God; as we ought to be. Now it is well to note this, because it seems to many people, when they are among thorns, that they are thereby acquitted and fully excused; and if afterwards they are corrupted, if they are hurled among wolves (as they say), that it is all right, and that God will pardon them. On the contrary, here is Job who is called a God-fearing man. In what country? It is not in Judea, it is not in the city of Jerusalem, it is not in the Temple; but it is in a polluted place, in the midst of those who were entirely perverted. Being then, among such people, yet he was preserved, and he lived in such wise that he walked purely with his neighbors, although all were then full of cruelty, outrages, pillaging, and like things. Let us note that this will return to us with all the greater shame, if on our part we do not consider how to reserve ourselves purely for the service of God, and for our neighbors, when he gives us such occasion for it as we have, namely, that daily[8] the Word of God is preached to us, that we are exhorted, that it sets us right when we have failed. We surely must, then, be attentive to what is here shown us.

Now in conclusion let us note well what is here added to the text, *"He kept himself from evil."* For this is how Job surmounted all difficulties and battles which might have hindered him from serving God and from living uprightly with men: it is because he recalled to himself that he well knew that, if he had given himself license to do like others, he would have been a man completely addicted to vice, he would have been an enemy of God. Job, then, did not thus walk in the fear of God, in such openness and integrity without many battles, without the devil's having schemed to pervert him and to lead him to all the corruptions of the world; but he withdrew from evil, that is to say, he held himself back. What, then, must we do? Though we are in the Church of God, yet we shall see many evils; and (though it should be) there will never be such openness or purity, that we would not be mixed among many despisers, debauchees, who will be firebrands from hell, deadly pests to infect everything. We must, then, be on our guard, seeing that there are great scandals and all manner of lewdness, by which we would be immediately debauched. What must we do then? We must withdraw from evil; that is to say, we must fight against such assaults after the example of Job; and when we shall see many vices and corruptions ruling in the world, though it may be necessary for us to be mixed among them, nevertheless we must not be polluted by them and we must not say, as is customary, that we must howl among the wolves; but rather we must be advised after the example of Job to withdraw ourselves from evil, and to withdraw from it in such a way that Satan may not be able to make us give ourselves to him by means of all

---

8. The 159 sermons on Job were preached daily on weekdays, 1554-1555.

the temptations which he will put before us; but we must allow that God should purge us of all our filth and infections, as He has promised us in the Name of our Lord Jesus Christ, until He may have withdrawn us from the stains and pollutions of this world, to join us with His Angels, and to make us partakers of the eternal felicity to which we ought now to aspire.

Now we shall present ourselves before the face of our God.

SERMON 2

The Lord Gave; The Lord has Taken Away*

Then Job arose, and tore his robe, and sheared his head, and threw himself upon the ground, and worshipped, and said, "Naked came I out of my mother's womb, naked I shall return there; the Lord has given it, and the Lord has taken it away; blessed be the name of the Lord." In all this Job sinned not at all, nor attributed anything unreasonable to God
—Job 1:20-22

WE MAY well say that patience is a great virtue, as indeed it is; since there are very few who know what the word "patience" means; from which fact it might be concluded that we slightly value being patient and having this virtue at which we grab so long. Now God, seeing such indifference on the part of men, wishes to put before their eyes that which is so needful for us. For if we are not patient, our faith must have vanished; for it cannot be maintained apart from this means. This being so, God wills that amidst the miseries of this world we may always have a peaceable heart, and that we may be so assured of His goodness that we may rejoice and content ourselves therein, and that we may be able to glory against Satan and against all our enemies. And how is it possible, unless we regard ourselves as higher than this world, and we consider that, although our condition is miserable with respect to the opinion of the flesh, yet, since our God loves us, we surely must suffer? Now this passage is also the most excellent there is in Holy Scripture to show us what the word "patience" implies. We must be taught by it if we wish that God should acknowledge us as patient in our afflictions. We commonly say that a man is patient, although he may not have any true patience; for whoever suffers evil is called patient;

---

* Sermon in *Calvini Opera, Corpus Reformatorum*, volume 33, pp. 91-103.

but however much we may hold back being patient, we must abate our sadness. If there is some evil, may it be sweetened by recognizing that God never ceases to procure our salvation, that we must be subject to Him, and that it is entirely right that He should govern us according to His will. That is how patience is shown. But there is nothing better nor more useful than to behold the mirror which is here held up to us. We have seen that Job could have been overwhelmed,[1] having heard so much bad news. Now it is said that he has arisen, and has torn his robe, has sheared himself, and has thrown himself to the ground to humble himself before God. Here we see in the first place that those who are patient bear well an affliction, that they feel displeased and anguished in their heart; for if we were as a tree trunk or a stone, there would be no virtue in us. Is a man who is not aware of his illness worthy of being praised? We shall surely see a feeble-minded person who laughs, who mocks all the world, and yet he is at the edge of the grave, but he is not aware of his illness. This, then, does not deserve to be held or accounted as virtue, for it is stupidity; brute beasts sometimes feel nothing, but they are not virtuous on that account. So then, let us note that the word "patience" does not mean that men should be drugged,[2] that they should have no sadness, that they should not be at all offended when they experience some affliction; but the virtue is when they are able to restrain themselves and so hold themselves in bounds that they do not cease to glorify God in the midst of all their affliction, that they are not troubled by anguish and so swallowed up as to quit everything; but that they fight against their passions until they are able to conform to the good pleasure of God, and to conclude as Job here does, and to say that He is entirely just.

This is what we have to note when it is said, "Job has torn his robe, and has shorn his head." For such fashions were customary in oriental countries, as we know that there were more ceremonies in those regions which do not exist at all in the cold countries where we live. For when something hap-

---

1. Fr. *abysme,* cast down to the depths.
2. Fr. *eslourdis,* weighed down (mentally).

pened which could move men to great anger, as a sign of
grief they tore their clothes. So much for one item. Then,
in that country, where they were accustomed to letting hair
grow, they sheared themselves to display grief; on the other
hand, where they sheared themselves, when they displayed
grief they let the hair grow. They are, then, signs of the grief
which here overtakes Job when he tears his robe and shears
himself. Now it is certain that his act was not in any sense
feigned, as quite often those who wish to disguise themselves
assume masks in order that no one may guess that they are
in great sadness and that they may not cease to laugh in their
heart. Job has not used such hypocrisy. Let us know, then,
when he has torn his robe and he has shorn his hair, that it
was anguish and unlimited displeasure, and when he threw
himself to the ground, it was yet another testimony. But
it seems that Job here releases the bridle to his sadness, which
would be a vice to condemn. For we know that men are only
too excessive and overflowing in their passions. For although
they restrain themselves and correct themselves as much as
they can, yet they do not cease to go out of bounds, and there
is nothing more difficult than to so restrain ourselves that we
keep rule and compass on ourselves. We see that men cannot
rejoice without being too gay. Grief or sadness is a much
more violent passion which carries men further away than
does joy. So then, we have to be on our guard always and
whenever God sends us some adversity, for this is where we
are accustomed to overflowing the most. Now it is here said
that Job tore his robe; it seems that he wishes to spur himself
to be more sad than he was (for a man who sees himself so
disfigured is astonished at himself) and then when it comes
to his hair it could be said that he sought aids to needle himself and add to his grief, and that he was as it were driving
himself to despair. And this (as I have said) would surely
be condemnable; but in the first place let us note that the
Scripture here wished to express to us that the sadness of
this holy person was so great and so vehement that he was not
able to satisfy himself, that he went beyond ordinary custom
by tearing his robe, to show that he experienced such anguish

that it had grieved him to the bottom of his heart. This is what the Scripture wishes to express to us. Now although men ought to be on their guard lest they be swallowed up by sadness when they are afflicted, yet whenever God sends us some evil we must think about it. For the common manner of repulsing every trial is very bad; and yet this is the way men have been in this respect; when they wished to be patient they extinguished all thoughts of their maladies, they pushed them far away, and they withdrew from them; briefly, they wished to be so stupified that they might know or discern nothing. Now entirely on the contrary, when God afflicts us it is not to give us blows of the mallet upon the head in order that we may be dazed and drowsy, but He wills to induce us to think of our miseries. How? Beyond the necessity for keeping in memory our sins in order to ask pardon for them and to be all the more careful to walk in the proper way, we are also instructed it is part of our life, in order not to please ourselves, in order not to be inflated by vanity, nor by presumption as we are, and then to acknowledge the obligation that we have to our God in that He treats us so tenderly, in that He carries us, as it were, in His bosom; and then when we see that He cares for our life, let us look further, that is to say, let us reach toward the eternal kingdom, wherein is our true joy and rest. This, then, is how God does not cease to be pitiful toward us when He sends us some affliction; for it is in order that, examining what is in us, we may also acknowledge our condition. Also it is good and useful that believers, when God afflicts them, are incited to think to themselves, "Who am I? What of me? Why am I thus afflicted?" Let them think (I say) of all these things. Now this is how Job was able to tear his clothes and then to shear his head without offending God; not that he wished to be precipitated in too great anger, but it tended to humility; as also it was to the ancients a sign of repentance; for if God sent pestilence or war, they wore sackcloth and threw ashes on their heads. Why that? It was not to nourish an evil sadness, of which Saint Paul speaks (2 Cor. 7:10), which he says is according to the world (we must flee from that), but that was of another

sadness which he says is according to God, when men, after
having known that they are poor sinners, come before their
Judge; that they are there condemned, and they show that
they deserve to be confounded. For he who wears sackcloth,
who has ashes on his head, protests that he no longer has any
basis to glorify himself, that he must keep his mouth closed,
that he is as if he were already buried, as if to say, "I am not
worthy that earth should sustain me, but it ought to be on
top of me; and God should cast me down so low that I should
be as it were trodden under foot."

This is what Job meant by it; seeing that God invited him
to humility, he surely wished to conform; and for this cause
he tore his robe and sheared his hair. Now though we see
(as I have already mentioned) that patience is not without
affliction, that it is very necessary that children of God should
be sad, experiencing their pains; nevertheless they do not
cease to have the virtue of patience when they resist their passions in such a way that they do not fret against God, that
they do not go out of bounds, that they do not kick against
hope, but rather that they give glory to God; as immediately
follows in the text, *"Job threw himself to the ground, he did
it to worship."* Now it is true that this word means "to re-
cline" or "to lie down," but the purpose of humbling oneself
before God and doing him homage is implied. We see some
who throw themselves on the ground, but they continue to
be so angry that, if it were possible, they would ascend above
the clouds to wage war against God. We see those who are
so carried away by spite, but it is because they cannot rush
against God as they wish. Now Job, entirely to the contrary,
throws himself on the ground, in order to worship, indeed
looking to God to humble himself before His high majesty.
For when we experience the hand of God, it is then that we
ought to do Him more homage than ever. It is true that if
God treats us kindly we ought to be moved thereby to come
to Him, as in fact He does invite us. The great goodness He
uses — what is it except that He wishes to draw us to Himself? But since we are so lazy about coming, He has to summon us and show what right He has over us; as when a prince

sees his vassal who is slow to do his duty, he sends him his officer to summon him.   So God, seeing that we do not take into account coming to Him, or perhaps that we do not come with such ardent affection as would be properly required, invites us and calls us.   Job then, knowing the purpose and true use of afflictions, threw himself on the ground, in order to do homage to God, as if to say, "Lord, it is true that until now I have served and honored Thee, while I prospered, and I was in my great triumphs, I delighted in doing Thee service. But what of it?   I did not fully know myself; and now I see my weakness, that we are miserable creatures.   So then, Lord, I come now to do Thee a new homage, when it pleases Thee to afflict me in the world; Lord, I voluntarily yield myself to Thee, and ask not unless it be to render myself subject to Thy hand, whatever may come of it."   So much for the saying "Job threw himself to the ground, having the aim of worshipping God."

We come now to the saying, namely, that Job recognized man's condition.   "Naked came I out of my mother's womb," he says, "and naked I shall return there."   When he says "there," he implies that he is from elsewhere, namely, from the womb of earth which is the mother of all; or perhaps, like a man who has a heart ailment,[3] he does not express all the words, but he speaks half, as we see that those who are extremely sad do not express all their words.   Yet this protestation is clear enough, namely, that Job wishes to say, "Well, I must return to the earth, just as I came out of the womb of my mother."   It is true that this passage could be taken in a double sense: namely, firstly, that it was as a general statement.   Behold men who came naked into the world, and when they return it is likewise; they do not take their riches, nor their honors, nor their pomp, nor their delights; they must go away in decay; the earth must receive them.   But the other exposition is more suitable, that Job applies this to himself, as if he said, "Naked I came out of the womb of my mother; for a time God willed to enrich me, that I had a great quantity of livestock, I had a large family, I had a multitude of chil-

---

3. Fr. *qui a le coeur serré.*

dren; in brief, I was well-adorned with gifts and blessings with which God had enlarged me. Now He wills that I go away entirely naked; He had enriched me with all these things, and He has taken them from me, in order that I may return to my first estate, and that I may now get ready to go to the grave." Now this sentence is good to note. For Job could not better prove his patience than by resolving to be entirely naked, inasmuch as the good pleasure of God was such. Surely men resist in vain; they may grit their teeth, but they must return entirely naked to the grave. Even the pagans have said that death alone shows the littleness of men. Why? For we have a gulf of covetousness, that we would wish to gobble up all the earth; if a man has many riches, vines, meadows, and possessions, it is not enough; God would have to create new worlds, if He wished to satisfy us. But what if we die? Six feet under we decay and are reduced to nothing. So then, death shows what our nature is; nevertheless, we see many who fight against such a necessity; they build worthy sepulchers, they have triumphant funerals; it seems that such people wish to resist God, but they do not succeed at all. Now such is the general condition of men; but as for us, we must suffer patiently to be despoiled when we have been clothed with goods and riches; we must allow (I say) that God should deprive us of everything, and that we should live entirely undressed and naked, and that we should be prepared to return to the grave in such condition. This (I say) is how we shall prove that we are patient. And it is what Job wished to indicate in this passage. Thus however and whenever we shall lack the goods of this world, we shall be hungry and thirsty, we shall be pressed by some afflictions, and we shall not have any help, let us think of our origin, let us look at ourselves and who we are and where we are going. For men abuse the fatherly care of God toward them when He proves to them what must happen to them. Surely we ought to have this very well imprinted on our hearts: namely, that God does not will that we lack anything, that He would not have put us in the world unless He was willing to feed us; yet we must always acknowledge that this comes from outside ourselves, and we should not suppose that we have by our own right what we possess by the gratuitous goodness of our God. If a man should feed me out of his pure liberality and should say to me, "Come every day; you shall have so much wine, so much bread; I wish to entertain you; and it is not that I would oblige myself to you, but I would give you this;" if thereupon I wished to bring suit to collect what I ought to beg for each day, receiving substance from his hand, if I wished to gain an income by what he gives me out of his pure liberality, would it not be too villainous an ingratitude? I would deserve that someone should spit in my face. All the more are we bound to receive the goods which God gives us with all modesty, knowing that He owes us nothing and, because we are poor, we must come to Him to beg every day from His infinite liberality. So then, when we have some need, let us run to Him (as I have said) and acknowledge, "Whence came I out? From the womb of my mother, entirely naked, a poor, miserable creature; I needed help and to be cleansed from the poverty in which I was; I would have utterly perished unless I had been helped from elsewhere. It pleased God, then, to feed and preserve me until now and to do me an infinite number of favors. And howsoever now He may will to afflict me, it is very right that I should bear everything patiently, since it comes from His hand." This is what we have to note from what is shown us by Job, "Naked I came out of my mother's womb, and also naked I shall return to the grave." In summary, we think, when God shall have placed in our hands some goods, that the ownership of them ought to remain ours, that we shall be so accompanied by our riches that they will come with us to the grave, that we ought never to be deprived of them. Now let us not reckon that way; for we deceive ourselves; but on the contrary let us know that if the good pleasure of God is to take away from us the goods with which He may have enlarged us, the next day we must be ready to be deprived of them, that it would do us no harm to be despoiled in a minute of everything that we may have been able to acquire in our whole lifetime.

Besides Job leads us still further, saying, *"God had given it, and He has taken it away; yet blessed be the Name of the Lord."* When he says that God had given it, he shows that it is reasonable that God should dispose of what He has put in our hands, since it is His own; for when God sends us riches, it is not that He gives up His title, that He may no longer have lordship (as He ought to have), since He is Creator of the world. For the word "Creator" implies that He has done everything in such a way that all power and sovereign dominion must remain His. And although men possess each one their portion according as God has enlarged them by the goods of this world, yet He must always remain Lord and master of them. Job, then, acknowledged this, entirely subjected himself to the good pleasure of God; and all of us confess this thing to be more than equitable; however, no one is willing to conform to it. Though this may be, as soon as God shall have let us enjoy for three days some blessing, it seems to us, if He takes it away from us, that He greatly injures us; we shall murmur against Him. And what is to be said of this? Recently I discussed ingratitude, that it seems to us when God has shown Himself one time liberal toward us through His gratuitous goodness that He ought never to fail us, no matter what we do. This then is a statement which is common enough but so poorly practiced that it is clearly seen that it is understood by a very small number. So much more must we think over the meaning of "The Lord had given it, and the Lord has taken it away;" that we may acknowledge what liberty our Lord has to give us enjoyment of His goods and also, when it may please Him, to deprive us of them in a minute. And this is why Saint Paul exhorts us (1 Cor. 7:30) that, inasmuch as the face of this world passes away and all things wear out and vanish, we should possess as though we possessed not, that is to say, we should not bind our courage;[4] as is said in another place (1 Tim. 6:17), "We must not trust in the uncertainty of riches;" we must always be ready to say with Job, "When God will have despoiled us

---

4. Fr. *que nous n'y ayons point nostre courage attaché.* Perhaps he means we should not set our hearts on things.

of what He has given us," or perhaps, "Lord, Thou has exercised Thy right, Thou hadst given it, and Thou hast taken it away when it pleased Thee." Here, then, is the summary of this passage, namely, whenever we think of the goods of this world we should remember that we hold everything from God. And on what condition? It is not by property right, that He should not longer wish any claim over it, and that He should no longer have any mastery over it; but if it pleased him to put it in our hands, it is on the condition that He may take it back when it seems good to Him. Let us acknowledge then, that we are so much more obligated to Him when He shall have caused us to enjoy some benefit, a day, a month, or some space of time, and afterwards, if He despoils us of it, that we should not find it too strange; but that we should run back to that acknowledgment which I have said, "May God always retain such superiority over us that He can dispose of His own as seems good to Him." If it is awful for mortal men to control their wealth as they wish, ought not much more control to be attributed to the living God? Seeing then how God ought to have mastery not only over what we possess but also over our persons and over our children, we ought to humble ourselves before Him by subjecting ourselves entirely to His holy will, without any contradiction. But what do we see? There are very few who do this homage to God. It is true that everyone will surely say that it is God Who has given them all that they possess; but what do they do about it? They claim Him, and raise themselves as it were in defiance of Him. And what is this? I pray you, is it not a mockery? Indeed it is unbearable hypocrisy, when, after having protested that we hold everything from God, we nevertheless are never willing that He should dispose of it, we are not willing that He should change anything, but wish that He would leave us in peace and go away from us, as if we were separated from Him and exempt from His jurisdiction. It is just as if someone said, "Oh, I am content to acknowledge that such a one is my Prince, I shall do Him enough homage and obedience; but He should not enter my house, He should not come to ask for anything, He should not cause me any trouble."

The world could not suffer such villainy. Nevertheless this is how they frolic with God. And what is the meaning of the confession "Let us hold everything to be from Him" while we are not willing that He should touch anything? We see, then, how the world openly mocks God; but we must always follow what is here shown, namely, since God has given us what is in our hands, He may claim it back and take it back when He wills.

Furthermore the final implication is added. "Blessed be *the name of the Lord.*" For by this Job so submits himself to God that He confesses Him to be good and just, although he is harshly afflicted from His hand. I have said that this implies more, inasmuch as one might still be able to attribute to God entirely sovereign power by saying, "Very well, since He has given it, He can surely take it away," but nevertheless he would not confess that God did it justly and reasonably, as there are many who when they are afflicted accuse God of cruelty, or of too great a severity, so that they cannot reserve for Him the right to take back what He has given to them; and they do not consider (as I have said) that they should possess wealth in such a way that they could be stripped of it the next day. There are very few who hold this consideration in such a way that remain peaceable in it and confess that there is nothing better than to be entirely subject to the majesty of God and to recognize that if He let us do according to our desires there would be only confusion; but when He governs us according to His will, it is for our profit and salvation. This is the point of view to which we must come. So, we see now that the sentence implies more when it is said, "Blessed be the name of the Lord." For we must not only split hairs over words,[5] we must consider from what affection this proceeds, and that it is said in truth and without pretense. For how is it possible that we should bless the name of God, except by first of all confessing that He is just. Now he who murmurs against God as if He were cruel and inhuman thereby curses God and as much as is in him rises against Him; he who does not recognize that God is his father and that he is

---

5. Fr. *esplucher les mots,* pick words.

His child, who does not render testimony of His goodness, does not bless God at all. And why not? For those who do not taste the mercy and the grace which God performs toward men when He afflicts them must gnash their teeth, throw and disgorge some venom against Him. To bless, then, the name of God implies that we are well persuaded that He is just and equitable in His nature; and not only this, but that he is good and merciful. This is how we shall be able to bless (according to the example of Job) the name of God: it will be by acknowledging His justice and His equity, and then by acknowledging also His grace and His fatherly goodness toward us.

And this is why the text also adds in conclusion: *In all these things Job sinned not, nor attributed to God anything unreasonable.* Or literally: Job put forward nor imposed upon God nothing which was without reason; and it is a manner of speaking which is very worthy to be observed. Why is it that men fret so when God sends them things entirely contrary to their desire, except that they do not acknowledge that God does everything by reason and that He has just cause? For if we had well-imprinted on our hearts "All that God does is founded in good reason" it is certain that we would be ashamed to chafe so against Him when, I say, we know that He has just occasion to dispose thus of things, as we see. Now, therefore, it is especially said that Job attributed to God nothing without reason, that is to say, that he did not imagine that God did anything which was not just and equitable. So much for one item. But we must note above all the word "in God"[6] or "to God." This implies much, for we do not think that the works of God should be spoken of so abominably as we speak of them. As soon as God does not send what we have desired, we dispute against Him, we bring suit, not that we appear to do this, but our manner shows that this is nevertheless our intent. We consider every blow, "And why has this happened?" But from what spirit[7] is this pronounced? From a poisoned heart; as if we said, "The thing should have been otherwise, I see no reason for this."

6. Fr. *En Dieu.*
7. Fr. *de quel courage.*

Meanwhile God will be condemned among us. This is how men exasperate themselves.[8] And in this what do they do? It is as if they accused God of being a tyrant or a hair-brain who asked only to put everything in confusion. Such horrible blasphemy blows out of the mouths of men. Yet very few think about it. However, the Holy Spirit wished to tell us that, if we wish to render glory to God and to bless His name properly, we must be persuaded that God does nothing without reason. So then, let us not attribute to Him either cruelty or ignorance, as if He did things in spite and unadvisedly, but let us acknowledge that He proceeds in everything and through everything with admirable justice, with goodness and infinite wisdom, so that there is only entire uprightness or equity in all that He does. Now it is true that here is an article to deduce, namely, how Job recognized that God took away from him what had been carried away by robbers; which seems to us very strange; but what we cannot explain this hour we shall reserve until tomorrow. It is enough to have shown that if we are afflicted we must not think that it happens without reason, but God has just cause to do it. And whenever we are tried and anguished let us run back to Him, let us pray to Him that He will give us grace to acknowledge that nothing happens to us in this world except as He disposes; indeed, and to be certain that He disposes in such manner that everything always comes back to our salvation. And when we shall have this knowledge, it will cause us to bear patiently the afflictions which He will send us. It will also be to make us humble ourselves before Him, and that having tasted for ourselves His fatherly goodness, we shall ask only to glorify Him in everything and through everything, as much in affliction as in prosperity.

Now we shall bow before the face of our God.

---

8. Fr. *se iettent hors des gonds,* throw themselves off their hinges.

SERMON 3

Blessed is the Man whom God Corrects*

*Behold, the man whom God corrects is blessed; therefore
refuse not thou the chastisement of the Almighty. It is He
Who makes the wound, and Who binds it up; Who smites,
and Who brings life.* —JOB 5 :17, 18

PREVIOUSLY Eliphaz has declared what the power of God
is, that we may be better prepared to receive the doctrine
which he adds.   For we see why we are not as teachable as we
should be: namely, because we do not sufficiently know the
majesty of God to be touched by fear of Him.   Therefore we
need to know how God governs the world, and to consider
His infinite righteousness, power, and wisdom.   Now if the
wicked are confounded because God shows Himself against
them and so have their mouths stopped, what ought to be our
attitude?   For God should not have to constrain us to do
Him honor; it should be enough that He gives us occasion, and
that He shows how there is just cause for us to do it, and we
should come to it of our own accord.   So, then, let us bear in
mind what has been declared previously: namely, that when
God's judgments are laid before us, it is no matter to laugh
at or to dally with, but it behooves all creatures to tremble at
them.

And now it is said that *the man is blessed whom God
chastises, and that therefore we must not refuse the correct-
tions of the Almighty.*   If a man should tell us that God does
men no wrong when He becomes their judge and uses great
severity and rigor toward them, surely this ought to affect us
sufficiently; but yet we would be as astonished at this doctrine as if a man had hit us on the head with a hammer. What
is to be done, then?   There must be some sugar mixed with

* Sermon 21 in *Calvini Opera, Corpus Reformatorum*, volume 33, pp. 258-270.

it, so that we may taste what is going to be said to us, assuring ourselves that it is profitable for our salvation. So then, after Eliphaz has set forth God's judgments in general, to dispose us to fear Him with all humility; he now shows that God will manifest love toward us, however the world may go; and especially that when He chastises us He never uses such severity toward us that He does not make us feel His goodness and mercy with it, to the intent that we should approach Him and not be dismayed like those who are afraid they are going to be confounded. God, then, means not that His majesty should be so dreadful to us; but His meaning is to draw us to Him, in order that we should love Him not only when He does us good but also when He chastises us for our sins. So, we see in effect what we have to gather from this passage. But it would seem that this sentence is contrary to what is written elsewhere in the Holy Scripture: which is, that all the miseries and calamities which we endure in this earthly life proceed from sin and consequently from God's curse. How can these things agree, that we are blessed when God chastises us, and yet nevertheless that all the evils which come to us from His hand are so many signs of His wrath, and that we have offended Him, and that He curses us? For whence come our happiness and joy, except from God? And on the contrary, when God is against us we see that our life is cursed. Again when we feel that God is angry with us by His punishing us, it would seem that there is no happiness in that. But we have to mark here how Eliphaz has an eye to the intent and end at which God aims when He chastises men. True it is that God well indicates that He abhors sin, and indeed the order which He appointed at the creation of the world is troubled when He handles us not like a father. You see, then, how all the adversities of this life show us some sign of God's curse, in order that thereby we should understand that sin displeases Him, and that He hates and abhors it, and cannot bear it, since He is the fountain of all righteousness. But yet for all this, after God has so declared the hatred which He bears against sin; He will also have us to perceive how He draws, exhorts, and summons us to repentance. And so, does

God afflict us? It is a sign then that He is not willing that we should perish, and that He solicits us to return to Him. For corrections are as testimonies that God is ready to receive us in mercy, if we acknowledge our faults and sincerely ask Him for forgiveness. Seeing how the case stands, we should not think it strange that Eliphaz should say that the man is blessed whom God chastises. But we must bear in mind the two points that I have touched, of which one is that as soon as some evil befalls us the wrath of God must come before our eyes, so that we may understand that He cannot stand sin; and thereupon we must consider the severity of His judgment, so that we may be heartily sorry that we have offended. Behold at what point we ought to begin. And therewithal also let us moreover take hold of God's goodness in not letting us run into perdition without drawing us home again to Himself, and in that His meaning is to bring us back as often as He afflicts us. So you see what we have to conceive of in all our afflictions. But there yet remains one difficult point: for in the meantime we see that afflictions are common to all men. God chastises those to whom He is willing to show mercy; but we see also that He punishes reprobates, and will still let the same turn to their greater damnation. What availed all the rods that Pharaoh felt, except that they made him the more inexcusable, because he continued to be stubborn and incorrigible toward God even to his end? Forasmuch, then, as God afflicts both good and bad, and we see by experience that afflictions are so much fire to further kindle God's wrath against reprobates; it follows thereupon, that God chastises many folks who are not reckoned to be blessed thereby.

Whereupon it behooves us to note that Eliphaz speaks here only of those whom God chastises as His children to their profit, as he declares by that which follows, saying that *God binds up the wounds which He has made,* He bandages them, He puts plasters on them, and He heals the sore. You see Eliphaz restricts this sentence to those in whom God makes His chastisements to turn to true amendment. But this sentence will remain somewhat obscure unless it is explained more at length, so that you may be clearly and firmly persuaded of it. Let us mark how God works toward reprobates. True it is that He exhorts all men to repentance when He chastises them (as we have said) and it would be the same if He woke them up and said, "Know your faults, and continue no longer in them, but return to Me, and I am ready to show you mercy." But yet for all that, it is well known that the said chastisements do not profit all men, and also that He gives not all men the grace to return to Him. For it is not enough for God to strike us with His hand unless He also touches us within by His Holy Spirit. If God did not soften the hardness of our hearts it would happen to us as it did to Pharaoh. For men are like anvils; when they are struck their nature is not changed; for we see how they repulse the blows. Even so, then, until God has touched us to the quick within, it is certain that we shall do nothing but kick against Him and spit out more and more poison; and whenever He chastises us, we shall gnash our teeth at Him, and we shall do nothing else but storm at Him. And in fact the iniquity of men is so wicked, so headstrong, and so desperate that the more God chastises them, the more do they spew out their blasphemies and show themselves to be utterly incorrigible, so that there is no way to bring them back to reason. Let us learn, then, that until God has touched us with His Holy Spirit, it is impossible that His chastisements should serve to bring us back to repentance, but rather they will cause us to grow worse and worse. Yet it cannot be said that God is not righteous in so doing. And why so? For thereby men are convinced, insomuch that if God held them not at bay in that manner by punishing their sins they might plead ignorance, that they never knew it, and that they overshot themselves because God had not invited them to acknowledge their faults. But when they have felt the hand of God, so as they have perceived His judgments in spite of their teeth, and have been as it were summoned, and yet notwithstanding have not only gone onward from evil to worse, but also have been puffed up with open and manifest rebellion against God; hereby we see, that in effect they have their mouth stopped, and that they have not any more to say for themselves. You see then how

God shows His justice as often as He punishes men, notwithstanding that the same is not found to be a correction to their amendment.

Furthermore, when God chastises the reprobates, it is just as if He had already begun to show His wrath upon them, and that the fire of it were already kindled. True it is that they are not utterly consumed for the present time, howbeit they are signs of the horrible vengeance that is prepared for them at the last day. You see that many men are touched with God's hand, who notwithstanding are accursed. For they already begin their hell in this world, according as we have examples in all who change not their wicked life when God sends afflictions upon them, but a man will see them take a corner and stand barking like dogs, and though they are able to do no more, yet they do not cease to show a continual rage. Or else they are like restive horses, as comparison is made in Psalm 32:9, or else they are completely besotted, so that they know not their own harm, I mean, as to consider the hand that strikes, as the Prophet says, "They will cry alas, and they will feel the blows."[1] But what of it? They never think more about God's hand, neither know they how it is that He visits them. We see, then, before our eyes, that many men are the more unhappy for being chastised at God's hand, because they profit not in His school, nor yet receive any benefit from His stripes. But here is mention made particularly of those whom God chastises, touching them with His Holy Spirit. Therefore let us assure ourselves that when God makes us feel His hand, so that we are humbled under the same; He does us a special good turn, and it is a privilege which He gives to none but to His own children. When we feel the corrections which He sends us, and moreover are taught to be displeased with ourselves because of our offenses, to sigh and to groan for them before Him, and to flee to His mercy for refuge; I say, when we have such a feeling of God's chastisements; it is a sign that He has wrought in our hearts by His Holy Spirit. For it is too high a point of wisdom to

---

1. Amos 5:16-20.

grow in the mind of man; it must proceed from the free goodness of our God; the Holy Spirit must first have softened the
said cursed hardness and stubbornness to which we are inclined by nature. Let us understand, then, that this present
text is spoken particularly of God's children, who are not
stubbornly against His hand, but are overpowered and tamed
by His Holy Spirit, in order that they should not strive
against the afflictions which He sends to them. But yet will
this saying seem strange according to the opinion of the flesh.
Why so? Whatever circumstances turn out otherwise than
we would have them, we term "adversities." When we endure any hunger, thirst, cold, or heat, we say that it is so
much evil. Why so? For we wish to have our own appetites
and desires gratified. And in fact this manner of speaking
(to say that the mishaps which God sends upon us are adversities, that is to say things against us) is not without reason. Nevertheless we must understand the purpose of them:
namely, that God's afflicting us is because of our sins. And
therefore let us not be beguiled into flattering ourselves.

Furthermore, I have already told you, not only that it is
needful for us to consider that God's afflicting us is because
He hates sin, and that His summoning us before Him is to
make us feel Him to be our judge; but also that He needed
to reach out His arms to us, and to show us that He is ready
to reconcile Himself to us, when we come to Him with true
repentance. So then, we perceive that those whom God
chastises are blessed, notwithstanding that we flee adversity
as much as we possibly can. And so we shall never be able
to consent to this doctrine to receive it into our hearts until
faith has made us behold the goodness that God uses toward
His servants when He draws them back to Himself. And
that we may the better comprehend this, let us mark what
becomes of men when God leaves them to themselves, and
makes no countenance of cleansing them from their sins. Look
upon a man who is given to evil: for example, let us take a
despiser of God; if God lets him alone and seems not to chastise him, you will see such a one harden himself, and the devil
will carry him still further and further; and therefore it would

have been much better for him if he had been chastised sooner.
And so, the greatest misfortune that can happen to us is when
God lets us welter in our own iniquities; for then we must
needs rot away in them in the end. Truly it were greatly to
be desired that men would come to God of their own accord
without being spurred, and that they would cleave to Him
without any warning given them of their faults, and without
any rebuking of them; this (I say) were a thing greatly to be
wished, yea and moreover, that there were no fault in us, and
that we were as angels, desiring nothing but to yield obedience
to our Creator, and to honor Him and love Him as our Father.
But forasmuch as we are so perverse that we cease not to
offend God, and besides that act like hypocrites before Him,
asking only to hide our faults; and forasmuch as there is so
great pride in us that we would have God to let us alone and
to uphold us in our lusts, and finally would we be His judges
rather than that He should be ours; considering (I say) how
perverse we are, God surely must use some violent remedy to
draw us to Him. For if He should handle us entirely gently,
what would happen? We see this thing partly even in young
children. For if their fathers and mothers do not chastise
them, they send them to the gallows. True it is that they
perceive it not; however, experience shows it, and we have
common proverbs of it, as, "The more that fathers pamper
their children, the more they spoil them;" and mothers do
it still more; for they are fond of flattering them, and in the
meanwhile bring them to naught; herein God shows us as it
were small beams of that thing which is much more in Himself. For if He should handle us mildly, we would be utterly
undone and past recovery. Therefore He must, to show Himself a Father toward us, be rough with us, seeing we are of
so sturdy a nature that if He should deal gently with us, we
would not be able to profit by it. You see how we can understand the truth of this doctrine, that the man is happy whom
God chastises: that is, to wit, by considering what our nature
is, how stubborn it is, how hard it is to be put in order, and
that if God never chastised us, it would not be for our profit;
and therefore that it is needful that He should hold us back

in check, and that He should give us so many lashes with the whip that we would be compelled to consider Him. Then we shall at length come to conclude that the man is blessed whom God chastises; yea, truly if He adds the second grace unto it: that is, to wit, if He makes His rods and His corrections to avail, and causes the Holy Spirit to work in such wise in the heart that a man may no more be hardened to advance himself against God, but may have the care to think about his own sins, and be rightly tamed and humbled. So you see why I said that the greatest benefit which we can have is to be corrected at God's hand, in so much that when we have taken everything into account we shall find that the corrections which He sends us are more useful than the bread we eat. For if we die of hunger, God will have pitied us by taking us out of this world. But if we still live here below and cease not to provoke the wrath of Him Who shows Himself so good and liberal a Father toward us, is it not too shameful an unthankfulness? I pray you, had it not been better that we had been born dead, than that we should so prolong our life to our damnation. But if God goes before us and uses chastisements as preservative medicines, and tarries not till the disease has progressed too far; is it not a great benefit to us, and such a one as we ought to wish for? So then, as often and as long as His corrections are hard and bitter to us and our flesh provokes us to impatience and despair, let us learn to call this lesson to remembrance, that the man is blessed whom God chastises, although our imagination will not admit it; for on the contrary we surmise that nothing is better than to be spared and supported in it. Yet we know by experience that it is not without cause that the Holy Spirit has uttered such a sentence. However, this is not to deny that the corrections which we have to endure are always sour and painful in themselves, according as the Apostle says (Hebrews 12:11); and God also will have us to feel the prickings which give us pain. For if we endured no evil when God corrected us, where would be our obedience? And furthermore, how shall we learn to be displeased with ourselves for our sins? How shall we be afraid of God's judgment, to be tamed aright?

Then it behooves us to be grieved by the evil which God sends us. And although the evil be turned to our benefit, and God does thereby show that He loves us; yet it is needful that there be some pricking and painfulness in it, in order that we may perceive the wrath of God and be displeased with ourselves in our sins. But yet herewithal we must climb higher, and when we shall have learned that our nature is inclined to all evil; yet let us confess ourselves to have need that God should use some sharp punishment to purge us of it, as we see physicians who sometimes use some kind of poison in their medicines, after they see the malady to be great and deeprooted. The physician sees well enough that it is to weaken a poor man and to debilitate his veins and nerves; and especially when no gentler means will serve than the letting of blood, which is as much as drawing the substance out of a man, and yet must he use such violent means to remedy such a malady. Even so must God work in us, although it is an extraordinary means for Him. For when we say we are blessed to be chastised at God's hand, it must lead us to humility, seeing that God cannot procure our salvation except by showing Himself to be against us. Is it not to be said justly that there is a marvelous corruptness in men, so that God cannot be their Savior and Father except by handling them roughly? For His nature is to show Himself gracious and gentle to all His creatures. And He follows the order which He would keep as in respect of Himself; He does nothing else but spread out His goodness upon us in such wise that we should be replenished with His grace to be completely enraptured thereby. But now, if He handles us gently according to His own nature and inclination, we are lost. And therefore He must as it were half way change His mind, that is to say, to show Himself otherwise toward us than He would be. And what is the cause thereof? Our desperate wickedness. And therefore we have good cause here to be confounded with shame, when we see that He must (as you would say) disguise Himself, if He intends that we should not perish. So much for this sentence.

But because we cannot well apply this doctrine to our use without adding what follows, let us join them both together. It is said, *"Refuse not the correction of the Almighty; for He Who has made the wound binds it up,* and puts suitable plasters on it, and after He has sent the malady He heals it." Here we are exhorted not to refuse God's corrections. But the reason is fully given: that is, to wit, because God will give it a good issue. That is wherein consists the happiness which Eliphaz has mentioned. Let us learn here that when God wills to exhort us to patience, He not only tells us that we cannot avoid His hand, that we lose time by rebelling against Him, that in spite of our teeth we must pass that way, and that we cannot withstand necessity; for that would be "patience of Lombard," as they say, when we would so grind our teeth and meanwhile lift up ourselves against God as much as we could, so that we would not be patient except by force. Therefore if we wish to be patient with respect to God we must draw near to Him by another means: that is, to wit, we must finally be comforted, as Saint Paul says in Romans 15:4, where he puts these two things together as inseparable: that is, (1) that to the intent we may have patience in all our adversities, we must taste God's goodness, we receive joy through His grace, and (2) we must assure ourselves that His afflicting us is for our salvation. And this is the thing that is shown us in this passage when it is said, "Refuse not the correction of the Almighty; for it is He who is the Physician for all your wounds, it is He who will send you healing of all your diseases." God then shows us here that His meaning is not that men's subjecting themselves to Him should be by saying, "Since we cannot do otherwise, God must be Master, for we cannot exempt ourselves from His dominion." It is not a matter of coming to Him in such a manner, but our Lord says, "No; be patient, humble yourselves under Me, and take warning by My judgments that you murmur not against Me, nor set yourselves in defiance; otherwise you will have to be beaten down by My hand, indeed, in such a way that you will be entirely crushed. But if in all humility you acknowledge your faults and you come to me to ask pardon for them, you will experience such alleviation of your evils that in the midst of the greatest afflictions you will have occasion to give Me thanks." This, I say, is what we must meditate on in order to have real patience. Now, then, seeing that by nature we are rebels against God, that as soon as He touches us with His little finger we are offended, seeing also that we have such pride in us that it seems to us that God does us wrong when He chastises us; when, I say, we have these two such great vices it is very difficult to purge us of them. All the more ought we to meditate on the doctrine which is here shown us: namely, that our God by afflicting us wills to bring us under Himself, yea, for our benefit and for our salvation.

Besides we must surely note the promise which is here put, namely: *that God will heal the wounds which He has made.* It is true that this does not pertain to all, but it pertains to those who receive corrections graciously.[2] However, let us note that God wills that all should be admonished to return to Him, when they see that He shows them such gentleness.[3] But what do we see? There are many who do not taste what is herein contained; and that is also why we see such impatience, such murmuring, such blasphemy against God. Corrections are everywhere; but where is the repentance? There is none; but we see that it seems that men have conspired to resist God to the limit. Why is that? It is since there are very few who understand this doctrine, who receive this promise, saying, "Lord, it is Thy office to bind up the wounds which Thou mayest have made, and to give health to the sick." And yet let us well retain this lesson, indeed, seeing that it is so often reiterated. For it is not only in this passage that the Holy Spirit speaks thus, but we see that it is said, "The Lord afflicts us, and on the third day He heals us,"[4] so that if He has given us a crack with the switch, we should not therefore think that He is not willing to be propitious toward us when we come to Him. When such exhortations are made to us by

---

2. Fr. *benignement,* benignly.
3. Fr. *douceur,* sweetness
4. Hosea 6:1, 2.

the Prophets, it is as much as if God said to us, "It is true that I have afflicted you for some time, but My mercy will pursue you, it will be perpetual; that if you have felt some wrath, some sign of anger like a father enraged against his children, it was not because I have hated you, but you had to be made to experience the result of your sins and to acknowledge that I detest them; yet in the end you will experience that I ask only to heal the wounds and to give healing for the malady which I have sent." Now it is true that at first glance it does not yet seem suitable that God should take pleasure in healing wounds after He has cut us. Why would He not rather leave us in peace and in prosperity? But I have already shown that the sores which God makes are to us so many doses of medicine. Double grace, then, is here shown to us. (1) One follows from the fact that when God afflicts us He procures our benefit, He draws us to repentance, He purges us of our sins, and even of those which are unknown to us. For God is not satisfied merely to remedy evils which are already present, but He considers that much seed of disease is hidden in us. He anticipates, then, He puts it in order, it is a special blessing which He does when it seems as if He comes against us, sword unsheathed, to show us some sign of anger; whenever He does this, He shows that He is our Physician. That is the first grace. (2) Then, this is the second grace which is also clearly shown to us: namely, that God binds up the wounds which He has made and heals them. It is what I have already alleged from St. Paul (I Corinthians 10:13), that He does not allow us to be tempted beyond what we can bear, but He brings good issue out of all our troubles.

So then, although corrections are useful for us, even necessary, and though God must invite us in various ways to return to Him, yet He spares us, and considers not only what our sins require but what we are able to bear. And that is why it says that He will chastise us by the hands of men, that His wrath is not as great as His power. For what would it be like if God displayed His arm against us? Alas, what creature could subsist before Him? Indeed, He would need

only to show His angry face, and all the world would perish;
and although He does not do this, if He merely withdraws
His Spirit, everything must expire, as is said in Psalm 104:29.
But He treats us kindly,[5] and meanwhile He also withdraws
His hand when He sees that we are so crushed, and that we
are bent under the burden; He spares us, that is, provided
that we are of a humble spirit and in the right disposition.
For we know what He declares in His Law, that if we come
charging against Him, He will come likewise toward us, as
is said also in Psalm 18:27, "I shall be harsh with those who
are harsh." In vain do we think we are going to get anywhere with God by obstinate, rebellious, or furious means.
For He will be perverse with the perverse, that is to say, He
will be fierce when men employ such obstinate malice against
Him, and they must be completely crushed. But if we have
a good disposition[6] to subject ourselves to the strong hand of
God, it is certain that we shall always find in Him what is
here said. Let us follow, then, what is declared to us by the
Apostle (1 Peter 5:6). "Humble yourselves," he says, "under the mighty hand of God;" for whoever bows his head,
whoever bends his knees before God to do Him homage; if
he falls, he will feel the hand of God raising Him; but he who
raises himself against God must feel that His hand is against
him. Do we wish, then, to feel the hand of God under us to
assist us? Let us humble ourselves; but whoever shall raise
himself will of necessity come to bruise himself against the
hand of God, and to feel a bolt of lightning to cast him into
the abyss. So, let us well remember this teaching when it is
said, "Refuse not the corrections of the Almighty." When
we have caught the meaning of the goodness of God, when we
have known His fatherly love, it will sweeten for us afflictions
which otherwise would seem to us harsh and bitter. However, each one of us must apply this teaching to his own use.
For it will be very easy for us to say, "Blessed be God who so
chastises men," and yet when we are chastised He will not be

5. Fr. *Humainement,* humanely.
6. Fr. *une esprit debonnaire.*

praised by us, but rather we shall murmur against Him. Now we must never do such a thing; but when we are privately afflicted, let us receive corrections patiently, and let us take for ourselves the exhortations which we know so well how to give to others. Let us acknowledge, then, that there is not one of us who does not have many vices in himself, and that these are as many maladies which God cannot heal except by means of the afflictions which He sends us. It is true that if He willed to use absolute power, He might well do this otherwise; but we are not speaking of the power of God; we are discussing only the means that He wills to hold out to us. Since, then, God wills the arrangement to remedy our vices by afflicting us, each one must study for himself this lesson, in order that all of us may confess with David, "Lord, it has been for my profit that Thou hast humbled me." (Psalm 119:67). David does not there speak of others, as if to say, "Lord, thou hast done well to chastise those who have transgressed," but he begins with himself. That is how we must do it. And it is what is here shown us by the Holy Spirit, "Behold, blessed is the man whom God chastises." And why? For men cannot allow themselves to be governed by God; they strive and always remain incorrigible; wherefore it is needful and profitable for them that God should chastise them. Now, since we see today the hand of God raised, both in general and in particular; we ought to be so much more affected by this teaching. Such preposterous things are seen. So, ought we to be astonished if God should show such severity? Yet it is certain that He would spare us much if He did it. It is true that apparently He does not punish the wicked as He does us, although they are rebellious and obstinate as could be, and, no matter how they are admonished, they are in no wise willing to conform to God. But what of it? He warns them by the afflictions which He puts before their eyes in other persons, and indeed by these sometimes He makes them feel it in their own selves; and He will condemn their insubordination, inasmuch as they remain so rebellious and obstinate. Now on our part, let us pray to Him that He may not allow us to be so hardened, but that as soon as He will show us signs of His wrath He may so work in us by His Holy Spirit that He may soften the hardness of our hearts, in order to give place to His grace, when He will have received us into mercy, as we have need of it, and as we can perceive it if we are not too stupid.

Now we shall bow in humble reverence before the face of our God.

SERMON 4

How Shall Man be Justified in God's Sight?*

Job, answering, said, "I know it is true that man shall not be justified in God's sight. If he wishes to debate with Him, he shall not prove to Him one point out of a thousand. He is wise in heart, robust in strength. And who shall be opposed to Him and have peace? He transmutes mountains and they do not even feel it when He overturns them in His wrath. He removes the earth from her place, and her pillars tremble."
—JOB 9:1-6

ALTHOUGH men were compelled to confess that God is just and that there is nothing to find fault with in Him, yet their passions are so excessive,[1] that, if some one is afflicted, not only will murmurings against God be heard, but with throat wide open those thus pressed will blaspheme against God. Meanwhile they will not cease to be tormented, but it seems to them that they are in some manner revenged when they can thus defy Him with Whom they have to do. All the more needful is it for us to have premeditated upon the justice of God in the long run,[2] in order that when He afflicts us we may always remain humble enough to acknowlege what He is: namely, just and blameless.[3] However, it is not yet all, to confess in general that there is only equity in God. For we have previously seen that Bildad, supporting the argument that God is just, poorly applied it when he stopped with the statement that God punishes men according as they have deserved. Now (as we have already seen) this is not an equitable rule. God sometimes spares and supports the wicked; sometimes He chastises those whom He loves and

---

* Sermon 33 in *Calvini Opera, Corpus Reformatorum*, volume 33, pp. 406-418.
1. Lat. *ex orbita*, off the track.
2. Fr. *de longue main*.
3. Fr. *irreprehensible*.

treats them with much greater severity than those who are entirely incorrigible. If, then, we wished to reckon that God chastises men, each one as he has deserved, what would be the result? Anyone who tries to maintain His justice by this means proceeds poorly. It is, then, a vice when anyone wishes to measure the justice of God, as if to say, "He afflicts no one except for his faults; indeed, both in such quality and in such quantity as each one has offended Him, God must return to him in this world." Then the justice of God is not properly understood. For this reason, Job now gives a much better treatment of the justice of God and how it must be acknowledged than Bildad has just done. It is that, without looking at one sin or another but by taking men as they are from the wombs of their mothers, yet the entire world must be condemned, and it must be acknowledged that, although afflictions may seem harsh, yet no one can argue against God. Let us note well, then, that these are two different manners of speaking. One says, "God is just; for He punishes men according to what they have deserved." The other says, "God is just; for, irrespective of how He treats men, we must keep our mouths shut and not murmur against Him, because we can gain nothing by it." If we see a wicked man whom God afflicts (just as we have discussed before), then God wills that His particular judgment should be recognized, in order that someone may be warned by it. And the Holy Scripture speaks of it in this manner. We see that God will punish adulteries,[4] He will punish cruelties. He will punish perjuries. He will punish blasphemies, and like things; yes, either upon persons, or else upon nations, upon some place which has been addicted to some crime; God puts down His hand there, where He shows us a mirror to instruct us; as Saint Paul speaks of us, when he says, "God judges sinners,"[5] in order that each one may be on guard. For if He has punished rebellions against His Word, it is to make us walk in fear; when He has punished wicked greed,[6] it is in order that we

---

4. Fr. *les pailliardises*, an old generic word for sexual sins.
5. See Romans 2 and 2 Thessalonians 1.
6. Fr. *cupidités*.

may be held tightly in check; when He has punished adulteries,[4] it is in order that we may walk in all purity both of body and of soul. This, then, is surely how God wills that His judgments, when they are manifested, should be regarded and contemplated. Sometimes one may well say, "God is just. And why? For He has punished such a one, indeed, since he was a man of bad and dissolute life. He has exercised His vengeance upon such a country. And why? It was full of every infection and stinking odor." We can well speak thus, and we ought to do it; but not always. For as we have already mentioned, it is not a universal rule. What, then, must we do? We must come to the higher consideration that God is always just, irrespective of how He may treat men. Now this is very worthy of being noted; for today we see beasts, who always imagine that they are subtle teachers.[7] When they support the justice of God according to their fanciful interpretations, they wish that God should be accounted just. And why? Because (as we have already said) He treats men according to the demerits of each one. And to do this they must attribute to men free will; election by God must be ruined and annihilated. For they find it very strange to say that God elects those whom it pleases Him, and that He calls them to salvation by His free goodness, and that others are reprobated by Him. And that is why these troublemakers[8] who pretend to be great scholars upset the first foundations of our faith to prove the justice of God, indeed, to their fancy. And why do they do it? They cannot climb high enough to acknowledge that God is always just by comparison with men, however just they may be. It is true that we must watch the other extreme, which is vicious. For we shall see that those who are of a life as infamous as could be, if they are not discovered in their baseness,[9] will say, "Oh, as for me, I am a good man (yes, with respect to the world), but I confess that everyone is a sinner before God." They cover themselves with this common cloak. Look at an adulterer who

---

7. Fr. *docteurs*.
8. Fr. *belistres*.
9 Lat. *turpitudo*.

will have haunted the border for ten years; look at a blasphemer who ceases not to curse and swear, defying God; look at a nasty despiser of God and of all religion; look at a debauchee, a man without conscience who asks only to gratify his desire, without faith, without loyalty; such rascals[10] will say that it is true that they are sinners before God; for no one is just before Him. Thereby they will excuse their faults which are as enormous as could be, and they will hide under the cloak of human weakness; and they will say that there is no man who could be equal to God. It seems to them that they have done much by passing off such a confession. Now I have already shown that we must have both of these two articles. One is that in general we acknowledge that God is just in regard to all the world, and that men, however brilliant they may be, must not argue and debate with God, from which process no good can come; but both great and small must all be confounded. That is one item. The second is, let each one look at himself in particular, and let each one groan for his faults, and let each one detest them and condemn them. Whereupon, let us also learn the vengeances and punishments which God sends upon sins, in order to know how we may profit by it. If we are beaten by His rods, let each one say, "It is entirely right; I certainly deserved it." If God instructs us at the expense of another by correcting others before our eyes, it ought to affect us. Let us apply such examples to our instruction, in order to forestall God's being compelled to rush upon us, since we have profited by the chastisements which He has shown us in the persons of others. These, then, are the two articles which we have to note and to practice.

Let us come now to explain what is here said by Job. "I know," he says, "It is true that man shall not be justified with God." Thus it stands; but the word "with" is equivalent to "in the sight of God."[11] Now, when properly understood, this is a teaching of great weight. Why do men justify themselves so boldly? That is to say, they presume upon themselves, they are caught, and they are full of pride. What is

---

10. Fr. *canailles*, nearly calling persons "dogs" without actually doing so.
11. Fr. *envers Dieu*, toward God.

the cause of this, unless it is that they confine their attention to comparing themselves with their neighbors here below? This, then, is what we run back to. And that is why Saint Paul brings us back to the great Judge: "Each one shall bear his own burden,"[12] as if he said, "My friends, it is a mistake to make such comparisons." For instance: "I see that others live no better than I; and I have vices, everyone else has them." That is why it is, then, that men do not condemn themselves as they ought, but rather they flatter themselves in justifying themselves. But here it is especially said that with God man shall not be justified. What must we do, then? Let us learn that whenever our sins are spoken of and proposed to us, we must not keep our eyes focused here below, but we must consider the judgment-seat of our Lord Jesus Christ, where we shall have to give an accounting; we must acknowledge the incomprehensible majesty of God. Let each one, then, think of that, and then let us all wake up, to withdraw from our follies, that we may no longer have these vain imaginings and dreams by which sinners are put to sleep. If this had been observed, today there would not be the debates in christendom concerning the justice of faith. The Papists cannot be persuaded of what we say, that we are justified by the pure grace of God in our Lord Jesus Christ. And why not? "And what would become of merits," they say, "and of the good works of which the salvation of men consists?" And why is it that the Papists stop and get drunk on their merits, unless it be that they do not consider God? They dispute about them in their schools: "Behold the good works which merit recompense and salary, just as bad works deserve punishment; for these are opposite things. If the sins of men deserve to be punished, it must be that there is some reward for their virtues; for the justice of God would not be equitable, at least so it seems to us, and all argument about it would thus be reduced to shadow-boxing." But here is where the Papists are asleep in this dispute; for meanwhile God on His part does not cease to judge, and not according to their laws, but according to His majesty: that is to say, He will find in

12. Galatians 6:5.

men what we cannot perceive there. Now if our virtues were truly divine, that is to say, if they could suffice before God; that would be something. But what are they? Properly understood, they are only smoke; if they did come before God, they would have to be put down. Let us remember well, then, what is here said, that man will not be justified in the sight of God.[11] By which we are admonished that whenever we speak of our sins we must not stop here below, but rather each one must appear before God, that we may know what a Judge he is. For as soon as we wish to plead against Him we must be confounded and, as it were, cast down into hell.

Now Job adds furthermore, *"If man wishes to debate with God, he shall not answer Him one item out of a thousand."* It is true that this could be ascribed to God; if we have pleaded well, if we are able to conduct a long trial consisting of a thousand items, God will not stoop to open His mouth to answer such a thing. And this is very true; for all our pretended plausibility for justifying ourselves may well be convincing before men, because they cannot see as clearly as the situation requires; but when we approach God, all that goes away into nothingness. Let us not think, then, that God is impressed by our long and great trials, while we foam at the mouth, trying to excuse ourselves, and to commend our virtues, on account of which it seems that God ought to be, as it were, vanquished by us. Indeed, but meanwhile He does only laugh and mock all the fanfare that men bring forth; it is nothing. See, then, a good and holy sentence, that God will not answer a single charge when we shall have alleged a thousand. The reason? It is inasmuch as they are neither set down in God's ledger nor receipted by Him. Before men a thousand charges would certainly be taken into account. But before God? God will not be astonished in the least by them. However, the natural sense of this passage is that we shall be so impeded when we come before God (that is, in combat against Him) that we shall not be able to answer a single charge out of a thousand which He will have made against us. It is true that we are so weighed down in the first place, before having unsheathed our sword (as they say) to make

war against God. And we see that. I pray you, shall we not
have great difficulty in attacking a mortal man, or a creature
who is nothing compared to the living God? If we wish to
wage war against someone, we think, "Has he the means to
avenge himself? How shall we come out in the end?" These
thoughts can turn us to anger and despair. We raise many
questions about the matter of pleading against men; and if
we wish to strike against God, we make a terrible blunder.
We see, then, by this what rage there is in men, indeed, devilish rage, to so attack God; but if we do it, we shall know by
experience that we get the worst of the rub and that such a
Master does not play with us. This, then, is what Job here
shows. For he sets down such audacity as we see in men; and
then on the other hand, he sets down the trouble they have
when God makes them feel that He is just and that He confounds them. Let us note well, then, that men wish to plead
and debate against God, as we see; however, after they have
entered into combat, they must remain crushed thereby; and
God will then make them feel that they must remain confounded despite their teeth. This is very necessary; for I
have already shown that the foolish presumption by which
men are deluded proceeds from the fact that they do not consider God; but they state their case. "And indeed, I am no
worse than others, and then, if I have vices, there are virtues
which compensate." Men, then, sleep so, since they did not
acknowledge what the majesty of God is and they have not
a living apprehension of it to be humbled under it. Since it is
so, let us note well what is here said: namely, that men wish
to plead and debate against God. And why that? For we are
so blinded that we cannot look to ourselves, saying, "How
now? Look at God who can swallow us up and cast us down
to the lowest depths of hell; and yet we come to address ourselves against him?" If anyone speaks to us about pleading
against God, nature itself teaches us that we ought to hold
this in horror; I say the most wicked. We shall see pleasure-
mad people[13] who have neither conscience nor religion; yet

13. Fr. *gaudisseurs*.

there remains some feeling of nature engraved in them, so that they are astonished and ashamed when it is said to them, "Do you wish to plead against God?" However, those who seem to be both good and modest will bring suit, in such a way that there is no one who does not act like an escaped horse[14] by contesting against God. We see that even the Prophets have been assailed by such a temptation. It is true that they resisted it as was proper; but yet the apprehension that they were sometimes angry to see such strange judgments of God did not in anywise trouble them, and their reason carried them away, as it were.

Since it is so, then, that we are so inclined to plead against God, all the better ought this doctrine to be imprinted on our memory: namely, that we should contain ourselves when we are tempted to debate so against God, knowing well that we can gain nothing by it, whatever we may be able to do. Now, when we have been warned of this, we shall not be too much scandalized, seeing that there are many who thus throw themselves off their hinges. For this scandal troubles the weak. We should surely wish that each one of us confessed that God is just, and that His mercy fills the whole world, and therefore we must only glorify Him; but when there are wicked ones who provoke God, others blaspheme against Him, and no one dares open his mouth to blame or rebuke them, since they are in fashion and triumph according to the world; seeing this, the weak are troubled, and it seems to them that the power and justice of God are so far diminished that they cannot render to Him the glory which belongs to Him. Now we see that it is quasi-natural for men to plead so against God; and although it is a monstrous thing, and though we ought to hold it in great detestation, yet such a vice is common. Since it is so, let us not be too much troubled by it when it happens. This is what we have to remember. Now we must note well what is here added as the second article: namely, that if God makes a thousand charges against us, we shall hardly be able to answer a single one. Here we are admonished that when

---

14. Fr. *le cheval eschappé*, a common idiom for "an ungovernable person."

we shall have closely analyzed[15] all our vices, we shall not
have acknowledged the hundredth part, not one in a thousand.
It is true that if men well examine themselves without hypocrisy, they must find themselves wrapped in so much evil that
they are ashamed of themselves and that they are completely
beaten down; especially ourselves. For if one chose those
who are the most holy, even they must step into rank with
David, who confessed that no one could come to true knowledge of his sins (Psalm 19:12).[16] But if the most holy, who
seem like angels, are completely confounded in their sins, since
they are infinite in number; I pray you, what of the common
people? For even though we may have made much progress
in holiness, yet we are very far from those of whom I speak.
If, then, men sincerely examine their lives, they will find such
a depth of sins that they will be completely disheartened. But
what then? Still we have not knowledge of one one-hundredth
of what is required. And why? Behold David, who took
the examination of looking at his faults, cries, "Who can know
his sins?"[17] He confesses, then, that he knew a vast number; and then he adds, "Lord, purge me of my hidden faults."
And why does he say that? Why does he call faults hidden?
For our sins must be known, or we could not confess them as
sins. The answer is that David well knew that God sees more
clearly than we do. And so, when our conscience reproves us,
what will be the judgment of God? Behold, then, the order
that we have to keep: it is that each one has to enter into himself, and closely analyze his vices, as far as he shall be able
to come to the knowledge of them. Have we analyzed ourselves? Well, there is our conscience which is judge; and
what a judge it is! It is true that it is a judge which it is well
to fear. But does not God see much more clearly than a mortal man? My conscience will convict me of a thousand sins;
and if God enters into account with me, there will be found
many more.

15. Fr. *bien espluche,* plucked clean (as the feathers of a bird).
16. David did not pray to be kept from committing all secret sins, but
only to be cleansed from their power. He prayed to be kept from committing rebellious, deliberate sins, and from the unpardonable sin.
17. Fr. *qui cognoistra,* who shall know?

So then, we surely have to weigh what is here said: namely, that of a thousand points we shall hardly be able to answer to God for a single one; that if we have known one fault in us, God surely goes far beyond; for He sees those that are hidden to us. Now then, let us learn, following what has been said, to so think of our faults that we may be entirely persuaded that God will not be satisfied with what we are able to acknowledge; but He will wish to judge according to what He saw and knew, and not according to what we shall be able to find; for we pass over the live coal (as they say); but God strikes down to the bottom; to Him belongs the office of searching the hearts, as He attributes to Himself in the Scripture. And besides we do not distinguish between vices and virtues so well as we ought. This, then, must be reserved to Him. And do we not distinguish? If we wish to judge well and rightly all our works, we must recognize what perfection is. For without perfection there is nothing good before God; that is to say, there is only stink. And who deserves to be approved by God, unless perfection is declared? Now how shall we recognize what perfection is, seeing that our sight is so dimmed, seeing that we do not see except, as it were, by imperfect light?[18] For although God may shine upon us, we nevertheless have not such pure and clear sight that we could use the brightness He may show us. It is true that the Word of God enters the lowest depths of our hearts, that it penetrates bone and marrow and all that there is. It is true that it is a burning lamp; it is true that Jesus Christ is called Sun, and that He shines everywhere; but we do not cease to have our vision distorted, nevertheless. It is very necessary, then, that we know what perfection is. Now by this we are admonished that when we find things good and perceive no vice, the vice does not cease to be there nevertheless, because we do not recognize the perfection which God demands. Briefly, God alone knows what perfection or integrity is. And why? It is in Him, He knows it, and we are too feeble to arrive at it. That is why it is said that what we do will be in vain; yet we shall not be able to answer Him a single point when

---

18. Fr. à demi jour.

He will have proposed and set before us a thousand. Now I have already mentioned that men are admonished that if they wish to plead against God they will always find themselves confounded, to their perdition; but it will be too late. And yet this warning is very useful to us. The reason? In order that before the blow, each one may retain himself in sobriety and modesty, saying, "Alas! What use is it to plead against our God? Do we think we shall win our case? On the contrary, God will cast us down." And for each one to condemn himself is the only means of being absolved by Him. But if we go at it heedlessly, God will punish us for such pride. May be at first He will not show us our confusion; but yet we shall finally be so wrapped in it that we shall not be able to get out of it.

Behold, then, how God puts into a labyrinth all presumptuous persons who attack Him, and who undertake the fight spoken of here. While it is true that God may well do to some so that He will corner them[19] and that they will finally amend their ways; yet we must not therefore assume that He always works in the same fashion. We see some who are full of pride, self-righteous, and they wish to obligate God to them; very well, God checkmates them, and tames them, He puts them in extreme confusion and He draws them out of it again. We shall surely see that God does not always work along the same track. Yet we must always listen to what the Scripture says to us, that is, that God displays His hand against the proud to cast them down. And this is how He proceeds. I say that hypocrites are so inflated with pride and presumption that they surely think that their virtues merit being received, indeed, and of their getting salary and payment. Well, they please themselves in that opinion for a time, and God leaves them there; Satan, on the other hand, coaxes and wheedles them and gets them bound tighter and tighter; they admire their feathers like peacocks, saying, "I have done this and that," and it surely seems to them that God ought to be satisfied with them. However, after they are very pleased with themselves and all their virtues, if God brings them to account

---

19. Fr. *il les mattera*, He will checkmate them, as in chess.

and He puts forward that everything they think is virtue is only vice, indeed, only stink and abomination before Him; then, they find themselves confounded, and justly, in a way that, when they will have deceived not only the world but also themselves, confiding in what had beautiful show and appearance outside; what is said in St. Luke 16:15 will have to be manifested every time: namely, that which is esteemed high and excellent among men is only villainy in the sight of God. Let us guard well, then, against raising ourselves to the point of fighting against God and bringing suit to justify ourselves. For otherwise God will have to confound us, and so hurl Himself against us that we shall be oppressed and crushed by a thousand crimes, and we shall not be able to answer a single charge; when we shall be accused of a thousand mortal sins, that is to say, of an infinite number, if we wish to defend ourselves against a single charge, our case will be dismissed for lack of evidence.[20] Let us guard, I say against coming into such a position. Now, in order that we may be so much more affected, it is said, *"God is wise in heart, and He is robust in strength."* This doctrine has already been discussed; but it is not without cause that it is here spoken of once again; for it is a lesson upon which we ought to meditate each day. I have already said that men deceive themselves and are carried away in their frivolous imaginations, since they do not think of God; but they confide in themselves.[21] It is an evil.

Now let us go further. If men thought of God, would they not be touched in a lively way to acknowledge Him according as He declares Himself to them? Would they not be moved by such fear and reverence that they would glorify Him as He deserves? But they do not do it. The reason? It is that they do not understand what God is like. Well, we surely say, "God, God;" that trots out of our mouths; however, His infinite majesty is not known by experience; everything that is in God as we see Him is like something dead. In fact, it is seen by the blasphemies, perjuries, and like things. If men were in anywise affected by the majesty of God, would

---

20. Fr. *nous en serons deboutez,* the judge will nonsuit us.
21. Fr. *ils s'appuyent sur eux mesmes,* they lean upon themselves.

we hear a thing so holy and so sacred thus torn to bits.   If
men are angry, they have to compare it to God, as if He were
their valet; as if a master, when he is enraged, will (if he is
giddy) punch his valet; or a hairbrained husband, his wife:
or perhaps a horse, if he angers his master.   So we do to God.
When we see men throw all their anger at Him as if God were
their inferior, must we not say that we are quite besotted?
And indeed, we do not have to be angry to act that way.   For
we see that dogs[22] have no scruple against slashing to bits the
name of God.   And although there may be no occasion to
incite them to do it, yet they do not cease to all intents and
purposes to blaspheme, which is something monstrous and
against nature.   It is, then, a sure sign that the majesty of
God is unknown to us, although the word may fly easily
enough out of our mouth.   There are perjuries as well.   Today it is horrible that one cannot draw out a single word of
truth without some ceremony to induce those who are called
upon for testimony to refrain from perjuries; of all who will
be examined, hardly one in ten is found speaking the truth.
In fact, they have a common proverb among them, that they
have won their case when there are no witnesses; that is to
say, when there is no one who dares to speak the truth.   And
that is how they defy God.   And, I pray you, what is the good
of the Holy Scripture, all religion, and things as sacred as
we have today, with respect to them?   Men ought to be
restrained in fear by them; as it is said that the true mark of
a child of God is that he trembles under His Word.   Now we
see that God is talked, chatted, and babbled about enough,
and all the secrets of His majesty are indeed, as it were,
laughed over; are not these infallible arguments that we do
not know what God is, although His name is in everyone's
mouth?

Let us note well, then, that what is here added is not a
superfluous point: namely, *God is wise in heart and robust
in strength.*   Now it is true these words do not seem to have
all possible vehemence; but if they are well explained, they

---

22. Here Calvin actually calls such persons "dogs", as does the Scripture,
i.e. Matthew 7:6, Philippians 3:2, Revelation 22:15.

are calculated to make us pull in our horns.   For when it is said that *God is wise in heart,* it is not human wisdom nor anything comprehensible to our senses.   When it is said that *He is robust,* it is not only robust as if He were a giant or like a mountain; but we must so glorify Him that we may know that there is neither like power, nor force, nor strength in all that we see in creatures; that it does not partake at all of anything we can see here below; but we must seek all force and strength in God alone.   That is what this word means. True it is that it cannot be dispatched now as it deserves; but we had to mention it in order to see the procedure that Job followed here, or rather the Holy Spirit Who speaks by his mouth, in order to show ourselves what the justice of God is. Do we really wish, then, to know what we are?   We must accept this general conclusion, that when no open sins are found in us, when our life is not dissolute, when we have walked honestly and above reproach in the sight of men; that is not all.   Why not?   Such as all creatures are, God could condemn them, and He would remain just; and if we attempt to reply against Him, it is true that according to our fancy we could surely find things to say for some time, and God may allow it, and, indeed, not resist us at first; but yet in the end we must bow our heads to receive sentence of condemnation; and when men have applauded us, indeed, when they have absolved us, we shall not cease to be condemned and to remain confounded when we come before this great Judge. For He surely sees more clearly and more sharply than all the men in the world.   And so, let us know that there is no other means to obtain grace before God, and to cause our sins to be covered, indeed, after having confessed freely that there is only every odor and infection in us, except that we have our refuge in our Lord Jesus Christ.   For in Him we find full and perfect justice, and virtue by which we shall be acceptable to God and we shall find Him propitious toward us.

Now we shall bow in humble reverence before the face of our God.

SERMON 5

Though He Slay Me, Yet Will I Trust in Him*

*Does not His majesty astonish you? Does not the fear of Him fall upon you? Your memoir is like ashes, and your bodies like bodies of clay. Hold your tongues in my presence, and let me speak, and let happen to me what may. Wherefore should I take my flesh in my teeth, and put my soul into my hands? Though He slay me, yet will I trust in Him; nevertheless I will argue my ways before His face.—*JOB 13:11-15

WE HAVE to pursue the statement that we began yesterday: which is, that the Scripture shows us many things which are beyond our understanding. For when a man speaks to us after that manner concerning God, there is such scornfulness in us that it seems to us that we are not bound to perceive anything which we do not find good. Hereupon there have been some who wish to play wise men by disguising things in order to please everyone; like the two examples we alleged yesterday. The one concerns free-will. For behold what the Scripture tells us: namely, that men can do no good at all, but are held entirely captive to evil. It seems to many that, if this were so, sinners would be excused and acquitted, since they have no power in them to do good. Now there are forgers of lies who row between two streams and say that it is better, then, to grant men some freewill, in order that they may be blameworthy when they have done amiss. Indeed, but the Scripture speaks otherwise. Why is it that they flee to such a subterfuge, unless it be that they tell lies in behalf of God? Has He need of their lies? Must His truth be maintained by that means? As much is to be said of those who darken the grace of God in that He has elected those who seemed good to Him before the creation of the world, and in that He rejected the others. And how is that? It is a very sore point, and we see that many men have stumbled upon

---

* Sermon 50 in *Calvini Opera, Corpus Reformatorum,* volume 33, pp. 617-630.

it. You see what these sages allege and how they contrive, saying, "Indeed, we say that God has elected those who ought to be saved. And why is that? Because He foresaw that they would be well disposed thereunto. Knowing, then, that they were ready to receive His grace, He marked them out, that He might say, 'These are mine.' " But does the Scripture speak so? No, it speaks entirely to the contrary. But it says that God finds us all alike, and that it is He Who distinguishes us; and one is no better than his companion, unless God of His infinite goodness draws us out of death.

You see, then, the pure and simple doctrine of the Holy Scripture. Why do men come to smear it? As I told you, it is because they think they excuse God by it. Indeed? Must God borrow our lies, and must we be His attorneys full of quibblings, as we see that evil cases need to be colored and completely disguised in order to so blear the eyes of the judges that they may know nothing? Is it needful to work after this manner in behalf of God? Let us note well, then, how it is said here that when we shall have applied all of our wit to disguise what men would otherwise reject and condemn, in order that no article in all the Holy Scripture should be disliked, God will condemn us for such sophistical inventions. This extends yet further. For we see how many there are at this day who wish to concoct a mean between us and the Papists. "Indeed," they say, "it is true that there are many abuses in the Church (they confess all) and things are too heavy and unbearable; it is needful to have some reformation." They will confess this. But meanwhile, if they are asked what it is that we preach, they find not the slightest fault with our doctrine, but that we follow the pure simplicity of the Gospel without adding or diminishing; notwithstanding, they see that it is rejected by many, and that men cannot agree on it, and that it would be a very difficult thing to reform all things rigorously, and men are not so easy to handle. Hereupon they find and invent a lie, saying, "It would be better, then, to accept a middle position, at least temporarily." Why do they bring us this deviltry, unless they who have contrived it wish to play alchemists and to find some quintessence, and I know not what? For they were fully convinced that in the Papacy there is only horrible confusion, and that all things have gone far overboard. Idolatry there is as gross as could be; then, the service of God is completely destroyed; we see that men put their trust in their own merits; that they have imagined that Jesus Christ is as it were buried, that they trot to this saint and that saint, to have their patrons before God; that the sacraments are put up for sale; that they buy and sell souls; that they attribute to bits of trash and to ceremonies more than is proper, so that they make idols of them. You see, then, these straddlers know all this well enough, and that it needs to be remedied. But in what way? "O," they say, "what the Lutherans have wished until now is, as it were, impossible; the world cannot allow such a change. There must, then, be some middle position. Very well, it is true that men have corrupted the service of God by confining themselves to that which was commanded by men; it must be said, then, that for obedience's sake men should be bound to do so still, but not bound by such obligation nor so strictly as before. Again, men have trusted too much in the merits of works; it must be said now that we ought to begin with the grace of God, and that it is the principal thing upon which we must rest. If Jesus Christ has been as it were annihilated, and men have not had their refuge in His grace; now He must be declared to be our Attorney, indeed our chief Attorney, but not our only Attorney. Meanwhile men mix their own merits with the grace of God, and the commandments of men must always be observed in some manner. Also men must not cease to have the deceased saints as attorneys, so that they may be fellow-commissioners with Jesus Christ. As for worshipping images, men will no more be so besotted, but it may well be said that images are to stir up the devotion of the ignorant and simple sort, and verily it is an overly gross folly to run after them on pilgrimage, but yet in the meanwhile men may still keep some devotion to them for the weak and ignorant. As for the sacraments, men may well show that they ought not be held in such great esteem, but men ought to know that they ought not to make account of them except for the remembrance of Jesus Christ; but yet men may always retain I know not what. As for the Mass, well, that will no more be so exposed for sale, men will have no more particular Masses for the departed dead, nor in honor of such a saint, nor for this thing or that; but there will be a common Mass; and men will always say that it is a Sacrifice; not that Jesus Christ is not the true Priest Who offered Himself to God His Father; but the Mass will represent the death and passion of Jesus Christ." See how it seemed to these builders of falsehood that they had worked subtly when they made such a mixture, in order that the Gospel might not be too harsh for the world. On the contrary, it is said that God will neither be aided nor served by our lies. What is to be done then? Let us walk in integrity and simplicity, and let us have our mouths shut, that when He has spoken we may hold ourselves to what proceeds out of His mouth without any reply. Behold (I say) how we shall be approved by Him; but He will condemn us with all our subterfuges, when we shall have thought Him to bear favor according to our own fancy, and we shall have stepped ever so little aside from the purity of His word to disguise His judgments, though they be strange to the human senses.

And now let us come to what is added. *"Does not His majesty astonish you? And does not the fear of Him fall upon you?"* says Job. And then he adds, *that their memoir is like ashes, and their bodies are like a body of clay.* Hereby he means that when we lie on behalf of God, it is as much as if we did not apprehend His majesty, and that we would make Him like ourselves, and pull Him down here below, as if we were in like degree with Him. Behold (I say) what drives men. Why are they so impudent in falsifying the truth of God? Because they would measure it by their own span. And what distance is there between God and us! Then let us learn, therefore, to conceive what the majesty of God is; and thereupon let us be no more so foolish as to wish to attempt anything either against His word or against His judgments. Let us bow our heads, and let God say what pleases Him, and when we have heard His word, let Him also do what He thinks good, and let us adore Him in all His works; especially when we enter into the consideration of our feebleness and frailty, saying, "What are we?" You see, then, the two things that Job here compares. First he says, "Does not the majesty of God astonish you?" When he speaks of majesty or dignity, he shows that men ought to be somewhat better advised when they talk of God. But what? We proceed to do it stupidly, and it seems to us that God will allow men to play with Him, as he adds immediately. Therefore when we speak of God, let us learn to conceive the infinite glory that is in Him. For when we have once conceived that, it is impossible that we should not be humbled to say, "Alas, it is not a matter of speaking of God after the manner of men, nor making any comparison with Him. For what should be made of Him? Where would we set Him? Or in what degree would we place Him? Would we have Him matched with His creatures? Is not that as much as to make Him, as it were, nothing? And what shall become of His majesty when men have so abased Him? Then if we had the wisdom to contain or even only to taste what the infinite glory of God is; it is certain that we would learn to humble ourselves under it, and not be any longer so presumptuous as to make ourselves believe this or that. Furthermore, let us consider what we are. For the feebleness and poverty that are in the nature of man give a far greater glory to the majesty of God, so that He must be magnified the more, when we know thoroughly what we ourselves are. If we had in us the glory of angels, we would approach nearer to God; but yet we would be obliged to do as the angels do, according as it is said of them under the shape of cherubim, that they had to hide their faces, and were not able to look upon God perfectly. It is true that the Scripture says they see the face of God; but how is it that they see it? They are not able to abide it without casting down their eyes, and as it were without covering their faces with their wings; that is to say, without the modesty of worshipping God as their sovereign, unto Whom they are not able to attain, and without acknowledging the highness of Him by humbling themselves. See how it is with the angels of paradise.

And now what are we but rottenness? As for our souls, they are like little sparks which would soon be quenched and pass away into a shadow, were it not that God preserves them in their state, and that He does it of His pure goodness.

We have not, then, in ourselves the power to stand a single minute; but God must preserve us, because there is nothing in us but smoke and vanity. When we know this; it is certain that all presumption will be well beaten down in us, so that we shall no longer have the foolish desire to dispute after our own manner, to paint God with our colors, according as we see Him disfigured and torn in pieces by men. We shall no longer be so presumptuous or bold, when we know what His glory is, and have thought of the weakness that is in us. That is how we shall be astonished with fear of Him, as Job speaks here. For it is impossible that this knowledge of God should be idle in men, and that it should not cast them down in such wise that they would any longer be so bold as to babble against God. For when they have spoken at random, it is a sign that they have never known Him nor felt what His majesty is. And why? As I have said, it is a lively feeling when we once understand that it is God Who has created us, and that we are from Him; and that whether we look up or down, all things are in His hand, and that there is in Him a wonderful righteousness, there is in Him a wisdom that is hidden from us, there is in Him an incomparable goodness. When we have known all these things, it is impossible that we should not be astonished and abashed in ourselves so that we shall utterly abase ourselves before Him and adore His highness, which is infinite. So then, let us learn to know better what God is, in order that we may be trained in all modesty and sobriety, and meanwhile let us also examine what we are. When we see our own flesh does tickle us to applaud ourselves, so that we are inclined to flatter ourselves, and seek to stand in our own conceit; let us stir ourselves to say, "Whence comes this vice? It is because thou hast not yet known thyself. Consider who thou art, do only enter into thyself, and be judge of thine own condition." There we shall find that we have a bottomless pit of sin in us, and that we are wrapped in such ignorance that it is horrible to behold, which is as it were so thick a darkness that it utterly chokes and strangles us; and so far off are we from having our eyes open to know

God that we see not the thing that is before our nose. Therefore when men shall have so thought about themselves, it is
certain that they will be so touched by the majesty of God
that, whereas it was seen that they were full of pride, and as
it were hairbrained in speaking of God, so that there was not
any reverence or modesty in them; then the fear of God will
fall upon them. Instead of the great and strange rashness
that is to be seen in the world men will find reverence of God.
And Why? For (as I said) when we once conceive what
God is, we shall stoop under Him. Again on the other side,
when we see what we are, we shall have no more occasion
to be pleased with ourselves, or to advance ourselves in any
manner whatever. So you see what Job meant to indicate by
these two sentences.

Now for the greater confirmation, he says, "Indeed, but
think you that He will bear with you if you play with Him
as a man?" He shows that men are beguiled in that they,
not knowing the majesty of God to honor Him as they ought,
do play with Him. Although we ought to honor Him, we
play with Him as we are accustomed to doing in dealing with
one another, as he who can deceive, does it boldly, and all is
well, provided he is not caught. Now according as we apply
our wiles among men, so also would we commend our craftiness to God, but that is too great an abuse. Therefore let us
not think we can play with such a master, and escape unpunished. For although God may allow men to run riot for
a time, yet in the end He must show them that He is not the
party they took Him for, but another manner of person. He is
not the party they took Him to be, because He is not like
creatures who ought to be obedient to the common rule in
such manner that they may be brought to account and measured
by the Law which He has given to us; to us, I say, for He has
squared out His Law to be our measure, and not to be subject
to it Himself. So also men must understand that He is totally
other than they have imagined Him to be; for they have not
had an eye to the infinite glory which is in Him. So then,
let us guard against this playing. For God shows us that

whenever we discuss either His word or His works, we must be well aware what we are doing.

And now Job says, *"Hold your tongues before me; I will speak, and let happen to me what may."* Here Job shows that he is not like these babblers which skirmish with God's word and with His judgments from a great distance . As you will see, some have their tongues well sharpened to talk, but that is only to debate frivolous questions far off from practice. But Job shows that such is not his case. And why not? *"You see,"* he says, *"how I carry my flesh between my teeth,* as if I were torn to pieces, and that I am obliged to take up my flesh and my skin in my teeth to carry them. *I have,"* he says *"my soul between my hands.* Since you see me in such a plight, do not think that I prattle like a parrot in a cage. No, no; I am forced to speak from my heart. For God examines me by holding me as it were upon the rack. Then I must display my feelings. For as for me I speak as one who has experience, and God examines me in such a way that it is well seen that I have no leisure to disguise things and to say one thing when I mean another. So then, let me speak. For you will not bear my burden; it is God with Whom I have to deal, and it is He also to Whom I have to answer; and so as for your disputes I leave them there for whatever they may be worth, that is to say, for utterly useless and frivolous toys. But as for me, I will speak according to what God shows me, and what He shows me in fact." You see in summary what Job means to say.

Now let us here note the manner of speech which he uses: namely, *that he beholds his flesh between his teeth* to carry it. For he was as it were all torn to pieces, as if a man's skin were torn off, and he knew not what to do except to take it up between his teeth. You see, then, that Job tells in what plight he was; and thereby he shows that he was in so pitiful a condition that he was no longer like a living creature. When he adds that *he holds his soul* (or his life) *between his hands,* it is as much as to say that it was fleeing and as it were abandoned and left to the spoil. Herein a man may see the silliness of the Papists, when they supposed that *to hold one's*

soul between his hands signified to have power to do good
or evil. "Let men devise what they wish," they say, "I have
my soul in my own hands,[1] that is to say, I can do what I
think good, I am in a free condition."[2] To be short, they
meant to build their free will upon this sentence, *"I have my
soul between my hands."* But we know that when God threatens men, if he tells them He will leave them in their own
hand, it is the most grievous affliction that can come upon
them.[3] Behold, God thunders at us when He says He will
leave us in our own hands. And why? For unless God
holds us back, there is no remedy for our running headlong
into destruction. We see, then, the silliness of the Papists
when they so twisted the Holy Scripture. But the sense is
very clear in this context, where Job says that he carries his
soul between his hands, as if it had already expired. Our
soul is hidden within our body as in a chest, and that is the
means of preserving it; but if we have it in our hand, it is
as if it were abandoned. Job, then, declares that he is more
dead than living, and that God handles him in such a manner
that he is like a wretched, rotten carcass, so that there is no
more life in him, but he has become loathesome to all men.
"See," he says, "I know well that I am no longer considered
to be of the company of men, but I must be esteemed as a
dead body.[4] Hereby, as we have said, Job shows that he is
not a speculative teacher but a true practitioner of the things of
which he speaks, that is to say, of the judgments of God. And
undoubtedly, without this experience, we can know neither God,
nor His hand, nor His power, nor His justice, nor anything
else. It is true that all men will not be examined as Job was,

---

1. Cf. the American poet, William Ernest Henley (1849-1903), "Invictus,"
"I am the master of my fate: I am the captain of my soul." Thank God,
this mood is gradually passing.

2. Fr. *i'ai une condition libre.*

3. Cf. Judges 6:13. Gideon said . . . "Did not the Lord bring us up from
Egypt? But now the Lord hath forsaken us, and delivered us into the hands
of the Midianites." Also the words of the Lord recorded in Jeremiah 12:7,
"I have forsaken Mine house, I have left Mine heritage; I have given the
dearly beloved of My soul into the hand of her enemies." And the prayer
of Lamentations 5:20, "Wherefore dost Thou forget us forever, and forsake
us so long time?"

4. Fr. *un corps trespassé,* a body from which the life or soul has departed.

that is to say, with such severity; but yet we must come to the touchstone, which will show that we have nothing but vain speculations. If God does not sometimes summon us, so that we may feel what our sins and what endless death are, and understand that we are destitute of salvation, and that we are shut out from all hope, with respect to ourselves; we shall never know how to discuss the truth of God; I say, we shall not know a single word about Him with hearty affection. For these babblers who play with it may well put on a beautiful show, and they may make their boasts before men; but there will be no steadiness in them. Do we, then, wish to speak of God earnestly and as we ought? It is needful that we should have been previously exercised, and that we should have come to the practice of it: that is to say, that we should have been pressed, in order that we may know both Him and ourselves. You see in summary what Job meant in this passage.

Besides, let us note well, that our Lord leads us into such trials, we need superhuman power in order to subsist. When we hear some of the words Job pronounced, we would condemn him, and rightly so; however, we ought to consider well the extremity in which he was, in order that we may not find it strange if some temptations were too dominant in him. Though he finally resisted all combats, yet he had some feebleness mixed in, by which he was as it were terrified; and although his faith did not actually fall, yet it was shaken, and he surely felt the power of certain vices. It behooved him, then, to overcome such temptations, though they were very grievous to bear; therefore let us not find his language strange. For what man today can say like Job that he is like a poor desperate soul, that he holds his flesh and his skin between his teeth, and that he has his soul in his hand? It is true that David speaks after the same manner in the hundred and nineteenth Psalm;[5] but yet in comparison, Job was even at the abyss, as we see. If we consider only what he endured in his body's being so rotten that no one would condescend to look at him, indeed, that the very sight of him was enough to

---

5. Psalm 119:109, "My soul is continually in my hand."

make a man's hair stand up upon his head, and that he had
become so hideous a thing that people were ashamed of him,
indeed, that they hated him — now then, if Job had endured
no more than these pains in his body, would it not have been
very much? But the chief point, as we have said, was the
feeling of God's judgment, and how God persecuted him, that
he found no favor at His hand, that it seemed to him that God
meant to add continually plague upon plague, until he had sent
him to the bottom of death and damnation. When then, Job is
assailed so severely, let us not think it strange if there were
some too exorbitant temptations in him. For it was necessary
that God should here show His perfect strength by comparison
with the weakness of man. But let us on our part apply this
to our instruction. And in the first place, if God sends us
such great excessive afflictions that we are as it were swallowed
up; let it not cause us to despair (as will be declared more
fully soon again) but let us resist it, knowing that God still
reserves His mercy ready for us at the proper time. And if
we languish more than we would wish, let us know that God
will let the illness ripen in order to heal it better. If a man has
an abscess, or perhaps a stinking score, so that it is enough to
impair the entire health of the man, yet the physician or sur-
geon will not lance the abscess at once. And why? He would
cause an inflamation, because the matter is not yet ripe. But he
will put some drawing plaster on it first to make the abscess
ripen, and then he will boldly apply the lance. So it is that God
deals with us. For He sees that we have some very bad ab-
scesses; but what of it? Let us not think it strange if He does
not heal them at once; for the disease must first be made ripe,
and then God can apply His hand, and find suitable remedies.
Let us know, then, that God knows what is good and proper for
us, and let us wait for Him in patience. But if we are too eager
to make haste, when we endure any afflictions, what excuse can
there be for us? When we see that Job has come to the gulf of
hell and nevertheless humbled himself before God, that although
he endured such grievous torments that he was in such excessive sorrow, yet he restrained himself; I say, if a man who was
so afflicted still bridled himself, I pray you, shall we not be too,

too inexcusable, if we chafe and fret in our adversities? Then let us consider these things, and let every one of us look at himself. When we see that such a servant of God has been thus tried to the limit, we ought to be so much more controlled in our adversities and not to fret against God as we have been accustomed to doing. You see what we have to remember concerning this passage.

Job says that *if God would kill him, he would trust in Him; nevertheless he would argue his own ways before God's face.* It is true that the Hebrew word *lo* (which we translate *in him*) may be taken for *not,* and so does it signify properly. Notwithstanding, it is sometimes taken relatively, as they call it, and one letter is changed into another, which is a common usage among the Hebrews. Nevertheless the meaning is the same either way. For if you read *not,* it must be by way of asking a question, "Though He kills me, shall I not hope? Yes, I will hope." Or else if you read "I will trust in Him," we see that the substance is not changed. In summary, then, Job indicates that although he is overthrown and as it were enraged in his passions, that he has not lost all hope; it is not that he pretends to plead against God, or perhaps to alienate himself from Him, or that he wishes to vex Him by having no more to do with Him. Why not? He protests that he hopes, whatever may come of it. "Although He may kill me," he says, "and confound me, yet will I not cease to trust in Him; nevertheless I will argue my ways before His face. Behold, I must mix this vehemence which you see and which you perceive, I must mix it with the hope which I have in God. And here we have a beautiful and excellent mirror of God's working. For he lets the faithful fall, in order that their faith may be so much better tried. These things seem to be incompatible in themselves; but God Himself makes them agree. At the first sight a man would say, "Lo, here are fire and water;" but at last God brings all things to such an end that there is no disagreement at all. There have been some who in their disputations, would always wish conclusions after the manner of the philosophers, and that all things should be so put in order that there should be no disagreement, but a certain peace pact among all things; but such men never knew what it is to have been sifted by God and to have passed through His judgments. And why? For, as I have said, God handles us in such a strange fashion that all things are hereby confounded. In fact, there are also things in us which can never be made to agree. For sometimes we desire to live, and sometimes we desire to die; and these are contrary things, indeed, but the considerations are different; for, as Saint Paul says, naturally we covet to be, and consequently we flee death. Death is horrible to us, because it is contrary to our nature. It is the thing that frightens a man.

On the other hand, we see that we are held here as in a prison; as long as this body surrounds us we are in bondage to sin; therefore we are constrained to groan, and in so doing to aspire to the eternity which is promised us when God shall have taken us out of this world (for when we approach death, we come to it; as death is also the entrance to life), knowing that since Jesus Christ has passed the same way, we need not be afraid that death will have any power over us; for it is as a blunted sword, or one off which the point is broken, so that it cannot wound us; and although it may draw some blood from us, yet notwithstanding the same will be but to deliver us from all our weaknesses. It surely seems that these affections are contrary, and so they are; but God causes them to agree in such wise that what we have apprehended by our natural sense is put down, because faith is the governess. As much is to be said of what Job discusses in this passage. For you see that believers are fully persuaded upon this point, namely, to hope in God, and to obtain salvation from Him, howsoever the world may go. This thing they could not do, unless they held Him for their Father and had in Him their refuge, as if to say, "Behold, God has been my Father to the uttermost, and then He has given me liberty to come to Him. Therefore must I call upon Him, put myself into His keeping, and not doubt but He will always be merciful to me. Indeed, but He afflicts me, and when I am minded to come near Him, I shall not perceive that He has heard me. Truly this knowledge is hard and grievous to bear; but yet must I wait for my God in silence and do Him the honor or resting myself upon His promises." See, then, how the faithful are fully resolved on that point. But on the other side, it behooves them to know themselves; and it is impossible that they should know their own infirmities, except they also make their complaints and say, "How now? And these things are contrary. For if we ought to wait for God in silence, is it fitting for us to raise disputes and to enter into complaints? For to do so is contrary to faith." It is true that it is contrary at first sight, but God makes them agree entirely. For after we have been agitated with some foaming at the mouth, behold, faith draws us in such wise into silence that finally we conclude thus: "Undoubtedly the goodness of God will never forsake us, howsoever the world may go; but we shall always find Him favorable, although He may not show Himself so at first." So you see what we have to gather in summary from this passage. Now we see at what Job aimed when he said, "Although God may kill me, yet will I hope in Him; nevertheless I will dispute with God, and argue my ways." For the Hebrew word that he uses means *to reprove;* it also means *to dispute,* or *to plead.* So then he says and protests that he is not the man whom the parties who had spoken took him to be. For it seemed to them that he was a man who would have played double or quit, that he would have no more hope in God, and that he had spoken those things as it were in spite. He declares that he is not such, for he always kept hope in God. Now, since he trusts in God, he must of necessity submit himself to Him. For to trust in God is not to shrink away from Him, and to hold oneself aloof. On the contrary, to hope in God is to come to Him, and when He seems far away from us even then to strain ourselves to get to Him; and then, moreover, to know what the Holy Scripture tells us, namely: to hide ourselves under the shadow of His wings, and to return to Him, in order that He may receive us into His bosom, as a child is received by his own father. You see, then, what is contained here.

For when Job says that *he will always hope in God,* he shows that he is not like one of these loiterers who suddenly leap,[6] because they want to play they are escaped horses. "It is en-

---

6. A French pun, *ces esgarez qui s'esgayent.*

tirely contrary," he says, "for I ask only to be near Him and
that He should have His hand upon me." Hereby, then, he is
cleared of the false slander with which he was charged. Nevertheless, he says afterwards, *"Behold, yet must I dispute with
God concerning my ways;* that is to say, the hope that I have is
not such that it is utterly unmixed with complaints, so that I
would not lift up myself nor murmur against God at all." It is
true that this proceeds from weakness, indeed, from vicious
weakness worthy to be condemned; but though such is the case,
God does not altogether let him go; for, as we have said, faith
overrules our passions. When we hope in God, and call upon
Him, that is not to say that we should never have any conflicts
in ourselves; but faith must get the upper hand, the peace of
God of which Saint Paul speaks[7] must win the victory; that is
to say, it must overcome in our hearts. When he speaks of the
peace of God and attributes victory to it, he shows that we shall
have turmoils in us and that we shall be tossed to and fro. But
what remedy is there for it? The peace of God must have such
power that it may control in the end and that all our passions
may be held in check. Then let us note well that in confessing
that he will hope in God, Job also confesses his own weakness
and shows that he is not so perfect that there is never any fault
to gainsay in him. Yet, nevertheless, he always has his refuge
in God. Since the case stands so, let us also on our part understand that when we are shaken by the provocations of our flesh
and our own affections somewhat carry us away, we must not
therefore despair or imagine that God will help us no more; but
let us be advised to hope in Him; and although we do it not so
perfectly as is required, yet let us be sure that nevertheless He
will cause us to feel that our waiting upon Him is not in vain;
He will strengthen us continually more and more in the faith
and cause it to be victorious over all the temptations of the
world and of this present life.

Now we shall bow in humble reverence before the face of our
God.

---

7. Colossians 3:15.

SERMON 6

If God Were Our Adversary*

O that Thou wouldest hide me in the grave, that Thou hadst locked me up until Thy wrath had relaxed, and that Thou wouldest set an end to the time in which Thou wouldest remember me. Shall the man that is dead live again? All the days of my struggle I will wait until my change may come. O that Thou wouldest answer me when I call to Thee, O that Thou wouldest favor the work of Thy hands.—Job 14:13-15

THE PROPHET Isaiah,[1] showing how horrible and how heavy to bear is the wrath of God, says that those who experience it would be content to hide in the mountains, and indeed they would wish that they might fall upon their heads; our Lord Jesus Christ also made this statement.[2] Now this is to show us that we must not be so stupid as we are; for we do not know what it is to have God against us. It is true that we shall sufficiently experience the evil we endure when He persecutes us; but this is neither all nor the principal thing. It is needful to weigh thoroughly what the wrath of God is. And why so? For when we understand the hand of God, we think of our sins; and thereby we are confounded, and we know well that we must perish unless God had pitied us. Though we flee this feeling, our Lord exercises us in it to make us wide awake when He wishes to show us mercy. You see what ought to be understood by the statement of Job when he says, *"O that Thou wouldest hide me in the grave."* For he prefers death to his life, such as it was. And why? Because he would escape the hand of God if it were possible. For he knew well that it is a thing far more terrible to have God for his judge than to die a hundred times. And this surely ought to touch us to think more carefully about

---

* Sermon 55 in *Calvini Opera, Corpus Reformatorum,* volume 33, pp. 680-92.
1. Isaiah 2:19, cf. Hosea 10:8.
2. Luke 23:30.

75

our sins than we have done, in order that we may know that, when we shall have endured all the evils of the world, it is nothing in comparison with appearing before the judgment-seat of God, when it comes to rendering an account. If we have some slight malady we cry out, "Alas!" If we have an accident, we are heard making complaints; yet our sins remain there as it were buried, and never come into our thoughts or memory. Hereby we show how perverse we are in judging things. Therefore whenever we hear that those who have been afflicted by the hand of God have desired death and to be hidden in the grave, let us know that this is what we ought to fear above all: namely, that God should declare Himself as it were our adversary. When we are persuaded that this is the greatest danger that can happen to man, we shall try by all means to return to Him. When our sins come to our mind, "Alas!" we shall say, "what is our situation? For if God declares Himself our enemy, what shall we do? What will be our condition?" Let us anticipate it, then, and behold how solicitous we shall be to seek God to obtain grace from Him, so that we shall never be at rest until He be reconciled with us. You see the usage to which we ought to apply this doctrine.

We must note well the saying, *"I would wish that Thou hadst hidden me in the grave, and that I had been locked in it, until such time as I had been cut off."* He shows why he desires death: namely, because he finds himself confined under the judgment of God, and he can find no way to escape. Hereby we are warned that our subterfuges will do us no good in the end; and that when we have bustled often here and there, we must be as it were confined. We shall have profited well for one day if we have retained this lesson. Why? Although God may threaten us, yet it is seen that it takes nothing to make us believe that we can get out of it, as each one of us imagines this or that, so that our hypocrisy is the cause why we are not touched by the threats of God, as would surely be required. There is nothing that more quickly provokes the extreme vengeance of God than when He sees that we do not take account of His wrath; that is what provokes Him to the limit. So then, let us learn by what is said here, that when God knowingly wills to press us it will not be a question of escaping by one means or another, but we shall have to be confined. On the other hand, if God should give us some respite, and especially if He should show us how we may obtain grace at His hand, let us use that opportunity. It is said immediately, *"I would that Thou hadst hidden me in the grave."* Here it could be asked, "And is not death a sign of the wrath of God and of His curse? Is our coming to it any relief? What does it profit us?" Indeed it seems that it is the extremity, and that God could not execute any greater severity toward us than to put us to death. But Job has here conceived death without a proper apprehension, as we have declared previously; and we ought to remember that. He was anguished there, since God made him experience his misery. Thereupon he thinks how he could be rid of it. "At least," he says, "I would wander in the dark, but as long as I bear my flesh (as he finally says in conclusion), as long as my soul is in me, I am in pain, I am tormented, I have nothing but distress. If God had taken me out of this world, I should have some respite, it would be the end;" and (as he has said before) he would have his end as a hireling, whom you see at rest when his term has expired, and his agreement run out. You see why he desires here to be entombed in his grave. Furthermore, let us note that he well knew that men do not cease to be under the hand of God by dying, and that they must be judged by Him, and experience Him. Job knew that well enough; but meanwhile he considered the misery by which he was pressed, and is as it were attached to it, so that he does not think of all the rest. You see, then, that when God persecutes a poor sinner he has no other consideration but to say, "Alas! must I be inclosed here without remedy? and must my misery increase, and I perish in the end, because God will always pursue me?" The sinner has no consideration except for the thing that is so hard for him to bear. For this cause he thinks death is nothing to him, but it seems to him that it would serve him as a medicine. After that manner Job spoke in desiring to be covered in his grave, and to be as it were locked in there.

When he says, *"Until Thou remember me, and until Thou assign me a term;"* thereby he shows how there is some apprehension even after death, but it seemed to him that according as he was carried away and ravished, there would be some respite for him to take his breath; that when he will have gone out of this world, then he will not be in such confusion, neither so hard nor heavy as he experienced here. But I have said Job could not but know that even after death we have to render account; for he says, *"I will wait in the grave until thou assign me a term to remember me."* This *remembering* here is nothing else but God's calling of His creatures to judgment. But Job was so confounded and this passion did so agitate him that he did not judge from a settled mind, as we ought to do. And why? First, as long as we are in this world, what should we more desire than that God should remember us? For if He forgets us, what shall become of us? Peter said, "Get Thee away from me, O Lord, for I am a poor, sinful man."[3] Indeed, but we must go the opposite way, saying, "Lord, draw near us; for without Thy grace, we are nothing." So then, it is very needful that God should remember us. And why? To maintain and preserve us, in order that He may sustain us and have pity upon our feebleness to relieve it, and that He may guide us by His providence. You see, then, how necessary it is that God should remember us, or our condition is very miserable. For there is nothing man ought to fear more than to be forgotten by God. This is one point. Again, although God may take us out of this world, yet He does not forget us, though He may seem to; for He always keeps His own in His hand and under His care; and as for those who are damned, they are held as it were in chains until the day of executing the sentence. You see, then, that God does always remember us; and when the Scripture says He has forgotten us, it is because we do not experience His present help; as if a poor man languished and asked God to help him and did not feel His help, it would seem that God had not heard him. You see how it is said that He has forgotten us: namely, according to what we perceive; but yet He remembers us continually. Job, then, was mistaken to surmise that if he were dead he would be as it were forgotten until God should call up to all his creatures at the last day, and summon

---

3. Luke 5:8.

them to His judgment-seat. Job, therefore, did not consider this mindfulness of God toward us as he should have; but we can contemplate it, provided we are persuaded of what I have said: namely, that God does not cease to think of us, though He leaves us there for a little while, so that our bodies rot in the earth, and our souls abide in suspense, waiting for the day in which all the world shall be restored.

Moreover, as long as we live let us be fully persuaded that there is nothing better for us than when God thinks of us; indeed, even if it were to punish us. If God thinks of us in order to make us experience His favor;[4] therein consists all our joy and glory, as is said in the eighth Psalm.[5] "Alas! what is man, that God should condescend to look upon him, and to watch over him?" We are as a little shadow; we are nothing at all; and yet God is willing to have a fatherly care of our life. And ought not we to acknowledge a wonderful goodness in Him on that account? So then, we must highly prize the mercy which God shows us in being mindful of us, even making us feel His goodness; but (as I said), although He chastises us for our sins, yet He is gracious to us; for thereby He shows that He is not willing that we should perish, seeing that He calls us back again to Himself when He sees us on the road to perdition. For are not all His chastenings as many warnings which He gives us to come to repentance? You see, then, how we ought to prize more highly the grace of God in that He is mindful of us, and not to desire Him ever to forget us. This is in summary what we have to remember from this verse.

Now it follows, *"Shall the man who is dead live again? For I look for my change all the days of my struggle,* or of my travail." Here Job shows how far he was troubled in mind, better than he did previously. For he was in such distress that he did not know what the end of men is, or whether they should be raised again or not after they are dead. Truly this seems strange at first sight; but we must note what I have already said: namely, that Job speaks of his former temptations which he resisted. There is great difference between being utterly

4. Fr. *sa grace.*
5. Verse 4.

beaten down by a temptation or fully experiencing it, and being
shaken by it and yet in the meanwhile resisting it. What a
number of evil opinions and fancies will come into our head. As
we know that men receive many deceptions from Satan. Behold, one wicked fancy that comes into our head is that we
greatly mistrust God, as if we should say, "How do you know
whether or not God thinks of you? How do you know whether
or not He has abandoned you? How do you know whether or
not He condescends to look favorably at His human creatures?"
Behold all the thoughts that strike men; and it is in order to
make us humble ourselves. When we see that we are so full of
vanity, all the more have we need to walk in fear before God,
saying, "Alas! What is this? I ought to dedicate all my wits
to glorify my God; and behold part of my intelligence is applied
to such thoughts. Indeed, there come enormous blasphemies
into my head." Greatly, then, ought men to be displeased with
themselves, when they conceive such fancies. But believers
repulse them immediately; for as soon as the devil comes to
trouble us in that manner, we are armed with the word of God,
we make a buckler of faith, as the Scripture says. Although
Satan casts fiery darts at us, as St. Paul says;[6] yet they do not
enter into our souls so as to wound us; the poison of them is
not applied to us. It is true that Satan will assault us mightily;
but yet that sting of his shall be neither deadly nor poisonous.
We shall repulse, then, all these wicked fancies when we are so
assailed. But others are entirely seized by it, and are so mistaken that some doubt the providence of God; others think that
God has utterly rejected them, and they are as it were entirely
cast down. There is, then, great difference between a fleeting
fancy that comes into our head for a while, and which we resist;
and a persuasion that settles itself and takes root in us. It is
true that we do not cease to be guilty when we shall have fought
against all the temptations of Satan, and overcome them; yet
shall we not come to a full end, but we must still mourn before
God, because we have not glorified Him as perfectly as is required; nevertheless He accepts such constancy, when we resist
evil in that manner. See how Job did it. He recites the temp-

---

6. Ephesians 6:16.

tations with which he was assailed, but yet he was not overcome by them. In fact, there are three degrees to be noted. For
sometimes there come fancies to our mind, and we drive them
away immediately. Sometimes we shall be in pain and distress,
so that we shall be in great toil, saying, "How shall I come to
the end of this temptation?" But yet in the end when Satan
presses us with it, God does still strengthen us. The third
degree is when we are utterly borne down and overcome. As
for Job, he not only came to the first degree of having the fleeting fancy to ask whether or not men shall rise again; but he
also came to the second step of temptation. For when he saw
himself so pressed with misery, he thought to himself, "Alas!
What does God intend to do with me? It seems that He wishes
to scrape my whole body. And since He is my enemy, what
will become of me?" Job, then, was tormented with that temptation (which was evil) because he considered that God was so
against him. Yet he was not overcome. Although the battle
was rough and hard for him to endure, yet he was the winner.

You see how we must take this passage. For had Job settled
in that opinion, it would have been a cursed blasphemy to ask,
"Shall man rise again, or not?" But surely he was assailed in
such a manner that he persisted in the faith that he had conceived, and the Spirit of God gave him the victory. We must
not, therefore, charge him with blasphemy; neither must we
accuse him of unbelief on account of it. For faith is never without battles; it behooves her to be thoroughly exercised. And
how is that done? When the devil proposes to us many occasions for unbelief. You see, then, the true test of our faith. Job,
then, must not be cast out of the number and company of believers for having been assailed. Also it is to be noted that he
did not simply doubt, but he was so carried away because he
was pressed by God's hand. If Job had been asked, "Do men
utterly perish in dying?" he would have answered, "No. For
although the body may rot away, God will raise it again; and
the soul is reserved until the last day, at which time we shall
be wholly restored." Job would surely have answered so, if he
had been examined about death in general. But since he had
the special problem of God's pressing him so sorely that he did

not know what would become of him, that it seemed that God
had determined to confound him and completely destroy him;
being so frightened by it, that is why he doubts. Let us note,
then, that Job considered what was in his own person; namely,
God's severity, so great that it surely seemed that there was no
probability that he would ever get out of the misery in which
he was.

For this cause he says, "Shall the man who is dead rise
again?" Verily he means that aspect of death in which God
displays all his powers to bring a man to nothing. And what
is that? It is as if he should say, "Alas, Lord, it seems that
Thou art minded to exclude me from the hope which Thou hast
given us of our rising again. For seeing Thou handlest me so
severely, does not this strange dealing which Thou usest toward
me tend to my utter destruction? And when Thou hast destroyed me, who can restore me?" He surmises, then, not that
God wills to restore him at the last, but that He wills to utterly
root him out of the number of creatures. That is why he asks,
"Is it possible for a man to come to life again when he has
passed away?" It is because God dealt so strangely with him
that it seemed that He willed to bring him utterly to naught.
And hereby we are warned to pray to God that He may handle
us so moderately that we may always have the hope to assure
ourselves that our miseries will not endure forever, but that
God will remedy them, and that it is His office to raise those
out of their graves who are in them. For if we do not believe
that, we must fall into horrible despair, which will confound us,
as we see it would have happened to Job, if God had not held
him up by His strong hand. And you see also why it is said,
"Lord, chasten me, but let it be with reason."[7] Not that God is
ever unreasonable; but by the word "reason" or "judgment"
Jeremiah means a moderate fashion agreeable to our infirmity,
when we are not tempted so strongly that we may not always
perceive that God will have pitied us in the end, and will have
remedied our miseries. You see, then, whereof we are admonished in this text when it is asked, "Will a man come back to
life after he has passed away?"

---

7. Jeremiah 10:24, "O Lord, correct me, but with judgment."

Concerning the following saying: *"I will wait until the day of my changing may come."* Some expound it that if Job thought that God would raise the dead, and that there was some hope of the resurrection and renewal, he would wait for that day. But it must be taken more simply; namely, "Lord, comfort me; for I am now confounded, I see Thou usest nothing but force, I see Thou executest nothing but violence against me; and so must I still fight and strain myself, and I have no other comfort except to wait for the day of my change." See then, in summary, how Job understood that saying. He reasons with himself rather than with God whether a man shall return to life again when he is dead. As if he said, "I see myself here in so wretched a state that it surely seems to me that I ought to remain confounded, and there is no longer any means of my being restored. For since God is against me, and He wills to destroy me, what is there to say?" Whereupon, however, he forces himself, and struggles hard, and comes to the conclusion, "Yet will I wait for the day of my change." Hereby therefore we perceive that Job was victor and won that battle.

For notwithstanding that he entered into debate whether or not he would rise again, yet in the end he says, *"Behold, I will wait for the day of my change,* indeed, *all the time of my travail."* As if he said, "It is true that as long as my time lasts, I wish that God would keep me shut up in my grave, that He would cast me into some pit, and that he would cause the mountains to fall upon me; but yet I must wait for Him, even in the midst of the afflictions in which I am. Although they are hard and unbearable, yet since there is a change, that fact surely ought to give me some comfort, and to nourish me in the obedience of God." We see now what the meaning of Job's words is. We have a good and very useful doctrine to gather from this passage. In the first place, whenever we are assailed by Satan, and tormented by evil imaginings, and especially when there comes any distrust to lead us into despair; we must not enter these disputes, but quickly and briefly conclude to find our solution in God's truth. And how? Some take pleasure in surrounding themselves by evil imaginings; and there will come into their heads some opinion, indeed a wicked opinion which tends even to push them against God. Whereupon they dispute and imagine, "Is it possible or not? Why is it so?" When, then, we entertain such fantasies, and we chew our bits,[8] having evil opinions which are entirely contrary to faith; it is as if men came to terms with enemies who came to besiege their city. For if men listen to them and applaud what they say, it is the destruction of the whole city. Men will not open their gates to them; but it is just as if they did. So it is with those who surround themselves in their own evil opinions which Satan proposes to them; for if they remain in them, the result will be to lead them to destruction. What is to be done, then? Let us follow the experience that is shown us here by Job. Truly he was assailed dangerously when he doubted whether or not he could ever rise again, since God had brought him so low. If he had continued in that frame of mind to the end, what might have been the result? But after he had been so assailed, he broke contact quickly. "No," he says, "I will wait for the day of my change, whatever may come." This is what we have to do: it is to conclude according to God's truth. Also, when we conceive any wicked imaginings which could turn us from the faith and from the way of salvation, we must soon come back to take some sentence from the Scripture; and when we see that we are warned by God's truth, let us conclude that we must not dispute about it, when God pronounces it. Thus you see the sovereign remedy that we have to beat back Satan, in this place, that is to say, when he tries to turn us aside from the faith and from obeying God's word.

Besides, when Job says that *he will wait for his change,* this word deserves to be weighed thoroughly. Truly he speaks of the resurrection, inasmuch as we must be completely renewed, the corruption which is in us by reason of Adam's sin must be destroyed, and God must receive us into the immortality of His kingdom. This is the change of which Job speaks. And that is also where we have to look. For without the resurrection we can in no wise comfort ourselves; all that may be alleged will not be sufficient to cheer us. We see also that the Holy Scripture directs the faithful there when it wishes to satisfy

8. As a horse chews the metal mouthpiece of a bridle.

them, and to give them a certain and firm rest. "Now, let us acknowledge," say the servants of God, "that we are called to share the heavenly glory which God has promised to His own; therefore, be glad in it." However, to be well assured of this last change, we must consider the changes that God makes today even during the course of this life, how God makes many changes in us by which He gives us already some taste of the last change. For example, we are in some affliction, and surely we are as it were confined. When we look for the end of it, we see none, there is no remedy, it is past recovery, and we are lost; and suddenly God has such pity on us that we are delivered immediately. Do you not see a change that ought to lead us further? It is that we may understand that there is a much more perfect deliverance than all these which we perceive at this day particularly. Then, let us learn to acquaint ourselves well with the changes that God makes daily, that we may be lifted up on high, and by this means we may be quiet until the time that we may be renewed in the kingdom of heaven. Also here you see how David spoke of it.[9] For when he speaks of the changes from God's hand, whether it be rescuing men from trouble or casting them into it, that saying is of great weight though it may not seem so. For men have always this fond opinion concerning fortune, as if to say, "See what ill fortune has befallen me," or, "See what good fortune has happened to me." No! These are the changes from God's hand; and to that point we must always be brought. But among all the changes that are made in the world, the liveliest image of the last renewal is God's quickening us by His Holy Spirit, His enlightening us by faith, and His making us new creatures in our Lord Jesus Christ, as the Scripture says. Let us consider what the birth of men is. It is true that when we come into this world, we bring some remnant of God's image in which Adam was created; but this same image is so disfigured that we are full of unrighteousness, and their is nothing but blindness and ignorance in our minds. You see then what the state of men is at their birth. But God enlightens us by His Holy Spirit, in-

9. Psalms 78:42.

deed in such wise that we are able to behold Him, in so far as is expedient for our being transformed into His glory and for our being reformed by His Holy Spirit.

Therefore when God will have so changed us that we feel that He dwells in us, and by this means we fight against our wicked lusts; whereas other men do ordinarily delight in their vices, and bathe themselves in them; when we seek just the opposite, so that whatever evil is in us displeases us, and we mourn on account of it, also we follow the good, and we desire to give ourselves wholly to serving God; is not that a wonderful change? For such emotions will never come from ourselves. When we taste God's goodness, so we that are assured of His fatherly love toward us, and we even have the certainty of our salvation in order to call upon Him as our Father; do you not see a change that can show how powerful God's hand is? For men by their own nature can never open their mouths to call upon God in truth. It is true that they may well have some ceremonies, as pagans pray to God, as the Papists also do babble and make prayers that are long enough; but all this is nothing because they are not assured in their prayers, or fully persuaded that God should be their father. Do we then see that God is willing to hear us? Are we desirous to serve Him, and to honor Him? It is as if He had changed us and cast us in a new mold, as if He had made us a new creature. In fact, it is not without cause that the Scripture calls us new creatures in our Lord Jesus Christ. In other passages we are said to be His workmanship, because He has created us to good works. Saint Paul does not mean that God has created us only to be mortal men, but he says that God has created us to good works. Therefore when God does so change His faithful ones, you see a special work of His in which He displays His power over all nature. And here you see why I said that we must take hold of such changes, that we may have certain hope of the resurrection. If we doubt whether God will renew us at the last day when we must come before Him, how has God changed us already? He has now put His grace into us. To what purpose will He have given us courage to serve Him and honor Him, and to what purpose also will He have given us the spirit of adoption, unless to assure us of the hope we have of the everlasting glory? All this would be useless. So then, the change that we perceive today in ourselves is an infallible witness of the heavenly glory which we do not yet see and which is hidden from us. But God gives us a good earnest of it, according as it is said that the Holy Spirit is the earnest and pledge of it. And why? It is because of the effects. For the Holy Spirit is not idle in us, but rather shows openly that He dwells in us, in order to make us children of God. And we cannot be God's children, unless we immediately take pains to do good works and to follow His will. You see then how the faithful ought to practice this lesson.

Job says particularly that *he will wait for that change all the days of his travail.* This saying still ought to be well noted. For if we are agitated with many afflictions, it is not enough when we are moved and affected to say, "Now we must trust God"; for that is nothing unless we continue, indeed, in the midst of all our battles. First of all, therefore, let us note that hope is not for a day or for a month, but it must continue until the end. In fact, when we are leaning upon God's promises, He maintains us thereby, in order that we may not faint every day, but that when we have passed some time, we may always be more and more fully persuaded until God accomplishes the things which are as yet delayed until another time. You see then that it profits nothing to have had some good emotion, to have hoped in God, unless there is perseverance. Job expressed this yet more fully by the word *"travail"* or *"battle."* And why so? For he means that we should not come to God at our ease, as we may well wish. If we suffer nothing, we shall be satisfied to live yet in this world, and to double our lifespan if it were possible. Our desire is then that God should handle us without any tribulation, and please us in all respects, and obey us in all our desires. See how easily we would pass the time if we could only go at our own pace, if we could have no temptation, and if there were no sadness or anything whatever to fear. But it is said that we must wait all our days, and with fighting.

In the words *"all the days"* it is shown us that if the time lingers and seems long to us, we must not take it as an excuse to do evil, and to be grieved, and to quit everything in the middle of our journey; but we must continue until the end. Under the word *"battle"* is expressed to us the condition of this present life, which is that being only pilgrims in this world, we must fight, be besieged on all sides, be in continual peril, be tempted now with cares, now with some affliction, now with some danger. We must, then, think about it. However, let us understand also that we must fight against the lusts of our own flesh. But notwithstanding all these difficulties, yet must we wait for our change. You see what we have to retain from this passage.

Now in conclusion Job says, *"O that Thou wouldst answer him that calls to Thee, and that Thou wouldst accept the work of Thine own hand."* This is only a more ample declaration of the proposition that we come to hold. He wishes to show what the change is that he has waited for. It is that God should be gracious toward the work of His own hands. It is true that some expound this passage as if God would press down the work of His hands. But that is strained. He wishes, then, to indicate only that he will quietly abide God's leisure until He shows in effect that He will accept him as His creature. And that is why he says here, *"I will answer when Thou callest me."* For Job protests that he will no longer flee God, nor shrink back from Him when He calls him, but will be ready to come, indeed with a ready courage. And why? For he knows that God will show Himself pitiful toward him. Thus you see that the thing which we have to note in summary from this passage is that even in the midst of our troubles, when it seems that God is displeased with us, that we shall no longer come to atonement with Him, indeed that He will not reckon us any longer in the number of His creatures; when all this has come to pass, yet nevertheless we must fight against such despair, until we have gained this point, to hope for the change that we wait for. See, then, how this text ought to incite us to be comforted in our adversities, and to pray to God that He may so strengthen us by His power that, although we are tossed to and fro by many storms, yet we may not cease for all that to keep on our way toward Him, and that we may find no obstruction against coming to Him, however the world may go. For although He may seem to have cast us off and to be angry with us, yet if we return to Him and call upon Him, He will answer us and confirm the hope of our salvation by making us taste the love that He bears us, in order that we may be entirely persuaded of it.

Now we shall bow in humble reverence before the face of our God.

SERMON 7

When Will Windy Words End?*

Job, answering, said, "I have often heard such things; you are all tiresome comforters. When will be the end of windy words? And from whom wilt thou strengthen thyself to answer? I could speak like you; if your soul were in place of mine, I could keep you company by arguments, I could shake my head at you. I could strengthen you with words, and my arguments would be that you should accept sorrow. But if I speak, my sorrow will not be at all diminished; and if I refrain, how is the burden lightened? He has loaded me down with agonies; He has made desolate all my company. He has dried me up with wrinkles as a testimony, and leanness has come upon me which shows in my face. He has torn me in His wrath, He has treated me furiously, He gnashes His teeth upon me; and my enemy watches me and sharpens his eyes against me."—Job 16:1-9

AFTER Eliphaz has said that wicked men and those who defy God must be confounded. and their condition is reversed; as a conclusion he adds, *"They conceive only sorrow which brings forth pain, and their belly nourishes fraud and deceit."* By which he indicates that all the show that wicked men put on does not gain them anything, but God reverses their plans, by which means their efforts are frustrated. It is true that this sentence is expounded as if it were a reason which Eliphaz gave: namely, that not without cause God afflicts and confounds wicked men and hypocrites. And why? For they only plot evil against all the world. According, then. as they are a trial to their neighbors, it is done to them in like measure. In fact, Holy Scripture often uses this manner of speaking, as in Psalm 7:15;[1] likewise says Isaiah in 59:4.[2] When

---

* Sermon 62 in *Calvini Opera, Corpus Reformatorum,* volume 34, pp. 1-13

then the Holy Spirit wishes to declare that men in all their counsels, in all their thoughts and affections are given to evil and to sin, He uses this simile: that they are like a woman who conceived to bring forth a child. When they have conceived punishment, that is to say, torment against their neighbors, to harass them, to oppress them somehow, they give birth to iniquity, that is to say, they execute the evil which they have thought of. Now this sense would not be suitable to the passage. For (as we have already said) Eliphaz has already given good reason why God was thus against the wicked; but now he wishes only to say that, although they are led on by good hopes and it seems to them that they will obtain by some means the reward of all their undertakings, they will find themselves confounded in the end. And why so? Inasmuch as only the blessing of God makes us to prosper. These, then, will gain nothing when they will have nourished some hope in their hearts. For God will upset the whole thing. And it is not only here that Scripture speaks in this manner. It is said in Isaiah 26:18, "Lord, we have been in labor before Thy face, and yet we have conceived and given birth only to wind." It is true that these are believers who speak and lament before God; but they recognize their sins and confess them; for during the time that they say that they have been in travail like women, God was persecuting them justly for their faults. Now they say that they have conceived wind, and have given birth to it, that is to say, that when they expected some alleviation of their trials, it all went up in wind and in smoke, and that after having languished a long time their trouble is not corrected. Eliphaz here goes further, that is, that the wicked conceive only travail, and that they give birth only to trouble for themselves, that their belly nourishes deception, that is to say, of vain hopes and frustrations which will be deluded in the end. It is also the threat that God makes in Isaiah 33:11 against the despisers

---

1. "He made a pit, and digged it, and is fallen into the ditch which he made."

2. Isaiah 59:1-8 shows how sin separates people from God.

who have not taken account of His Word, even being hardened
against it. "You conceive (says he) straw, and give birth
to filth." As if he said, "There you are obstinate against My
Word, inasmuch as you cannot recognize the evil which you
have committed, and how you have provoked My wrath
against you! In vain you flatter yourselves; for with all your
flatteries you will know that you have conceived only straw
and thatch, and that the wind will blow it all away; and you
will know that all of your flatteries will have profited you
nothing." Now, then, we see in summary the intention of
Eliphaz; namely, that the wicked may well be for a time at
their ease, and that God will not press them so hard that they
are not nourished in some effort. But then what? God
(though they hold Him in contempt) will press them, they will
have to have a worm which gnaws at their insides, their consciences will always bother them, they will have remorse and
points of needles will torment them in secret; indeed, in the
end God will send them such powerful and excessive agonies
that they will give birth outside to what they have nourished.
And why? For their belly conceived only deception; that is
to say, although they may not have experienced their troubles
at the beginning, yet they are only ruining themselves when
they do not seek God's favor. They promise themselves this
and that, but in any case there will be only delusion.

We come now to the answer of Job. He says to them in
the first place that he has often heard such things and further
that they are tiresome comforters, even to address themselves
thus to Job with such boring words. In saying that he has
often heard such things, he indicates that they must not bring
him common, ordinary remedies, since his sickness was so
great and so extreme, that they must surely bring some gentle
comfort which could help him; and they must not hold up to
him these propositions, as one would do as a matter of form
to one not too seriously afflicted. We see, then, to what Job
objects in saying that he has often heard such propositions.
Now it is true that, when someone brings us some comfort
which is already known to us, we ought not to despise it. And
why not? If today we are taught about the goodness of God,

that we may be exhorted to patience, it does not release us
from thinking any more about it. It is true that the proposition will not be obscure to us; but if we are afflicted, and
someone reminds us of what has been said to us, let us not
think that it is superfluous language. And why not? For it
is a matter of practicing what we have already heard, what
we have already understood; but we may not have been
touched to the quick by it, since the occasion for it may not be
presented. But if God presses us by some agony and sadness,
then He makes us to taste the comforts which someone will
have drawn and produced from His Word. In fact Job was
not like these dilettantes who always desire I do not know
what as long as it is new and who cannot allow anyone to
say to them the same proposition twice. "O, I have heard
that," or "I have not," they will say, until they beat your ears
in with these answers. Indeed, but they certainly need to meditate, and when someone reiterates something to us, it is to
our great profit and our advancement. Now Job was not
thus, he was not defiant so as not to take account of a teaching because it was common, He was not a mere curiosity-
seeker; but simply (as already we have said) he shows that
his illness was so serious that he had need of being comforted
in an extraordinary manner. As when there is a common
malady, also a light remedy is used; but if the malady is painful, the medical doctor must investigate further. For if he
wished to apply the same remedy for all sicknesses, what
would happen? So it is with afflictions. We shall see a man
who will be afflicted by the death of his father, or of his wife,
or of his children, some injury will happen to him. Perhaps
someone will bring him some moderate comfort, such as God
has proposed. But if there is someone who is tormented in
not only one manner, but he experiences that the hand of God
persecutes him from all sides — when there will happen to
him one evil, there will be the second and the third, and he
will be afflicted not only in his body, in his person, in his
goods, and in his friends; but he may have (as we have seen
from Job) spiritual temptations, as if God wished to cast him
into the abyss — then one must proceed in a more delicate

manner. For when one wishes to molest a poor man who
has his heart cast down, all one could bring to him will be of
what use? It is much better to hold your tongue and let God
work to supply what is lacking from men. That, then, is
what Job intended.

Here is Eliphaz who proposes to Job that God punishes the
wicked in order to show Himself Judge of the world, that
they will be armed in vain, that they will not escape His hand;
although they may have a great train and a great band, God
will destroy all. But for what? When this proposition is
applied to Job it is in order to make him believe that God is
his enemy, inasmuch as he is wicked, as also there was only
hypocrisy in him. Here is a proposition which is misapplied.
It is not without cause, then, that he says, "Very well, these
things are known to me, and if I needed them now I would
apply them to myself; but these things are beside the point.
"For Job knew that he was not afflicted because of his sins,
that such was not the purpose of God; not that he did not consider himself guilty and worthy to endure any more, when
God wished to examine him strictly; yet he knew that God
was not treating him thus because of his sins, that there was
some other purpose. Job, knowing this, rejects the propositions that are held out to him. And why so? Since they are
ill-timed. "You are to me," he says, "tiresome comforters."
The reason? It is because they do not bring him suitable
remedies at all. By this we are admonished, when we wish to
comfort neighbors in their sorrows and trials, not to jump to
conclusions; as there are many who are forever harping on the
same string and they do not consider the person to whom
they speak, for we must treat one person differently from another person. For if there is someone who is obstinate against
God, we must speak in a style and language different than we
would toward a poor creature who innocently wandered. And
then according to what the evil is, there is also need to be
warned how to proceed against it. For example, if men are
stupid, we must cry out and rebuke their indifference, in order
that they may learn about the hand of God, in order to humble
themselves under it. There is, then, need of great prudence

when we wish to properly comfort those whom God afflicts. This is what we have to remember from the passage, when it is said that those who attempted to comfort Job were tiresome, since they did not bring to him anything from which he could profit. This, then, is what we have to remember especially.

Now Job adds, *"When will be the end of windy words?"* He calls words "windy" when there is no substance, that is to say, which cannot edify a man; as Holy Scripture uses this metaphor, for when it is a matter of a man's being taught for his salvation it is said, "He is edified." How so? Since he is founded, and then someone builds thereon, so that he is confirmed in the Law, he is confirmed in patience to bear steadily his afflictions, and then he is resolved to pray and to call upon God, to have recourse to Him. On the contrary if the propositions are only to agitate the brain, and that a man may chatter and babble, and yet no one receives any good instruction to apply to salvation — all these are windy words. Also let us note, when we wish to propound some exhortation or doctrine, that above all we must hang on to this conviction: namely, that those who listen to us should receive some good instruction, so that they may become accustomed to walk according to God, and that they may be established in confidence in His mercy, that they may apply themselves to call upon Him, not in doubt or suspense, but knowing that they will be heard. This, then, is how we must study to instruct our neighbors in such constancy that what we have learned may not scatter like wind. Besides each one of us ought also to hang on to such doctrine that we may not desire to be filled with wind; as we see many curious people who would like the preacher to give their own kind of amusement, to feast their ears, and to satisfy their vain fancies. They imagine this and that, and they would like the preacher to amuse them as they pleased, to discuss things which are of no edification. The human spirit is too much inclined to this vice, and even entirely given to it. For if each one of us wished to follow his appetite, it is certain that it would only be a matter of holding useless propositions about this and that, which would have no substance — there would be only wind. So let us learn to seek what is good and proper to edify us in the fear of God, in the faith, and in patience, and in all things good and useful. This is what we have to remember with respect to the passage where Job mentions windy words.

It is true, however, that we must also consider ourselves, that we should not reject all propositions held out to us as if they were wind; but we should learn to distinguish between something vain and good instruction, which we should learn to apply to our use. Then, let us pray to God that He may give us grace that, when someone presents to us some good doctrine, it may not evaporate through our indifference, that it may not go away with the wind. For when someone comes to propose to us the Word of God, we should know that here there is always some good instruction. Now many hardly profit by it. And why not? For they do not apply all their senses and their minds, but their brains rattle, and the Word of God goes away as if on wind; but it is inasmuch as there is no solid substance in them. However, to better apply this sentence to our use, each one of us (as I have already said) must look at himself closely.

Now it follows in Job: *If his friends were in his condition, he could speak like they do, and keep them company in arguments, to contest with them, and to shake his head against them.* It is true that some expound this passage that Job would not wish to render the like to them if he saw them thus molested, that he would try rather to sweeten their sorrows and to bring them some alleviation, rather than add to their sadness, as they do toward him; just as we have seen their cruelty, just as it was not a matter of putting this holy person into despair unless God had sustained it. Those who take this passage thus are moved by this reason: that it would not be a decent thing that Job should wish to avenge himself when God should have withdrawn His hand from him; and when he should be at his ease, that he should wish to mock these poor people who would be in similar calamity; for when only he has endured affliction, still it should teach him to have pity and compassion on those who would need it. But when everything is properly considered, Job does not wish here to declare what he would do, but what a man could do, when he should be in such condition. He does not imply, then, that he would render the like to those who knowingly molested him, but simply that He could take pleasure if he were as they. He indicates, then, in summary, "You speak well at your ease, you here shake your heads against me, it costs you nothing to condemn me, even to plunge me into the depths, you do that like people who do not know what it is to endure evil. If I were in your condition, could not I do as well? And how would you take it, if I came to shake my head at your calamities, seeing that the hand of God had pressed you to the limit? When I should say, "Oh, it is very useful. God must chastise you and cause you to experience how He afflicts sinners; when there would be only confusion in you, if I spoke of it thus, could you not say that I was a mocker and a cruel man? Now, then, think what you would do in my place." This, in summary, is the intention of Job.

Now we see that he is not here out for revenge, as those who have no fear of God, when they are angered, wish to have the power in hand to render double the evil that is done to them. Job was not thus. In fact, the children of God must surely hold themselves in check; although we are tried and tormented, it is not proper to kick back at those who have so unjustly persecuted us, for God may send them to humble us. We must know that they are rods which proceed from His hand. But we surely can after the example of Job remonstrate against those who without reason come to molest us that we could do likewise to them. And why? For a man will never properly know his fault until someone treats him as he has treated others. But when a man perceives that the evil could return upon his own head, then he may restrain himself and come to say, "How is this? What am I doing?" Here is God who, to lead us to right judgment, says, "Do not do to thy neighbor except what thou wishest done to thee."[3]

3. This is based upon a reference to the Apocrypha in Tobit 4:15. "And what thou thyself hatest, do to no man." Note that the Golden Rule is stated positively in Matthew 7:12 and Luke 6:31. When Calvin preached this sermon in 1554 he had officially quit quoting the Apocrypha, but we notice that he occasionally fell into it.

In fact He might well have said, "When you have dealings with your neighbors, be advised to treat them in all equity and uprightness, be advised not to be given to wicked covetousness to carry away the goods of others, be advised not to desire to get rich at the expense of this one or that one." And it is true that He speaks thus in Scripture; but in conclusion He offers this saying, "Do what you wish to be done to you."[4] For there is no one who would not be chief clerk for his own profit. Then we know how to argue, "How is this? So and so has done me this injury. Did this come from a Christian man? Is there no equity? Is this not from a cruel cowardly man?" Each one, then, will know how to advance his reasons about equity and uprightness when it is a matter of his profit. And this is what Job points out to his friends, inasmuch as they are blind, saying that if they were in such an extremity as he was they would surely wish to be handled more gently. He cannot do anything else but lead them to this natural equity, and to compare themselves with him. So, he says to them, "Come now, if you were in the condition in which you see me, would it be reasonable for me to hold out to you the propositions that you are bringing to me? If someone wished to treat you in such a manner as you are proceeding against me, how would you take it?" Then they ought to be moved. And why so? For (as I have already said) while we are outside ourselves, that is to say, when a thing does not concern us and does not properly belong to us, we look askance at it; but if the case concerns us, oh! we learn how to advise ourselves better. This, in summary, is what Job wished to say.

Now we can gather a good doctrine from this, following the sentence that I have already quoted from our Lord Jesus Christ: that we should not do to others except what we wish to be done to us. For we have the Law of God imprinted on our hearts, we have general principles which remain in us. Why is it, then, that we have such a corrupt and perverted judgment that we always misconstrue things? It is just this, that after God has given us a good rule, we are moved by ambition, hatred, pride, avarice. That is how everything is per-

---

4. A paraphrase of the Golden Rule.

verted. If, then, there is some ambition in us, in order that
we may make the most of it, we come to despise our neighbors; if there is some rashness, we may quickly toss away a
sentence before having properly considered the merit of the
case; if we are led by pride, we may wish to advance ourselves by knocking down those who are seen getting ahead
of us; when we are incited by hatred and ill-will, shall we not
be blinded to what we must do out of love or kindness? Let
us examine ourselves, and let us pray to God that He may
work in our hearts to judge uprightly, "How now, if it were
thy problem, what wouldst thou say?" This is how we shall
be both wise and prudent and settled: namely, when we shall
have applied to ourselves that which we cast against another.
For we are so given to our appetite and profit (as I have said)
and nature keeps us that way, that each one loves himself,
indeed too much. For this cause we shall be so much the less
excused for this vice when it will be found in us, seeing that
we are so often exhorted to follow uprightness and equity.
Now let us pray to God that He may so work in us that by
His Holy Spirit this vice may be converted into virtue. Let
us consider the implication of the saying, "Thou shalt love
thy neighbor as thyself." Why does each one go out of
bounds? Why do we love ourselves too much by despising
our neighbors? Unless inasmuch as we do not practice diligently enough what is said to us, that we ought not to be so
given to ourselves that we may not love our neighbors as our
own persons. For we ought to consider that God has created
all of us in His image, and then we are of the same nature.
By that also He shows us that we must agree in true brotherhood with those who are joined with us. This is what we
have to remember from this passage, when Job remonstrates
against those who were accusing him unjustly, that since
they would not be willing that someone should do likewise to
them, they must not thus abuse his patience. This, in summary, is what we have to gather.

Now it is said further, *"I would hold my tongue now, but
what will it profit? If I speak, what alleviation shall I get by
it?"* Job here anticipates the reply that could be made to him,

for his friends could say, "Comfort thyself now, since thou art such a clever man; and since, if we were in such a condition, thou couldst work wonders; come now, display thy faculties toward thyself." But he says, "Behold me in a condition as miserable as could be. So then, I do not know what hope I ought to conceive of; for God presses me in such a strange manner that, if I speak I do only increase my sorrow; if I hold my tongue there is no alleviation for me. Behold me, then, as a man swallowed up in all afflictions." This, in summary, is what Job wishes to say: that whether he speaks or whether he refrains, he is not alleviated in any manner whatever. That is also how David complains in Psalm 32:3 that his evil has so pressed him in anguish that he does not know what is to become of him nor what remedy to look for. "When," says he, "I have lamented and I have supposed by this means that I would have some softening of my sorrow, more fire is lighted. If I have kept my mouth closed, and though I was willing as it were to be beaten before God, my heart is both tormented and cut in pieces; and then my sorrow has pressed me so sharply that it is not relieved by this." And in the other passage (Psalm 39:2) he says that he had concluded that while the wicked held sway he would not utter a word but be there like a mute. But why? Says he, "I cannot hold myself to this proposition;[5] for when I wished thus to restrain myself, in the end hot words had to burst out." Like a pot when the fire is hot — although it is covered the foam comes out some place. Now this is well worthy of being noted. For when God sends us some sickness or some reversal of fortune, then it seems to us that no man has ever been treated as harshly as we are; and this is the cause of putting us into despair or of inciting us to every impatience, and that we come also to raise ourselves against God, or perhaps it seems to us that the believers who have been before us, although God afflicted them, were not as infirm as we are, even that they had no sufferings. And this also is the cause of adding to our torment. Yet let us remember what is here

---

5. That is, in the presence of his enemies, David could not confine himself to saying good things.

said, namely: God had so pressed His own, those (I say) whom He loved, and whose salvation He held dear and precious; yet He has led them to such extremity that they could bear no more, they did not know what to say nor how to keep quiet. David does not make such a confession without cause, but it is for the teaching of all the children of God. For when we see that a man filled with such virtue, having such constancy from the Holy Spirit, nevertheless is put down to the depths, both that he does not know what to do and that he is at his wits' end — let us profit by it, and if God sends us such difficult trials[6] that we are at the limit and we cannot bear any more — very well — may it not be anything new, for we are not the first. David shows us the way, and he got out of such a mire, God extended His hand to him, and after he had more and more humility, so God assisted him. Yet let us not doubt that He still does us mercy, after for a time we shall have been beaten down.

This, then, is why it is good and necessary that we should have these examples before our eyes, and this will even cause our infirmity not to have too much power over us. For if temptations press us and we do not know what is to happen we remember just this, "Very well, here are the servants of God who have been before us; although they had great gifts, yet they had to sigh under the hand of God, and they knew not what would come of it, and God by this means wished to despoil them of all arrogance, He wished to teach them by experience how they had to bow their heads under Him." And if it pleases Him today to beat us down using the same means, provided that the purpose be such, although we may nevertheless have to suffer; we do not torment our minds by it, since every thing will come back to our great profit and salvation. This is what we have to note from this teaching which is here contained.

Now Job adds that God presses him so, that it seems that He wishes to cut him in pieces. Speaking thus he denotes what we have already seen: that He had afflicted him not only in his body, but that there were greater and more difficult

6. Fr. *des tentations si dures.*

temptations, indeed even bitter ones, namely: that he was tormented inside, because God was to him as it were a mortal
enemy. It is true that he says that the leanness of his body was
as it were a brand of shame and a testimony of the wrath of
God, that he was wrinkled, that all his flesh was as it were half
rotten. In this is surely seen the marks of a horrible affliction, and that God was not treating him in a manner common with those whom He chastises with His stripes; but his
sorrow is excessive. This, then, is, in summary, what Job
wished to express. Now we have to note that God wished to
give us examples in those who had some excellent virtues, in
order that we might be able to know in their personalities that,
according as He distributes the gifts of His Holy Spirit, also
to turn them to account and to make them all the more fruitful, He sends them great afflictions in their persons, and
proves them, briefly, He chastises them to the limit. For
example, there is Abraham who is governed by the Spirit of
God, not as a common man, but as an angel, as full of excellence and perfection as could be. And how is it that God also
handled him? If we had to endure one-tenth of the struggles
that Abraham sustained and surmounted, what would become
of us? We would be found wanting. But God spares us, inasmuch as He has not poured out upon us such excellent gifts
as He has done to him. Likewise is it with David. There
is David who was not only Prophet of God, but also the King
to govern the holy and elect people, who had in his person
virtues well worthy to remember and to praise, even to admire
— and yet what did God lead him through? We see the
complaints that he made, not only as a man contemptible and
rejected, but saying that on earth God kept him in torture,
that He had to show him the extremities to which he had
come. For it is not without cause that he says so often that
he has passed through fire and through water, and that he
has been cast into the very lowest depths, and that he has felt
all the darts of God, and all His arrows being shot against
him, that the hand of God has grown heavy upon him, that
even his bones have been affected,[7] that there remained neither

7. Psalm 32:3.

marrow nor substance in them. When we hear this proposition, it seems to us almost mockery; but God wished to put here a vivid painting, in order that we may know, following what we have said, that according as God gives a great virtue to men, also He works quickly in order that these virtues may not be idle, but that they may be known in time and place. Besides let us note, however, that the principal temptations which believers have endured have ever been these spiritual struggles, as we call them, that is to say, when God has summoned them in their consciences, that He has made them to feel His fury, that He has persecuted them in such a way that they did not know where they stood with Him. Also this is to cast them into the depths in ruin more than all bodily evils, even the worst that could happen. This is also why Job uses this metaphor, that God has gnashed His teeth upon him. We see also how Hezekiah speaks of it, because he had passed through this temptation (Isaiah 38:3, 14). He says, "God has been to me like a lion." He had also previously used the expression which is here: that he did not know how to speak, nor how to refrain. "For I am," he says, "like a swallow, I talk jargon, I murmur; but I make no statements by which I can express the sorrow of my evil, I have no language of deliverance." But thereupon he comes afterwards to declare that God has split and broken his bones, like a lion which would take him between his paws and between his teeth. And how can he compare God to a lion which is such a cruel beast? No, Hezekiah did not wish to accuse God of cruelty, but he speaks of the apprehension that he had, and of the horrible affliction which he experienced when the wrath of God was upon him.

So then, let us note that when a poor creature enters into this doubt, namely: how he stands before God, and that he has only apprehension whether He may wish to make him to experience His goodness — he must be in such distress and such great astonishment as if he were between the paws of wolves. We must not imagine that it is a small thing for a man to experience the wrath of God, and above all when we dread that He is thus against us, yet let us pray to God that it may please Him to support us, and to spare us, knowing that we are not capable of sustaining such a burden, unless He gives us shoulders to do it. Besides, we pray to Him that He may not use such strictness against us, that we may not experience Him as a lion; but rather that He may always show that He is our Father, and that He may not punish us as we have deserved; but that He may always cause us to experience His mercy by means of our Lord Jesus Christ, in order that after we shall have been led by His Holy Spirit in this present life, He may raise us into the eternal glory of His Angels, which He has bought for us at such a price.

Now we shall bow in humble reverence before the face of our God.

SERMON 8

I Know My Redeemer Lives*

My breath has been offensive to my wife, and so I have entreated her for the children of my loins. Even little children reject me, and when I arise, they taunt me. My friends have held me in abomination, and those whom I loved have turned against me. My bone clings to my skin and to my flesh, and I have escaped with the skin of my teeth. Have pity upon me, have pity upon me, you my friends; for the hand of God has struck me. Why do you persecute me like God, and are you not satisfied with my flesh? I desire that my statements should be written, that they should be registered in a book, with an iron pen in lead or in rock to eternity. I know that My Redeemer is living, and finally shall stand upon the earth.—JOB 19:17-25

INASMUCH as God has joined men, in order that one may support the other, and that each one may try to help his neighbor, and, when we can do no better, that we may have pity and compassion one for another; if it happens that we are destitute of all help, that we are molested from all sides, and that no one shows humaneness toward us, but everyone is cruel toward us, this temptation is very hard. And that is why Job in this passage complains that there was neither wife, nor friends, nor domestic servants who pitied him, but that all the world rejected him. Now when we see this, we ought to apply it to ourselves; for (as was discussed yesterday) God permits that men fail us, that everyone estrange himself from us, in order that we may run back so much sooner to Him. In fact, while we have some support from the world's side we shall not hope in God as we must; rather, we keep our attentions here below; for also our nature is entirely inclined that

* Sermon 71 in *Calvini Opera, Corpus Reformatorum*, vol. 34, pp. 114-126.

way, and we are too much given to it. So God sometimes, wishing to draw us to Himself, will cause us to be destitute of all human help. Or perhaps, it will be to humble us; for it seems to us that He surely ought to have regard for us, and that we are worthy of it; and everyone blinds himself with such presumption. Our Lord, then, sometimes wishes to instruct us in humility by this means; that everyone will hate us, that we shall be rejected by great and small. So then, we shall have to think that we are not such as we have supposed. But though that may be, if this comes, let us know that still we are not forsaken by God; for we see that Job still has recourse to Him, and that he is not disappointed in his attempt. God, then, extended to him His hand, although men had rejected him and surely supposed that there was no more hope for him; it is then that God considered to do him mercy. Let us confide, then, in this. Besides, may we be taught to do our duty toward those who are afflicted, following what I have said, that He has joined us together and united us in order that we may have a community; for men ought not to entirely separate themselves. It is true that our Lord has appointed the policy[1] that each one shall have his house, that he shall have his household, his wife, his children, each one will be in his place; yet no one ought to except himself from the common life by saying, "I shall live to myself alone." This would be to live worse than as a brute beast. What then? Let us know that God has obligated us to one another in order to help us; and at least when we see someone in need, though we cannot do him the good that we may wish to, let us be humane toward him. If we do not do this much, let us note that in the person of Job the Holy Spirit here asks vengeance against us; for there is no doubt that Job (although he was agitated by great and excessive sufferings) was always governed by the Spirit of God, and especially with respect to the general principles, that is to say, with respect to the sentences which he uttered; as we have declared that they implied profitable doctrine. Let us note, then, that our Lord here declares that

---

1. Fr. *police.*

we are too cruel when we see a poor, afflicted man and we do
not try to help him but rather we withdraw from him.

Let us also note that sometimes we can gather good doctrine even from things said incidentally in Holy Scripture: as
here Job, speaking of his wife, says that *she could not bear
his breath, although he entreated her for the sake of the children of his loins.* This shows that children ought to add to
the love between the husband and the wife. For when God
blesses a marriage with descendants, that ought to increase
the mutual affection to live in greater concord. Pagans have
known this well; but it is poorly observed by those who surely
ought to see more clearly. And what condemnation will be
for believers, who boast of having been taught in the Word
of God, if they do not recognize that which nature has shown
to the ignorant poor who are as it were blind! There are,
then, pagans who have confessed that children were as it
were earnests[2] to better confirm the love between husband
and the wife, to hold them in peace and union. Following
this, Job says that he entreated his wife for the sake of the
children which he had begotten by her. Now this did not
move her at all. It shows, then, that it is a thing against nature, and that his wife showed herself to be like a savage beast
in this situation. So let us note that those who cannot follow
such an order are here rebuked in passing, as if the Holy
Spirit had pronounced their sentence in explicit terms. Yet
we see many who have no discretion, though God has done
them the grace of giving them children. Here is a man who
will have lived with his wife; it is true that marriage is already a thing so sacred that this word alone ought to well
suffice, when it is said, "They will be two in one flesh," for the
man to hold the union which he should have with his wife
more precious than that which he will have with respect to
father and mother; but when God yet adds as a superabundant
confirmation of this grace, that the marriage produces children, if men and women are so brutal that they are not induced and incited by this to love each other still more, it is
certain that their ingratitude is too base. Now (as we have

2. Fr. *gages.*

already said) it is a thing very poorly practiced among Christians; but we must profit by this word, although it is here mentioned only incidentally.

Job, to add to the evil, says, *that friends, and the men of his counsel,* that is to say, those to whom he was accustomed to communicating all his secrets, *have turned against him,* or perhaps, have mocked him, that they no longer held him to be of any account; and that not only those who had some reputation or position despised him, but *the smallest,* the most ill-starred. He indicates, in summary, that he finds himself destitute of all help, seeing that his friends have failed him. Secondly, that he has been in such shame that the most despised of the world still have not deigned to consider him as of their rank. He surely had to say that his affliction was great, seeing that there was no one who recognized him as of the company of men; but that he was already more than exterminated. This, in summary, is what Job wished to say. Now (as we have already mentioned) God wished thus to train him, in order that he might be an example to us. If it happens, then, that those who are our nearest neighbors should be deadly enemies, and that they should persecute us, let us learn to run back to God, and to bear it patiently, seeing that it happened to Job before us. And let us remember even what is said of our Lord Jesus Christ, because He belongs to all the members of His Church, "He who ate bread at My table has lifted up his heel against me."[3] This must be fulfilled in all believers; and for this cause our Lord Jesus has shown us the way, in order that we may not be too much offended by being conformed to His image. We shall see, then, all the blows, that the children of God will be betrayed and persecuted by those in whom they had fully confided, and with whom they had had great intimacy. Well: this is a very hard thing, no one can deny it, and when we experience this evil, it is enough to make us lose courage; but since our God has declared to us that so it must be, and He has given us a witness to it in the person of His Only Son, let us overlook it and sub-

---

3. Psalm 41:9 refers to David and Ahithophel, but it is also fulfilled in Christ and Judas, John 13:18.

mit to this condition. This is still what we have to observe in this passage.

We come now to what Job adds. *"Pity me, pity me, you my friends; for the hand of God has touched me,"* he says. It is true, when we see that God punishes men, that we surely ought to glorify Him, saying, "Lord, Thou art just." But there was a special consideration in Job, who was not punished by God for faults that he had committed, it was for another purpose; and yet let us consider what would have been the case if he had been chastised according to what he deserved, yet when we shall see a poor evil-doer whom God will have led to his condemnation, so we must be touched in ourselves, indeed, for two reasons. The one is, that when each one will look at himself, we shall find that God ought to punish us even more severely, when it should please Him to visit us according as we have deserved. Whosoever, then, will think of himself, will find himself blameworthy to be punished by God as grievously as those whom he sees hard-pressed; and so we ought to regard them in pity and compassion. So, our vices and our iniquities ought to make us humble. There is a poor, miserable fellow; I see that God persecutes him; it is a horrible thing. But what of it? There is cause enough for which God could also punish me; I must, then, be humble, and ,I must look at myself in the person of this one. That is one item. And then, when we shall see a man who will have been afflicted as greatly as possible by the hand of God, may we know not only that he was created in the image of God, but also that he is neighbor to us, and as it were one with us; we are all of one nature, we have one flesh, we are mankind, that is to say, we came out of one same source. Since it is so, must we not think one of another, "Furthermore, I see a poor soul who is going to perish; ought I not to have compassion to relieve him, if it is in me?"? And though I may not have the means, I ought to aspire to do it. These are (I say) the two reasons which ought to move us to pity when we see that God afflicts those who are worthy of it. When, then, we think of ourselves, it is certain that we must be very hard and stupid, or we shall have pitied those who are like us, as when we shall

recognize, "Here is a man who is formed in the image of
God, he is a soul which has been bought by the blood of the
Son of God. If he perishes, ought we not to be touched by
it?"

It is why Job says now, *"Pity me, my friends, since the
hand of God has struck me."* To understand this still better,
we must take this sentence: "It is a horrible thing to fall into
the hands of the Living God."[4] When, then, we see some
punishment which God sends, we must be moved with fright,
even though He spares us. I shall be at rest, and God seem-
ingly will not touch me at all, but I shall see how He strikes
one, how He afflicts another; is it not something to be astonished at? Must we wait for God to strike our heads with
great blows? It would be too base. But when we see that
He wishes to instruct us at the expense of others, we must
consider the cause why He punishes men so, as Saint Paul
shows us (Ephesians 5:6). He does not say, "Fear ye, for
the wrath of God will come upon you;" but he says, "My
friends, you see how God punishes unbelievers, while He
spares you; so you must know that it is for your instruction
when He gives some sign of His wrath upon men." Let us
note, then, this sentence of the Apostle, namely: It is a frightful thing to fall into the hands of God; and whenever He does
some punishment, may we be moved. Now from this we shall
be fully instructed to pity those who endure, by saying, "Alas!
Here is a poor creature; if it were a mortal man who afflicted
him, he could be given some alleviation; but God is against
him; and ought we not to have pity as we see this?" If someone argues, "Is it not resisting God if we pity those who are
chastised for their faults? Is it not as if we wished to set ourselves against the justice of God?" No; for we surely can
have these two motives in us: (1) to approve the justice of
God, giving Him glory and praise for what He does; and
nevertheless (2) we allow ourselves to pity those who are
punished, since we have deserved as much or more, since we
ought to seek the salvation of all, whether those who are our
near neighbors or whether there will be some bond that God

---

4. Hebrews 10:31.

will have placed between us; as we shall approve earthly justice, which is only as it were a little mirror of the justice of God, and yet we allow ourselves to pity an evil-doer. When a criminal is punished, it is not said that he is wronged, nor that there was cruelty in the judge. It is said, then, that those who are constituted to enforce justice acquit themselves of their duty and that they offer a sacrifice acceptable to God when they cause a criminal to die; however we allow ourselves to pity a poor creature who suffers for his evil deeds; if we are not moved by it, there is no humaneness in us. If we recognize this in human justice which is only as it were a little spark from God; when we come nigh to the sovereign throne, I pray you, ought we not in the first place to glorify God in all that He does, knowing that He is just and equitable in everything and through everything? Nevertheless, this will not hinder us (as I have said) (1) from having compassion on those who endure, to care for them and to relieve them; and when we can do no better, (2) from desiring their salvation, praying God that in the end He may make their corrections profitable to draw them back to Himself, that He may not permit that they may remain hardened to chafe against His hand.

This is, I say, the basis upon which Job requests and exhorts his friends to pity him. He speaks especially to those who were closest to him; for although God has put some unity among men in general, that is to say, He has joined them all together (as we have said) and they ought not to separate themselves from each other; yet God obliges us doubly when we have either parenthood or some other bond, as we know that relatives ought to be incited to bear toward each other some more private friendship; for then God has put men, as one might put beasts under a yoke, saying after a fashion, "Brute beasts ought to teach us what we have to do." When two oxen are yoked together if one wishes to be balky, they will torment each other; and if they do not agree to work together with one accord, then afterwards both to drink and to sleep, they will have to be there as their own tormentors. So it is with men when God draws some near to others in any

manner whatever; it is as if He wishes to couple them under
the same yoke to help and to support one another; and if they
are balky, if they are worse than brute beasts, what condemnation do they deserve upon their heads? So then, let us note
well, that according as God draws us together, and gives us
means of communicating together, He obligates us to one
another, for a friend will be so much more attached to his
friend, although our charity must be general, and though we
should love those whom God commends to us, and who might
even be our deadly enemies; yet the husband will be more
attached to his wife, the father to his children, the children to
the father, the relatives also to one another; and in general we
must recognize all the degrees of friendship which God has
put in the world.

Now Job adds, *"Why do you persecute me like God?"* It
surely seems that this sentence is not very reasonable here;
for it is said (as we have already mentioned) that the just will
wash his hands in the blood of the iniquitous. We ought,
then, to rejoice when we see that God punishes the wicked;
now Job states here that one ought not to persecute those
whom God persecutes. But this question was already solved
when we said that we can well agree with the justice of God;
and yet we allow ourselves to pity those who endure, and to
relieve them, if it is in our power; for at least we shall be
moved to desire their salvation. It will be, then, a cruel thing
when we shall persecute men like God. And why so? For
when God afflicts sinners (I do not say the righteous like Job.
but those who will have lived in evil, who will have been of a
wicked life) it is not that we may raise our heads against
them, and that we may molest them still further; but He
wishes in the first place that each one of us may learn to condemn himself in the person of the other. I see that this one
is now beaten by the rods of God. And why so? For his
sins. Now is not God Judge of all the world? This includes
me, then; for am I innocent? Alas! There are only too many
faults, and only too base. This, then, is how in the person
of another, one ought to condemn himself, whenever we contemplate in the other the chastisements which God sends; and

then also God wishes to train us to pity and compassion. If we follow this order, we cannot go wrong; but if without regard to our faults we come to torment those who already have too much evil, is not this cruelty? We wish to usurp the office of God to be judges; and rather we ought to think of what is said, "We must all appear before the judgment-seat of God." It is true (as we have already said) that God must surely be glorified through all the punishments which He sends to men; but this is not to say that each one ought not to condemn himself, and to be held to some humaneness through this means; when we shall know that God must be the Judge of all. And that is why Job argues rightly with his friends that they persecute him like God. Let us note well, then, that if God displayed His vengeance upon those who have offended Him, it is not that He wishes to arm us to be inhumane, and to set us in fury against the poor patients who are entirely beaten down; but rather he wishes that we may have compassion on them.

Besides, Job here accuses his friends of cruelty, saying that they cannot be satisfied with his flesh. *"Why,"* he says, *"can you not be satisfied with my flesh?"* It is certain that this is a figure of speech which he uses; for when we are thus set (as they say) against our neighbors, it is as if we wished to eat them alive; and we also use these mannerisms of speech in our common language. So then, as a man will take pleasure in his meal, to eat, and to drink; also those who are cruel against their neighbors — it seems that they wish to make their repast, that they wish to eat and to gobble them alive. That, then, is why Job says, *"Why are you not satisfied with my flesh?"* For when we see that our neighbors have more and more evil, and still we are not satisfied, but we add to their evil, and still we are not satisfied, it is too great a cruelty, it is like eating them. This circumstance, then, is to be noted when Job says, "At least his friends ought to be satisfied to see him thus beaten down. What do you wish more? I am at the extremity, so that I can take no more." It is a natural thing, that when we shall have hated some person, and desired evil against him, and sought all the means to avenge ourselves; however if the worst possible affliction happens to him, then our rage is appeased. Now I do not say that this feeling ought here to be held as a virtue; for pagans, although they were wicked, though they supposed that vengeance was lawful for them, yet had the consideration to be appeased when they saw that their enemies were so molested that they need not inflict anything further with their hands. How so? Here is a man who will have done evil to some one; or perhaps, he who will be offended will wish to avenge himself, if it were possible to him. However, God goes before and sends some great calamity to the one who will have offended him; the man who previously was embittered, and asked only to ruin him whom he hated, will say now, "Indeed, and what more shall I do? He is so cast down that he is even to be pitied, he has had enough." This, then, is how the fire will be extinguished naturally, when we shall have been the most irritated man in the world against someone, if we see him in affliction. This (as I have said) is not virtue, and deserves to be counted neither as the service of God nor as charity. However, if it is a natural inclination, even among pagans, what about those today who are not satisfied when they see their enemies persecuted as much as possible, but they are insatiable and would still wish to have eaten them? And if it is condemnable when one is not satisfied with the afflictions that God sends upon enemies, how much more so will it be to act this way toward friends? So may those who are so cruel know that they are not worthy to be counted as of the number of men. Whoever, then, wishes to acquit himself of his duty, not only ought to be appeased by the evil and the affliction of his enemies; but he ought to be moved to pity; and instead of seeking vengeance, he ought rather to be ready to help them as much as he can; for there is no doubt when God sends some affliction to our enemies, and to those who have irritated us, that he wishes to soften the malice and the ill-will which is in us, that He wishes to change that which causes us to be ill-affected toward our neighbors. Now if God calls us to humaneness, and we go entirely the opposite way, is it not fighting against Him openly? Let us note well,

then, when God afflicts those who have done us some wrong
and injury, that it is to soften the spite that is in our hearts;
and if we have previously been angered and piqued, or we
have desired vengeance, that God wishes to moderate all these
evil affections in us, and wishes to induce us to compassion
and humaneness. This is what we have to note from this passage.

Now Job adds still new complaints of his miseries, saying
*that his bone was attached to his skin, and that he has escaped
with the skin of his teeth.* It is to better express the proposition that we already discussed: namely, that his friends surely
ought to be satisfied, though they were like beasts seeking only
to devour. And why? "For," says he, "you see in what
state I am. What do you ask more? Can anymore desire
more evil to one person than God has sent to me?" Now
when he says that his skin is attached to his bones, it is as
if he said that he is all dried up, that he is like a corpse, that
there is no longer juice or substance in him. When he says
that he has escaped with the skin of his teeth, it is to indicate
that there is no health in him except in his gums, or that his
skin looks like his gums, for if vermin have spread in a body,
the skin will no longer be dry; but it will look like the gums;
that is to say, when the rot will spread, all will be eaten, bloody
flesh will be seen, and there will come out half blood, half
water, as from a wound, as we see that a wound looks like
the gums. Here, then, is Job who declares that he was so
disfigured that the appearance of a man was no longer recognized in him. Now when he came to this extremity, was it
not reasonable that his friends should be satisfied? We are,
then, here admonished to have more consideration for the
afflictions of our friends than we do; and that when God will
send them some calamities, we should pray to Him that He
may give us grace to have our eyes more open to consider
them, and to note them well, so that it may induce us to pity;
that everyone may be employed in applying the remedy as
much as he can, and that even at the end we should hope that
when they are touched by the hand of God, He will show
mercy toward them.

Now because Job was accused by his friends of having blasphemed against God, in that he justified himself against all reason, and in that he was blinded in his vices, not recognizing them; he says, *"I would that my statements were written, that they were engraved with an iron pen, that they were engraved in lead or in a stone to eternity,* and as a permanent memorial." Job, speaking thus, declares that he has not maintained his innocence in vain, and that he fears only what would be a reproach to him before God; for he knows that he has just cause to do it. This is, in summary, what he maintains. Now it is very certain with respect to the statements of Job, that some were excessive, there were many extravagant sentences; for he did not keep himself in bounds, and though he had a good and reasonable foundation, and though his case was approved by God, yet he pleaded it poorly (as we have previously declared) and there escaped from his mouth many words which were to be condemned. Why, then, does he now say that he would like his statements to be thus written? Is it not to bring double condemnation upon his head? Let us note that Job considered the principle, and that he was not bound by each word that he had pronounced; but he makes here these statements to defend his case. Now this defense was just; and although it was overly labored, and though he wandered from one side to the other, nevertheless he maintains rightly that he was not afflicted for his sins, and they must not think that he was the most wicked man in the world because God showed such severity against him. Job, then, proposed this rightly; yet he was still at fault, since he did not so recognize all his vices and he surely did not always consider himself guilty before God. By this we are admonished to speak very prudently. It is said in Psalm 39:2, "I resolved to keep my mouth closed, to bridle myself while the wicked have dominion and they hold sway; but in the end I could not contain myself." David knew well that when the children of God are tempted, seeing themselves oppressed by afflictions. while the wicked achieve their victories and have clear sailing, it is such a hard thing that it is very difficult for us to contain ourselves, that we should not murmur against God. For this cause he says, "I have resolved to hold myself as it were in check, I have put a sling over my lower jaw, I have barred my mouth, in order not to sound a word; but in the end all these checks were broken, all the resolution that I had made could not keep me from showing the desire that I had conceived within; and the fire in the end is lighted and broken out." By this David shows that it is a virtue very great and very rare, that we should be patient in silence and in restraining ourselves when wicked men press us, and above all when we see that the wicked have their mouths wide open to glorify themselves and to mock us. So, by joining this passage of David with the example of Job, we ought to be instructed to keep our mouths closed when God afflicts us. And why? For according as our passions are violent, although we may learn to speak in such simplicity as we ought, and to praise God. and to bless Him; still we cannot be so prudent or so moderate that nothing may escape us, that some froth may not come out, so that we shall always be guilty in our statements. So then, although we may not intend to blaspheme against God, or to say something which may not be to his honor, still it can only happen that we have been too bold in our speaking; as when Job asked that everything might be recorded, that all might be engraved as a memorial, that it should be put either in rock or in lead, in order that it could never be erased. Rather, let us be advised to pray to God that, with respect to the statements that we suppose are the cleanest, He may still pardon us our faults; for he who will be able to hold his tongue (says St. James 3:2) will have a rare virtue. For we are as ready to speak evil as can be, and when we suppose ourselves to have spoken perfectly uprightly, God will find that there will still be some excess. This, then, is what we have to note from this passage.

Now in the end Job adds, *that he knows that his Redeemer lives*. It is true that this could not be understood as fully then as now; so we must discuss the intention of Job in speaking thus. He intends, then, that he was not acting the part of a hypocrite by pleading his cause before men, and by justifying himself; he knew that he had to do with God. This is what

we must know, for these sentences, if they were taken as out
of their context, would not be to great edification, and we
would not know what Job wished to say.   Therefore let us
remember what we have discussed.   What does Job maintain?
We know that men try as much as they can to excuse themselves, indeed, since they do not think of God; it is enough
that the world is satisfied with them, and that they be considered gentlemen.   This is the hypocrisy which engenders
impudence.   For if I do not know that God is my Judge, oh,
I shall be satisfied that men applaud me, that they hold me in
good reputation.   And what have I gained?   Nothing whatever.   Is it not a great impudence, when, though my own conscience rebukes me, though I am convicted of having done
evil, yet I put up a front and say, "Why am I accused?   What
have I done,   Have I not a good case?"   I shall make beautiful pretenses to cover my sin, and when I shall have so dazzled
the eyes of men, behold, my case won.   But it is what I have
said, that hypocrisy engenders impudence, that is to say, that
men are bold to maintain their case as good, since they have
no regard for God.

Now Job, on the contrary, says, *"I know that my God is
living, and that He shall stand in the end upon the dust."*   As
if he said, "I may be considered as a wicked and desperate
man, as if I had blasphemed against God, trying to justify
myself against him.   No, not at all, I ask only to humble myself and to rest in His grace; however, I maintain my integrity against you, for I see that you proceed here only by
slanderous words; I, then, defend myself in such a way that I
regard God and have my eyes fixed on God."   Now from
this we can and ought to gather good instruction: namely,
that we should not be as hypocrites, covering ourselves before
men, making believe to maintain a good case, and showing
ourselves to be gentlemen, while our conscience rebukes us.
Let us learn, rather, to examine ourselves, to know our sins,
and to humble ourselves before God; let us begin, I say, by
saying, Now, how is it with me?   It is true that I could easily
excuse myself before men, but of what profit would it be to
me before God?   Would he accept me?   No, not at all.   Ac-

cording to this, then, let all of us, both great and small, come
before this heavenly Judge, and let each one present himself
there to ask forgiveness for his faults; and let us not doubt
that when we come there sincerely, we are absolved by Him,
not because we deserve it, but through His grace and mercy.

Now let us bow in humble reverence before the face of our
God.

SERMON 9

From My Flesh I Shall See God*

Though after my skin worms have worn this away, from my flesh I shall see God. I, myself, shall contemplate Him, my eyes shall see Him, and none other; my reins have decayed in my bosom. And you have said, "Wherefore is he persecuted?" And the root of the remark is found in me. Fear the presence of the sword; for the wrath of affliction is with the sword, in order that you may know that there is judgment. —Job 19:26-29

WE SAW yesterday the protest Job made of having regard to God and not being at all attached to men; because those whose interest is confined to this world below do not voluntarily search their consciences to condemn themselves as they ought, and to realize their sins, in order that they may ask God to pardon them, confessing that they have trangressed. For we see, as soon as we are set on the approval of men, that we ask only to surpass them, whether by truth or by falsehood. This is the cause why we do not properly think of God, and consequently we take no pains to correct our faults, as we ought; briefly, there is only hypocrisy. Therefore Job says that *he knows that his Redeemer is living;* as if he said that he has not pleaded thus far to be thus justified before men that this was not his purpose; for he knew that he must come before God, and there be judged, and render account of all his life. Then he adds that *God will stand upright at the last day upon the dust;* as if he said, "When men will be decayed, as the world must perish, God is permanent; so I shall commit great folly by wishing to excuse myself before men while God condemns me, for those who are now my judges, or who wish

---

* Sermon 72 in *Calvini Opera, Corpus Reformatorum*, vol. 34, pp. 127-139.

to confer this honor — they must perish with me, and God
will remain always. So then, it is sufficient for me to surrender myself to him, and to hear that which it will please
Him to ordain."

Now when he says, *"God will stand upright upon the dust,"*
he signifies that He is not like men; for we must forfeit everything when we are annihilated, we know that we must return
to that from which we came, in corruption, in rottenness. "But
God," says he, "cannot forfeit in the manner of men, but he
will always be in His condition." Besides, let us note that
Job wished to signify that God will pour out the power which
is in Him upon the dust, that is to say, upon men who are
nothing, and who have no power in themselves. Now this
title which he attributed to God implies much, that He is his
guarantor, and He by Whom he is maintained. If God
wished, he could surely remain whole, and yet we shall perish;
but He wishes to make us partakers of His power, and to make
us experience it. So, He stands thus upright upon the dust,
He makes the dust to completely revive, and thereupon He
restores it; for without this, in vain He would be called both
"Redeemer" and "Guarantor." Let us note well that Job
wished to express that God does not only keep His power inclosed in His essence, but that it is poured out upon men.
This is a good doctrine for us. For in the first place we are
admonished what vanity it is to wish only to please men and
to be approved by them. What do we gain? For everything
here below must pass away. Let us learn, then, to have our
eyes fixed on God, in order that He may own us, and that we
may be able to be approved by Him. This is where we must
apply all our study. However, in order not to be attached to
this world, in order not to be wrapped up in the hypocrisy
which is by nature too deeply rooted in us, let us know that
God our guarantee, that is to say, that it belongs to Him alone
to maintain the integrity of men, when they will have walked
in pure conscience before Him; that He will be their Judge
once for all, and He will stand upright upon the dust; and although all that we see around us may be frail and worthless,
God is not that way, His condition is much higher; and not

only for Himself, but in order to put all creatures back in their condition, when they shall have expired. And it is an inestimable consolation for believers. when they are seen to be oppressed by slander in this world; and although they have tried to walk uprightly, they never stop annoying them and biting them falsely, then they can commit themselves to God and call upon Him for their guarantee, they lean upon the certainty that God will be standing when men will be annihilated. Well, those who today presume to condemn us and to speak against us, must fall down, and things will surely be reversed; for God will then be our Redeemer. Men today by their temerity usurp the power of God, they undertake what is not lawful for them; but it must be that God will show in the end His position, both that He may be exalted and that we may know that it belongs to Him to maintain us.

This is what we ought to keep in mind whenever anyone speaks against us falsely: both that we shall have good testimony before God, and that it will be sufficient that He approves us, although we may be rejected by all the world. We come to what Job says. He says, that worms (for although the word may not be expressed, yet it is clearly seen that He intends all vermin and corruption) — that worms, after they have eaten the skin, will nibble away and wear away what is left; but though he hopes to see God, and to see Him, he says, "from my flesh," that is to say, to be restored; "yes, I shall see Him, and no other, although my reins have decayed within me," that is to say, all my power is dissolved and abolished. Here is an affirmation worthy of being noted, when Job declares that he will have his attention fixed on God, and no other, indeed, although he may be entirely consumed; as if he said that the hope that he has in God he will not measure according to what he can see; but that when nothing appears. yet he will not cease to look to God. How so? If a man finds himself as it were forsaken by God, that he perceives only all manner of despair, that death threatens him from all sides, even that it swallows him up; and yet nevertheless he perseveres, he is constant in the faith, to say, "So, I shall call upon my God, and I shall still experience His power; only

His power can give me strength; and that will happen, even when it seems that I shall be lost." Here is a man who surmounts things present. He does not show then the faith and the hope that he has in God, because he can see and comprehend by his natural senses, but he passes beyond the world; as it is said, we ought to hope beyond hope, and hope is of things hidden. Now we see the intention of Job. It is true that he does not speak here explicitly and simply of the resurrection; yet these words cannot be expounded unless it is recognized that Job wished to attribute to God a power which is not seen today in the common order of nature. It is as if he said that God wishes to be known by us not only while He does us good, preserves and nourishes us; but when he apparently fails us and we see only death before us, we must be resolved that our Lord will not cease to be our guarantee, and that, being His own, we shall be maintained through His protection.

But in order to profit better by this passage, let us weigh well what Job says. "Although what remains here," he says "may be worn away after my skin, yet I shall see my God." This is not believing in God only because He causes the earth to produce corn and wine; as we see many brutish persons who have no taste or feeling that there is a God in heaven unless He feeds them and fills their bellies. When they are asked "Who is God?" they answer, "He is the One who nourishes us." It is true that we surely must understand the goodness and the power of our God in all the benefits which He bestows upon us; but we must not stop there; for (as I have already said) our faith must rise above all that can be seen in this world. And so, let us not say, "I believe in God, because He sustains me, because He gives me health, because He nourishes me;" but let us say, "I believe in God, since already He has given me some taste of His goodness and of His power when He cares for this body which is only corruption, in that I see that He declares Himself Father in that I subsist by the power of His Spirit; but I believe in Him alone, since He calls me to heaven, since He did not create me like a bull or an ass to live here some space of time; but He has

formed me in His image, in order that I may hope in His
kingdom to be partaker of the glory of His Son; I believe that
daily He invites me there, in order that I may not doubt that
when my body shall be cast into the sepulchre, that it will be
there as it were annihilated, nevertheless it will be restored at
the last day; and that meanwhile my soul shall be in safekeep-
ing and secure, when after death God will have me in His
protection, and that even then I shall contemplate better than
I do now the life which has been acquired for us through the
blood of our Lord Jesus Christ." This, then, is what ought
to be our creed in order to be well ruled. Now when we shall
be thus well disposed, we shall be able to say with Job, "Well,
it is true that I see that my body is passing away into deca-
dence; if there is some vigor, it is decreasing day by day, and
I contemplate death without going to seek it ten leagues away;
for I can see so little but infirmity in my flesh, that it is already a message of death; yet I shall see my God." And if
we can speak thus when we see that our power declines and
vanishes little by little; if it pleases God to afflict us, in such
wise that we are, as it were, half rotted (thus was Job; for he
says, "My skin is eaten and consumed;" he was, as it were,
a corpse, and nevertheless he protests, "So, I shall not cease
to behold my God.") ; let us not cease to hope in God according to the example of Job. This, then, is how the greatness
of the afflictions that God will send us will not be to astonish
us, provided that we are taught to recognize Him as He is
toward us: namely, to consider well to what end He has
created us and maintains us in this world.

Besides, when Job says that *he will see his Redeemer from
his flesh,* he intends (as we have already said) that he will be
restored in a new state, his skin having been so eaten. For he
says that even his bones will be consumed and that nothing
will remain whole; and then he adds, *"From my flesh I shall
see God."* And how will he see Him from his flesh? That is to
say, "I shall be restored as I was previously, and I shall yet
see my God." And so he confesses that God will be powerful enough to raise him up, though He has entirely consumed him and plunged him into the depths. This is the

condition for which we ought to hope in God: it is that when
He will have cast us into the sepulchre, we may know that He
extends His hand to withdraw us from it.   Let us not say,
then, "I hope in God, because I see that He assists me and He
fails me in nothing;" but when God fails us, that He is as it
were far away from us, let us say with Job, "I shall see Him
from my flesh; I am now nothing; it seems that I am a shadow, that my life is quickly vanishing; yet my God will declare Himself so powerful toward me that I shall see him."
So Job spoke thus from the time when there was not yet great
doctrine, when possibly the Law was not written; but let us
suppose it was written, the Prophets were not yet, there was
only Moses (for the Prophets mention Job as a man from
ancient time).[1] So, then, having only a little spark of light,
he was so strengthened in his afflictions, and not only when
he saw a species of death, but when it seemed that God had
given him a constitution like a monster among men, a terrible
and frightful thing, yet he could say, "So is it that I shall see
my God."   What excuse will there be today, when God declares the Resurrection to us so exactly and so explicitly and
He gives us such beautiful promises of it?   And even considered that we see the mirror and the substance of it in our
Lord Jesus Christ, that He was raised in order to show us
that we must not doubt that we are at once partakers of this
immortal glory.   If then, after such confirmations, we cannot have the knowledge that was in Job, must it not be imputed to our ingratitude? For if we could receive the promises of God in true faith, would they not have enough power
to make us surmount all the temptations which thus rule over
us.   So then, let us note well this passage, in order to be able
to say also with St. Paul (2 Corinthians 5:1), "For if this
hut, which is our body, goes away (for by a "hut" he means
something made of leaves, some hovel that amounts to nothing) we have a building which is prepared, much better and
more excellent, in heaven. If this exterior man, that is to say,
all that which is of the present life and which appeared, is
annihilated, yet God wishes to renew us, and to make us al-

---

1. Ezekiel 14:14-20.

ready somehow to contemplate our resurrection, when we see our body thus failing." As also Saint Paul in the other passage (1 Corinthians 15:36) reminds us of the seed which is cast into the ground, saying that it cannot germinate to have a live root and to bear fruit, unless it is first changed into rottenness. Do we see, then, that death begins to rule over us? Let us note that God wishes to give us true life: namely, the heavenly life which was acquired for us through the precious blood of His Son. Now without this we must be conquered by the least temptation of the world, for (as I have already said) all the miseries that we have to suffer are so many messages of death. Now, seeing death, and supposing that we shall be consumed by it, must we not despair entirely? There is, then, no other means to comfort us in our afflictions except this doctrine: it is that when all that which is in us will be consumed, we shall not cease to see our God, indeed, to see Him from our flesh.

And then it is said, *"My eyes will contemplate Him, and none other."* Job adds this, following the proposition that he had held: namely, "Since God has given me the certainty that He will restore me to power, I shall commit myself entirely to Him; I must no longer be bewildered, nor be distracted, this way, or that way; for I must commit myself to Him alone. *My eyes, then, will contemplate Him, and none other."* Here is still a beautiful doctrine. What he said not long ago, namely, *that he will see God from his flesh,* refers to the experience when God will stand him as it were upon his feet; what he says this time is spoken from another consideration, namely, from a consideration of hope; for God is regarded by us in two manners; (1) we regard Him when He shows Himself to be Father and Saviour by experience and when He gives us a noteworthy experience of it. There is my God who will have withdrawn me from such a sickness that it will be like a resurrection; it is a testimony that He has put His hand upon me to help me; I contemplate Him then, and I contemplate Him by experience. Now, while I am sick, though there is no more hope, I do not cease to contemplate God; for I put my confidence in Him; afterwards, I await in patience the

issue which He wishes to give me, and I do not doubt that,
though He may withdraw me from the world, I am His own.
(2) There is still another manner of contemplating God. Job,
then, said that He will contemplate God by experience when
he will be restored to his condition; he adds in the second
place that he will not cease to contemplate Him, though he
may be completely crushed by evils. "My eyes," he says, "will
be fastened on Him, I do not wish to turn them away." Now
here we see the nature of faith: namely, to so reflect on God
that it does not go astray, that it has no such distractions as
we are accustomed to having. I pray you, what is the cause
why we cannot rest ourselves in God as it would be required?
It is because we separate the office of God and all His virtue
into so many pieces and bits that there is almost nothing left
of Him. We shall well say that it is God to whom it belongs
to sustain us; however, we do not cease to traipse high and
low, before and behind, to seek the means of our life; not as
being given by God, and proceeding from Him; but we attribute to them even the power of God, and we make as it were
idols of them.

That is how we can regard God with pleasure and yet cannot also have rest or contentment in Him. Let us note well,
then, the word which Job uses; it is that his eyes will contemplate God, and none other; as if he said, "I will cling to
this, I shall no longer be so agitated as men are, but I shall
commit myself entirely to my God by saying, 'It is Thou,
Lord, indeed Thou alone from Whom I hold my life, and
when I shall decay now, Thou wilt restore me as Thou hast
promised.' " Now let us always make the comparison between Job and us, that if Job, not having such a testimony
of the goodness of God, not having a doctrine one one-hundredth as familiar as we have, nevertheless said that he would
contemplate God — and we, shall we be excused when we
shall have gone astray this way and that way, indeed, after
our Lord Jesus Christ presents Himself to us, in Whom
dwells all fulness of divine glory, and all the power of the
Holy Spirit is shown in Him when He is raised from the
dead? And it is not even necessary for us to extend our view

very far to contemplate Him; for the Gospel is a good mirror, where we see Him face to face. Since it is so (as I have mentioned) let us be advised not to be guilty of such ingratitude that we may not have condescended to look at Him Who presented Himself to us so meekly. This, in summary is what we have to note from this passage.

Job adds further, *"Although my reins may be decayed within me,"* that is to say, "though there may no longer be power or rigor in me." In summary (following the proposition that he had already maintained) he shows that he does not look to God because God has treated him gently, because God has granted him all his wishes, because he is preserved from afflictions; but it is entirely the reverse. "Although," he says, I am in such anguish, though it seems that God is beating down upon me, though there is no longer any vigor in me; yet I shall contemplate my God with my eyes and I shall cling to Him alone, and I know that I shall yet see Him as my Redeemer and Guarantor, after He will have thus consumed me."

Now he says in conclusion to his friends, *"You have said, 'Why is he persecuted?' or 'Why shall we persecute him?' For the root of the case (or of the proposition) is found in me."* This passage is a little obscure because the word can be taken in two ways: *"Why is he persecuted?"* or, *"Why shall we persecute him?"* If we take it *"Why is he persecuted?"* it is that the friends of Job are astonished because God had treated him so harshly, and yet they conclude that they must say that he is a man entirely reprobate. If it is translated *"How shall we persecute him?"* it will be that they have come out of deliberate malice to find fault and to bite at him. But although there is diversity as to the words, yet the sense comes out the same. Let us look at the doctrine that we have to gather from it; for it is the principal thing, even the whole thing. Job, then, reproaches his friends that they have judged poorly of his affliction. And why so? For from the very first they rushed there, saying: "Oh, he must be a wicked man; if he had walked in good and pure conscience, he would not be thus afflicted." Now on the contrary, Job

says that *the root of the proposition is found in him.* It is
true that this word sometimes means "thing" and sometimes
"word;" but Job here signifies that he has a good and firm
foundation, and that when he will have been properly sounded,
it will be found that his case is not such as the others had
falsely estimated it.

Let us look now to what purpose this tends, and what profit
we can receive from it.   When Job proposes to his friends
that they have said, *"Why is he persecuted?"* he shows that
it is cruelty in men to look for the sins of another as soon as
they see someone beaten by the rods of God, saying, "This
man must be wicked; let us, then, peck him to death." For
this is the end where we must begin.   It is true (as was said
more fully before) that in all the stripes and corrections that
God sends, we must always contemplate His judgment upon
the sins of men; but it is to condemn us.   We must not be
judges of another by sparing ourselves; let us begin, let us
begin with ourselves.   We see, then, the usefulness of this
doctrine: namely, that if a man is oppressed by evils, we should
not be so hasty to condemn him, and indeed we should not be
inclined on that account to find crimes in him; but rather we
should look to God, Who shows Himself Judge both of us
and of him, and Who constrains us to recognize that we must
have pity and compassion for him who endures, and that we
must do it willingly, although we may know his faults; but
we should be advised rather to bring him some medicine that
he may get well.   Let us guard against putting the plow before
the oxen, that is, against making judgment before having understood the case, as we are accustomed to do.   Already it has
been said oftentimes, that God will not afflict men always for
the same purpose; sometimes He will punish their sins, sometimes He will wish to prove their patience, or there will be
some other reason.   Then, let us not be too hasty or bold to
judge before we have known all the facts; for we see what
happened to the friends of Job.   As soon as they see him
afflicted they say, "He must be wicked."   But blessed is the
man who judges prudently upon the afflicted, as it is said in

the Psalm.[2] Was not David oppressed by the hand of God
as harshly as ever any man was? Yet He says, "I have found
David my servant according to My heart, I have anointed
Him with the oil of joy."[3] Behold God who takes David as
it were into His bosom, and yet we see how he is treated. If
we are bold to judge it, we shall condemn both David and
Abraham, and all the holy Patriarchs. And will not this judgment come back to the dishonor of God? Certainly. So then,
let us be sober and modest when we see that our neighbors are
afflicted, and let us recognize the hand of God, in order that
it may not happen to us as it happened to the friends of Job.

Now he says especially that the *root of the case is found in
him,* or root of the proposition, or effect and substance. By
this he indicates that we must inquire before we judge. Now
in fact, each one will surely confess that if we made this mistake willingly, it would be foolish presumption and arrogance
in us, and this proverb is quite common, "From a foolish
judge, a brief sentence;" yet let us not hazard such a guess
without having sounded and examined what the thing is. Let
us note well, then, that we must come to the root before passing any judgment; and let us not judge suddenly, fearing to
appear ignorant, for this is what compels men to be too hasty:
it is that they are ashamed not to be keen enough to judge immediately; for if I do not give my account of it, I shall not be
esteemed. Now God mocks this ambition. Let us contain
ourselves, then, in soberness and modesty until God has declared to us why He punishes one rather than another; let
us not get ahead of God. It is true, when we shall have in-
quired, when we shall have come to the root, we shall then be
able to judge freely; for the judgment will not be from us, it
will be taken from God, since it will be founded upon His
Word, and it will be governed by His Holy Spirit; but above
all we must come to the root which is here mentioned.

And then Job says, *"Fear the presence of the sword; for
the indignation of iniquity,* or of affliction, *of the sword is*

---

2. Psalm 106:3, "Blessed are they that keep judgment."
3. Not an actual quotation, but a summary of Psalm 89:20, I Chronicles
17:19, and Psalm 45:7.

near, in order that you may know that there is judgment."
This proposition is obscure enough, because the words are
chopped; but in summary Job wished to say, *"Fear before
the sword";* as if he said, "You speak here as in darkness, you
make sport like those who have nothing else to do, and who
are at their leisure." Such people will be able to dispute; as
there are no people who make war better than those who are
far from the front lines, they will direct the battle, they will
besiege cities, they kill, they pillage, they sack, it is marvelous;
but when they will have chatted well, and drunk in the market-
place, they need only hear the sound of a drum, they are
scattered. Job, then, reproaches his friends that they have
disputed about his case as it were at leisure, but that they must
apprehend the judgment of God and fear the sword, as if already He had showed Himself upon them.

And then he says, *"The indignation of iniquity."* This
word denotes the cruelty for which he had already previously
blamed them. *"The indignation,"* then, as if to say, "You
are here hot with anger against me, indeed, to afflict me." For
the Hebrew word can mean "iniquity" and also "affliction";
but Job here declares that his friends have not come to him
as having some compassion for his trouble, rather that they
have come to him hot with anger, indeed, to afflict him, and
to molest him further. And what does he mean by this? *"The
sword,"* he says; that is to say, "God will not leave such a rage
unpunished, for although I have offended you, yet you must
be more humane toward me; but by condemning me without
cause you show only greater severity toward me; the sword
of God, then, must be displayed upon you, indeed, in order
that you may recognize that there is judgment." Here is a
noteworthy and very useful sentence; for Job in thus rebuking
his friends is as it were a Prophet of God who addresses himself to all in common and in general. He warns us, then, that
we have to fear the sword of God, if we are so malicious as to
judge evil of the good, and if we are so inhuman as to torment and afflict those who are already miserable enough. It
is said, "Cursed are you who say evil is good, and good is

evil;"[4] and yet we see that this vice has reigned from all time, and still reigns today. Those who are led by their passions — what scruple will they have against defying God openly? They know well enough, "Here is a case good in itself, and yet I shall go against it." "Here is a man who asks to serve God, I shall hinder him." "Here is something that could be to the edification of the Church, which could serve the community of men, to the public welfare, and I shall ruin it completely." For there will be seen even those who are seated on the throne of justice who will be there like devils incarnate to defy God, to upset all equity and uprightness, and who will be full of corruption and excess. When we see this, what can we say, except that we have come to the top of the heap of every iniquity? So it is with others; it is seen that there is neither great nor small who does not defy God. So then, must we not say that the devil possesses men, when they are so given to upsetting the good, to maintaining the evil, even since this horrible curse has been pronounced by the Prophet (Isaiah 5:20) against all those who will call evil good, and good evil? And this is what Job here claimed, saying, *"Fear the sword."* To whom does he speak? To those who are inflated against God, and against all uprightness. For against whom do we wage war except against God, when we wish to change the light into darkness when we wish to oppress a good cause? Here is God Who is assailed by us. So then, we have good occasion to fear, even when we shall afflict a single poor man, and when we shall molest him anew. For here is God Who is opposed to it; He says that He does not wish to bear these acts of violence, these extortions. When someone wishes to commit some outrage and injury to poor people, He goes before, and shows that He is their Protector. When, then, we are tempted to offend and to molest the poor, and those who are already in affliction, ought not these words to make us tremble, when they come back into our memory, that the sword of God is unsheathed against all those who wish to afflict further those who are already too much afflicted? Here, then, is God Who defies all those who are given to injuries, acts of violence and

---

4. Isaiah 5:20. "Woe unto them that call evil good, and good evil."

extortion, or such things, and He summons them to fire and
blood. And so, when it is a matter of some poor afflicted
person, and who will have no support, let us fear to tread
upon him, and to molest him, and to put him to shame. And
why so? For here is God Who pronounces that He has His
sword unsheathed against all those who will have thus tormented the good and the innocent.

This is what Job says in conclusion, *that the indignation
of iniquity will bring down the sword;* as if he said, "It is
true that men, when now they burst forth to molest the good,
it seems to them that they will remain unpunished, they fear
neither God nor His judgment; indeed, but the sword," he
says, "is ready for them." Let us not, then, be so presumptuous as to promise ourselves that the hand of God cannot approach us, when we shall have so tormented poor people, who
asked only to be peaceable, and who have not offended us in
anything, when we shall come to sting them, and when we
shall act toward them in sourness, God will be to us a hundred thousand times yet more sour, and we shall experience
Him in such manner, when we shall have come before Him
as before our Judge. Now if this were well pondered, it is
certain that things would be better in the world than they are.
We see Princes who through their ambition will go to sack
the country, burn down houses, destroy cities, steal, ravish,
pillage and ruin everything, so that it is horrible. And why?
All this is lawful to them under the title of war. But they
ought first to consider whether they are constrained to stir
up such troubles and to wage war thus through all the world.
But since it is only their ambition which inflames them to it,
and since so many evils must be produced by this rage by
which they are moved — do they think that the sword is not
ready for them? And then those who serve them in their
cupidity, and who nourish them in it — do they also suppose
that God ought not to unsheath His sword upon them? But
let us consider not only those; for we see those who are neither
kings nor princes, and who will not have the power to upset
the country and to go there by force, who yet will not cease to
have as much malice, or more than the others; for they will

be like little scorpions which shoot out their poison through
the tail, when they can do no other damage; and we see that
each one asks only to sting and to molest. Must not, then,
what is here said be experienced, namely, that the sword is
unsheathed against all such people? And that is why Job
says especially, *"In order that you may know."* It is true that
these were not blockheads, that they knew that there was a
God in heaven Who was Judge of the world, they were learned
and well trained people, as we have seen by their statements,
and, as we shall yet see, pleasing to God. And why is it,
then, that Job says to them, *"In order that you may know"?*
It is that when men are blinded by their evil afflictions they
do not recognize God, that it seems to them that, when they
will have put up a veil of partition, God ought no longer to
see a drop, and that He ought not to punish them as they have
deserved. Let us contemplate, then, the sword, although now
we do not see it with the eye; that is to say, although God
does not yet show us such signs that He wishes to afflict us, to
make us recognize that He is Judge of the world; and let us
show us that He does not wish to use excessive strictness toward us, indeed, when we shall not have been strict toward
our neighbors. And besides, let us know that it is not yet
enough to abstain from every evil; but we must be advised to
help all those who are in affliction. For when a man will be able
to protest that he has abstained from every wrong and injury,
still he will not be acquitted before God on that account. And
why not? For he ought to aid and help those who had need
of his help. Now if those who have abstained from evil are
not absolved before God, but are held as guilty, I pray you,
what shall we say of those who invent only malice day and
night, who consider, "How shall I be able to sting now this
one, then that one?" When there will be such wicked people
who will sharpen themselves thus on deliberate purpose to
destroy their neighbors, surely must not the sword of God be
all the more sharpened against them? Let us consider, then,
ourselves, and not only let us be ready to relieve those whom
we see to be afflicted; but also since there are so many miseries
and calamities throughout all the world, let us have pity and

compassion for those who are far away, and let our view be extended that far (as charity ought to embrace all mankind) and let us pray to God that it may please Him to pity those who are so anguished, and that after having chastised them with His rods, He may lead them back to Himself, and cause that all this may be converted to their salvation, so that, instead of our now having occasion to groan, we may then be able to rejoice all together and to bless His name with one accord.

Now we shall bow in humble reverence before the face of our God.

SERMON 10

Man Profitable to God?*

*Eliphaz the Temanite, answering, said, "Will man be profitable to God? It is to himself that the wise man is profitable. What does it matter to the Almighty, if thou art righteous? or what will He gain, if thou walkest in perfection? Does God fear because of thee, to accuse thee, or to descend with thee into justice? Is not thy wickedness great? and are not thine iniquities without end? Thou hast taken a pledge from thy brother without reason; thou hast despoiled him who was naked. Thou hast not given water to drink to him who was thirsty; thou hast refused bread to him who was hungry. And the mighty man possessed the earth; and he who had authority dwelt in it."—*JOB 22:1-8

WHEN we have to do with men, if we can bring some reproach against our adversary, or we find some fault in him, it seems to us that we have won our case, I say even when we are wrong and also no other judge than our conscience is needed to condemn us. If a man accuses me and I feel myself guilty; I am also going to see if there is something to bite at in him; and that is what I shall put forward for my absolution. Why? For it seems to me that I shall distract those who ought to be judges of my case, in order that they may not confine their attention to me, and that the evil which I have committed may be as it were obscured and hidden. This, then, is the common way that we deal with one another: namely, we seek some subterfuge, and it will serve as a hole to creep out of when we can say, "And how so? I have done such a favor to a man; and when I should have then offended him, this ought to be put in balance." This is how we wish to minimize that fault which we have committed; or perhaps we allege, "And if I have failed in this matter, is he entirely innocent?" Now when we come before God, all these things are cast

* Sermon 83 in *Calvini Opera, Corpus Reformatorum*, volume 34, pp. 267-279.

down. It is true that we would like to use the same manner toward God as toward mortal men; but it is an abuse. Why so? What reproach can we bring against Him? What fault shall we find in Him? What service that we may have done to Him shall we allege, to say that He ought to be held in obligation to us? We must keep our mouths closed in all this, so that it will only be a matter of confessing the debt, and of pleading guilty with all humility without making any replies, and without bringing suit, since we shall have profited nothing. And it is the argument which is here discussed by Eliphaz. And so we see that from the proposition that he holds a good doctrine can be gathered, and he might have spoken very well, provided that he had applied this as he should; but he wrongly addressed it to the person of Job. That is wherein he was at fault. Yet this doctrine in itself and in general is very useful to us: namely, when God avows us before Him, and He invites us to recognize our faults, it is not proper to seek some reply, by saying, "If I have failed in this matter, God surely ought to pardon me; for I have done Him some service, and He ought to recognize such a thing, and this surely deserves to be recompensed." Let us rid ourselves, then, of all these bits of rubbish; for they have no place when we come to appear before God. Why not? For we bring Him no gain, He receives from us neither cold nor heat (as they say) and as we cannot be profitable to Him, also we cannot do Him any damage. This concluded and settled, we see that all presumption in us ought to be cast down, and that there is no other remedy except that in all humility we should plead guilty.

But in order that this may be better understood, let us deduce things in order, just as they are here contained. *"What profit,"* says Eliphaz, *"will man bring to God? It is to himself that the wise man is profitable."* It is true that at first glance it surely seems to us that we deserve much from God when we take pains to serve and honor Him; but we are too blind in this; for we imagine that God could receive some good from us, as if He lacked something. Now on the contrary He can neither increase nor diminish, He is in such wise the foun-

tain of all good that He will borrow nothing from elsewhere;
and that which men bring to Him is not at all to relieve His
need or to augment Him in any manner whatever. "If I had
work to do," says He, "would I go to thee? Are not all creatures in My hand?" Besides, we know that God seeks nothing
outside of His majesty. So then, let us put away the foolish
notion that we may bring some good or profit to God; but
rather let us confess with David in Psalm 16:2 that our goodness will not extend to Him. For, though men exert themselves as much as they wish, yet God can receive nothing from
their hands, even to say that He has need of their being profitable to Him. And, indeed, after God will have poured out
upon us so many gifts that we shall be satiated with them, we
cannot give Him any recompense, as is said in Psalm 116:12.
"What shall I render to the Lord for so many things as I
have received from Him?" I can do nothing unless I call
upon His name. It is so impossible for us to oblige God to
ourselves that, when He will have given us a vast number of
blessings, we cannot render unto Him likewise; and indeed
we would not know how to bring Him a single drop of service. This is what in the first place we have here to observe.
Now if someone asks, "Why, then, is it that God requires of
us that we be attentive to serve Him? It seems as if it were
for His sake." Now it is not a matter of us and our salvation; God does not regard what is useful to Him when He
gives us the rule of the good life and He commands us to
abstain from evil and requires that we do this and that. God,
then, in all His Law has not any consideration for His profit;
but He regards that which is good for us and expedient for
our salvation. If we do well, it will return to us; if we do
evil, it will be to our damage; as for God, He always remains
in His completeness. It is true that as much as is in us, we
violate His majesty, we destroy His justice, and are guilty of
this; but it is not to say that we can diminish anything of God,
that we can deprive Him of what He has, that we can reach
Him to do Him any injury. Not at all. So then, man will
harm only himself, and also all the profit which will come to
him will return to his person. And in this we see the inestim-

able goodness of our God; for He commands us carefully and declares to us how we have to live. And why does He do it? Is it that He wishes to be a good manager, saying, "Some profit from it will come back to me"? Not at all; but because He procures our good and our salvation. If I would serve without regard to my profit, and I would be so careful for the welfare of someone that I would go to entreat him, "You have to do this and that," that evening and morning I should be after him to goad him and to incite him to put his affairs in order, and nothing would come back to me from all this — would it not be a sign of a very rare and unusual love? And here is God Who does thus toward us. And yet what is it? When we apprehend His infinite majesty, and we consider that He surely condescends to think of our salvation and to be so careful about it — must we not be touched to the quick, indeed, must we not be as it were ravished and astonished by such goodness? And now what ingratitude will be in men, when God can gain nothing from them, that they are so hardened and stupid that when He will have shown them the way of salvation and He will exhort them to walk in it, that they do not condescend to walk a step, but rather recoil! Is there any excuse when we shall be so ungrateful for the goodness of our God? Now there is yet more: it is that our Lord, although He receives nothing from us, yet He makes it appear that He is obliged. "Have I to do," He says, "with all that you bring to me?" And though thus it may be, He can receive nothing from us. It is true; but what we do, God accepts, He puts it in His accounts, just as if it were worth something to Him; as we see that He compares Himself to a father of a family Who has a vineyard, from which, having cultivated it, He gathers the wine; or Who has a farm and He gathers the wheat from it. God, using such figures of speech, shows that He holds our works so acceptable that they are like sacrifices, pleasing and of good odor. And He even says that, when we do well to the poor, it is as if we did it to Him, that He accepts it as done to Himself; just as our Lord Jesus Himself says, "That which you will have given to one of the least of My members, I acknowledge it as if it had been done

to My Person."[1] When, then, our Lord descends so far that
He subjects Himself to a condition of mortal and corruptible
man, and says that He receives what we do to our brothers,
although we can bring Him nothing, and He voluntarily obligates Himself to us without being in debt to us; on our part,
seeing all this, must we not be ravished in admiration that the
Lord shows such humaneness toward us? So then, let us note
well what is said in this passage, that when man will have
taken pains to live in holiness, and in uprightness, according
as God commands him; it is not to say that he has been the
least bit profitable to God in his whole life; he has been profitable only to himself; but yet our Lord to give us courage to
do well surely wishes to accept that which in itself is of no
profit; He requires it as if He were improved by it, and He
declares to us that our efforts will be neither lost nor useless.

That, I say, is the intention of our God when He calls us to
the good life. Besides, let us also recognize to what end this is
said to us in this passage; for we must remember the circumstance that I have mentioned: namely, when we come to account before God, we should forget all the foolish thoughts
that we have of being able to bring Him some gain, of having
deserved something from Him; all that, I say, should be put
down. Any why? He is not like a creature who needs someone to help him, and to relieve, He lacks nothing, and is satisfied with Himself. Since it is so, then, that our Lord is not
obligated to us in any manner whatever; let us learn to humble
ourselves before Him, and let us be contrite for our faults,
indeed to be entirely confounded for them, and to ask God that
He may pardon us for them. But why will He pardon us for
them? It will not be in order to say, "He knows that I have
tried to live well, I have done this and that." For what does
all that we can allege amount to? Nothing at all. And so let
us forget all these subterfuges, pleading guilty; for when we
shall have used all such replies, they will not be able to reach
God. If we have to do with mortal men, we may use such
gingerbread work to cover our faults; yet we are confounded
with shame if our falsehood is exposed. What will it be, then,

---

1. Matthew 25:40.

when we shall come to our God? And in this we see how abusive the Papists are. For, although they cannot deny that God holds them all under His curse if He wished to be severe toward them; yet they will put forward their efforts at satisfaction, and they wish to parade them before God; that if they have failed in one place, they can surely repair the breach by some other remedy; indeed, they have their works which they call "of superabundance,"[2] that God has not commanded, which will be to fill the holes when they will have committed some evil, and God presses them. "Very well," they say, "if we have sinned, there is the recompense; and even if it is put in the balance, there will yet be a superabundance." This is where the Papists are, so that to them it is a great absurdity that the remission of sins should be free, that God should pardon us of His pure goodness. They will well confess that this is true with respect to the guilt, but with respect to the penalty it is up to us to atone for it. When men are carried away by such pride, must we not say that they have entirely transfigured God, and that they no longer know what He is? All the more ought we to note well what is herein contained: namely, that it is in vain for us to make believe that we can bring some profit to God; it is only pure foolishness, it is only vain imagination. And so when we shall have conceived what His highness is, let us learn to recognize our faults in all humility, not having any reply; for we cannot bring any reproach against Him, as also we cannot allege to Him that He has received anything from us, nor that He is in anywise obligated. So much for one item.

Now it is said further, *"It does not matter to God whether we do good or not, or whether we walk in perfection."* When Eliphaz speaks thus, he does not mean that God closes his eyes, and that there is in Him no discretion between good and evil; but he means that it does not matter to Him with respect to Himself. It is true that God, according as He is the fountain of all justice and uprightness, loves equity; and if we live righteously, it is like a reflection of God. For it is certain that

---

2. Today known technically in Roman Catholic theology as "works of supererogation."

we have not the good in us; but it is as we see the sun shine
here below, when it sends forth its rays. The light that we
see here below does not come from the earth; we see the light
upon the houses, upon the earth; and yet it does not proceed
from there; but it is a reflected light (as it is called) which
is thrown back according as the earth receives it; it then proceeds from the earth. As also when in a mirror we look at
ourselves, the mirror has no face; but the face of the man is
presented there, and the mirror shows it. So then, when we
do well, it is not of ourselves (for one would know how to
extract from us only every odor and poverty, as we are corrupt by nature) but our Lord pours out His goodness and
His righteousness upon us. If then, He performs this grace
by regenerating us through His Holy Spirit, that we may live
in holiness, we are like mirrors in which His image is there as
it were represented; it is a light which comes from on high,
but it shows itself here below. Now, since God recognizes
that all the good is from Him, that is why He loves the good;
as it is impossible that He should do otherwise, seeing that
He is the source and the fountain of it. Besides, it does not
matter to His consideration, that is to say, to His profit, or
advantage which He may receive by it, it does not matter to
Him how men live. When men do worse than they could,
do they take away the righteousness that is in God? Can they
subtract from His majesty? Can they annihilate His glory
and His honor? Can they shorten the boundaries of His kingdom? Not at all! That, then, is how it is said that it does
not matter to God what men do. But as for us, let us consider
whether or not it is our blessedness to take His side, and to
render ourselves His subjects in obedience. And seeing that,
having no need of us, nor of our life, nor of our works, He is
yet concerned that we should live in holiness — let us know
by this the love which He bears toward us, just as already it
has been said, that He condescended to join us to Himself,
and to join us thereto in such a way that, if we live well, He
says that His rule is established; if we live in an evil manner,
He says that He rules no longer. And why? Can we hinder the sovereign dominion of God from remaining forever?

Not at all. Why, then, does He use such language? It is (as I have already said) to declare to us how He loves us, just as it is said in Proverbs 8:31, where the Wisdom of God is introduced, that His pleasure and His delights are to dwell among men. God speaks thus, to show us that He does not wish to keep the good which He has in Himself as it were locked up and hidden; but He wishes that it may be poured out upon us, and that we may be partakers of it; and as He takes pleasure in enlightening us, so that we are not like brute beasts, but we recognize Him in conceiving of that which He shows us, in such a way that we are raised high in His kingdom. So is He also in everything and through everything: it is that He takes pleasure in stretching out His benefits to give us such enjoyment of them, that He joins Himself to us, and us to Him. God, then, has had such care for us, that it does matter to Him how we live; but not because He gets by it either profit or damage. This is, in summary, what we have to note.

Now it is said further, *"Will it be from fear that He may have of thee, that He will accuse thee, or that He will descend with thee into justice?"* Here it is shown still more clearly that we shall gain nothing by wishing to shuffle with God, as we have become accustomed to doing with our kind. For why is it that such cavils are used in trials and quarrels with men, unless to put up some rampart, and to pacify the party; or perhaps to intimidate him, so that he may not pursue further with such strictness? For example, when someone will be assailed, he will consider: "This man pursues me hotly. What must I do?" Then he will come to use some subterfuge; or perhaps he will sick someone on the tail of his adversary to put a flea in his ear, as they say: "Dost thou not think that thine adversary is stronger than thou?" Or perhaps, he will stir up against him something underground; so that the man withdraws himself, and gets the chills, and dare not pursue as he had begun; for he fears that the evil may return upon his own head. So then, because we have been accustomed to intimidating mortal men, in order to escape their hands, and we show them our teeth, we give them some sign that **we**

have the means to take revenge; it seems to us that we can do
likewise toward God.   And what foolishness! Must we not
surely be destitute of sense! But because men are so presumptuous that they scheme to practice toward God what they do
toward their neighbors — for this cause it is said, "And
thinkest thou that God keeps silence for fear He may have of
thee?" Now what is it that moves men to strike with such
terror against their adversary?   Because a man considers,
"This one wishes me wrong, I must hinder him, and yet if he
assails me, I shall repulse him; or perhaps, I shall have the
means of justice to repel him." This, then, is what hinders us
from pursuing one another: namely, when we wish to maintain ourselves, and the wicked wish to injure us, we have
justice which thrusts itself between the two; for the fact that
we have there our refuge hinders them from executing what
they have undertaken, and this is how we proceed when we
have to do with mortal men.   Now let us not think that God
is led by such an affection. And why not? What can we do
to Him? Can we make Him either hot or cold, as I have said?
So then, God does not pursue us for fear He may have lest
we should forestall Him, lest we should put our foot on His
throat; for if He wishes only to breathe, we must be put down;
and those who rise up so against God — what are they doing,
except breaking their necks? It is as if a man cut his nerves
and his veins in striving to climb, and he cannot; he must stop
short of the goal, and if he wishes to strive beyond limit, he
will break his whole body. This, then, is a fatal fall. So is
it, when men have the devilish arrogance to raise themselves
against God. We must not, then, think that our Lord suspects us; for He will mock such a presumption, as it is said
in Psalm 2:4. Very well; it is true that men will make a great
noise when they scheme together. And above all if kings and
princes have leagues and they plot together against the living
God, the people also agreeing with them, they will make great
noise; but it is only here below, and men are like grasshoppers,
as the Prophet Isaiah (40:22) says. Grasshoppers have such
long feet that they can jump; but they must fall down quickly.
So men surely stir around here; but will they jump above the

clouds? Not at all. However, He Who dwells in the sovereign places will only laugh. This is to show where the throne
of God is, namely, above the heavens; so that men can never
attain unto Him; He will laugh up there in His rest while
they make great noise here. And so let us learn, when God
summons us, and we plead our case, that it is not that we may
be able to injure Him, it is not that He may consider Himself to hinder us from forestalling Him; not at all. Why
then? It is in order to make us experience the evil which is
in us, and that we may be incited by that to seek the remedy,
and that with true repentance we may come to Him, in order
to be governed according to His will. God, then, in punishing men procures their salvation; in condemning them, He
wishes to absolve them; or better, when they are chastised, He
wishes to ratify and to confirm His justice, by showing that
no evil will remain unpunished. However, He wishes also
to destroy the pride which is in men, since they are pleased in
their vices, and they glory in them; God wishes to put down
all that when He leads them into judgment. And so let us
learn not to flatter ourselves any longer, whenever we shall
have some remorse within and we shall be condemned by the
Word of God, our vices will be shown to us, our manges will
be scraped; let us learn, I say, not to use any more subterfuges; for we shall only aggravate our walk. And let us know
that God does not fear us, lest we should be able to do Him
some damage; but He invites us to be mindful of our faults
to be displeased with them; and by this means He extends to
us His hand to lead us to salvation; or perhaps He wishes
that our condemnation may redouble, and that we may be all
the more inexcusable, when we shall have resisted Him, and
that with the malice which is in us there will have been the
obstinacy and rebellion not to bend when He will have tried
to convert us to Himself. That, in summary, is what we have
to consider.

Now Eliphaz adds further, *"Is not thy malice great? and
are not thine iniquities without end?"* It is true that this is
very poorly applied to the person of Job (as already it has
been noted) but, however, we must hold this general doc-

trine, in order to apply it to ourselves according as we have
need of it. Let us note, then, that through the mouth of a
heedless man who would not have such prudence as he ought
to appropriate the truth to his use, the Holy Spirit shows us
what we have to do when we come to account with God; it is
that we should know that we are obliged to Him in everything and through everything, and that He is not held by us
in anything whatever; furthermore, that we cannot do Him
any damage; and that when He condemns us and leads us into
justice, it is not for His profit, but for our salvation, and our
good; indeed, that even when we are condemned, it is in order
to be absolved by Him afterwards, in order that we may not
fall into the extreme condemnation, into which the wicked
will be constrained to come in the end. On the other hand,
that when God leads us thus into judgment, it is in order to
examine our sins, and to pick apart all our life, in order that
we may be displeased with our vices. However, when we shall
have thoroughly stirred all that is within us, and it will seem
that we have known what is there; let us know that we have
not yet perceived one one-hundredth of it, I say, even those
who see there very clearly, and who wish neither to flatter
themselves nor to nourish themselves in evil. For though
that may be, according as men are dull, and have a short and
obscure view, it is certain that they will not apprehend one
one-hundredth of their sins; but God, Who sees much more
clearly than we do, knows them. If we fall into a vice today
and we are entirely convicted of it, we shall still commit a fault
tomorrow morning once again; indeed, and the day will not
pass without there being a great number of offenses and transgressions. And then it will always be to begin again, for we
shall not be convicted of a vice only once, or twice, or three
times, but a hundred times. So then, where shall we be?
When man has well examined his conscience, and he finds
himself guilty in so many ways, and he comes to conclude,
"God knows yet a hundred times more" — where can he stand?
Ought we not to be greatly astonished by it? Ought it not
to make our hair stand on end to be as it were plunged into
the depths of death?

This is what we have to note from this passage: namely, whenever, by hearing the Word of God preached, the vices to which we are attached are there condemned; each one has to enter into himself, that each one should conduct his own trial and not wait for God to pursue him; but he should recognize, "Alas! I have failed in such a way, and not only once, nor twice, but innumerable times. And if I have failed in this way, there are surely others; that if God wishes to stir up my odors, what will it be? I would completely burst from it." This, I say, will lead us to humility and repentance; so that we shall no longer be so slow as we were to approach our God; for at least we shall no longer be so peevish as to chafe against His corrections. And let us be even so much more careful to do it, when we see that the majority are pleased and glory in their vices, and instead of groaning and being confounded with shame, they pretend to be good Christians, indeed, the most perfect that could be found. It is true that they will say in general: "Oh, I am a man, and all must confess their sins; yet there are none who do better than I do; I would not know who would wish to live better." And who are they who speak thus? Poor debauchees, indeed, so debauched that the air stinks from their iniquities; and yet they will come here to mock God openly. Now (as I have said) if we will analyze what we are, nothing will remain for us except to be entirely confounded, to plead that we are guilty, not of one sin, nor of two; but in everything and through everything, let us know that we are cursed of God, and more than miserable, so that He may only pity us. In summary, it is here shown that men must not confess their sins before God merely as a form; as those to whom it seems that it is enough when they will have said, "Oh, I do not deny that there are faults in me." No, let us not do thus; but let the burden be so heavy upon us that we could bear no more. For, in fact, this is how God will be truly glorified: it is not when men will say that they have some little infirmities and imperfections in them; but when with David they will speak of the greatness of their sins, and of the multitude of their iniquities (Ps. 38:4, 5). And it is also how Daniel speaks in His confession (Daniel

9:20); he who was like an Angel in comparison with others
— and yet he says, "I have confessed my sins and those of
my people." He does not speak as if of some little fault, but
he says, "Our sins are great and enormous, Lord." And so,
let us learn to recognize who we are, indeed, in such a way
that God may be truly glorified in everything and through
everything. That is one Item. Also, what hope have we that
God may receive us, and that He may be pitiful and propitious, if we are not as it were overwhelmed by the faults that
we have committed? Our Lord Jesus does not say, "Come
to Me all you who will say, 'I am sinner, there are some infirmities in me.'" Not at all. But, "All you who are heavy-
laden and who labor, who have your shoulders bent under
the weight of your sins." These are those who are called by
Jesus Christ, in order to find mercy in Him, and in His grace;
and not those who so mock God, making a frivolous confession without being touched in their heart. That is what we
have to note from this word. Besides, to come to such an
understanding, we must make a special examination of the
faults which we have committed; for a man will never say
sincerely, "I am as it were cast down into hell," unless he has
well analyzed himself and he has considered his faults, one
after another, that they may be well noted. If, then, we have
not made a special examination, we shall never appreciate the
fact that our iniquities are without end and without number.

That is why this order is here set down for us; for Eliphaz,
after having pronounced in general that the sin of Job was
great and his iniquities without end, says: "*Hast thou not
despoiled him who was naked? hast thou not extorted a pledge
without reason? hast thou not withheld bread from him who
was hungry? hast thou not refused water to him who was
thirsty? and yet hast thou not agreed with people full of violence?* That is why God now persecutes thee." Now it is
true (as we have already said) that Eliphaz does great wrong
and injury to Job; yet the Spirit of God wishes here to instruct us of the order that we have to follow to be properly
humbled before God, in order not to harden ourselves and provoke by this means His vengeance when we should wish to

set ourselves against Him. In summary, let us note that men will not feel their sins as they ought unless they consider them in particular and then count them item by item. It is true that we shall not be able to come to the end and that we shall always have to conclude with David (Psalm 19:12): "Who shall understand his sins?" However this is not to say we should merely pass over them and not open the packages. If an earthly Judge knows how to be keen and attentive for a trial, and one not only for the life of a man; I pray you, when we shall have offended our God, must we not have a much greater anxiety about it? And even when a trial will not be criminal but it will be only for some petty sum of money, yet a judge must consider closely if he has witnesses, if the trial is well conducted, that things may be verified; and yet it will be a matter of only ten or twenty florins, or a hundred crowns, or I do not know what. And if a judge does not do his duty, he will have to be held guilty before God like a thief; for he is worse than a thief, seeing that he robs the goods of another, and the substance which belonged to one to give it to another. And I pray you, when God does us the honor of constituting us judges of our own life, indeed, and He does it for our salvation — shall we be excusable if we are indifferent and we close our eyes to what is so profitable and useful? Very certainly not. So then, let us weigh well what I have discussed: namely, that men will never truly understand their sins as they ought, and as is required, until they have well examined their life in particular. In fact, we see how David does it; for a single sin leads him back to the womb of his mother, when he sees that he has committed such a villainous transgression before God that he had been the cause of a cruel murder, not only of one man, but of many, wishing to cause Uriah to die. After, then, he has seen the villainy of his sin, the enormity of it constrains him to think not only of this sin alone; but he considers himself more closely, he comes even to contemplate himself as far back as the womb of his mother, and he condemns himself in everything and through everything. That is also how we must do it. However, the Papal confession was a devilish thing, when they wanted men, confessing in the ear of a Priest, to disgorge their sins; as if a glutton went to vomit up wine, when he will have gotten so full that his stomach could not carry any 'more. God, then, does not wish that we should have such a manner of confession; as also it is entirely contrary and repugnant to His Word. On the other hand, He also does not wish that we should say in a word, "I have failed," that we should just pass over the hot coals lightly (as the proverb is in this country) but that we should think carefully about ourselves, and that each one should enter into his conscience, and that we should realize, "Here now, I am guilty before God of not only a single fault, but of such a one and such a one; and not only once, but I always return to it." When we shall do thus, examining ourselves in a special manner, we shall surely be able to conclude: "And. Lord, our iniquities are infinite, our transgressions are without end." That, I say, is wherein God wishes to be glorified. That is how poor sinners will be touched to the quick, and wounded in their conscience to be displeased in their vices. In fact, those who make themselves confess only in general by saying, "I am sinner like the rest of men," will show that they are not touched inside to the depth of their heart, and that they do not know what it is to realize their sins so as to be displeased with them. Now on our part let us learn to search well and to sound the depth of all our vices; and when we have recollected quite a number, let us know that there are a hundred times more, and that we ought to be confounded in ourselves, that we ought to plead that we are guilty, gasping before God, by saying: "Alas, Lord! It is true that our sins are in great number, that our iniquities are infinite; but that the multitude of thy mercy is poured out upon us," as David says (Psalm 40:12, 13). For this is the sole means of obtaining pardon for all our offenses: it is when it pleases God to cover them and to abolish them through His goodness, and to cleanse us of them by the power of His Holy Spirit.

Now we shall bow in humble reverence before the face of our God.

SERMON 11

The Majesty of God*

Then Bildad the Shuhite, answering, said, "Principality and terror is toward Him who makes peace in His high places. Can all His armies be numbered? And upon whom does not His light shine? What righteousness will be attributed to man, being compared with God? he who is nothing? And how would he who is born of woman be clean? Behold He will not shine as far as the moon, the stars will not be pure in His sight. And how much less the man of wind who is only rottenness, the son of man who is only vermin.

—Job 25:1-6

BECAUSE we are so given to prizing ourselves, and this folly proceeds from the fact that we do not think of God and the nature of His majesty; we have here a good and very useful warning that, however and whenever we are tempted to attribute to ourselves some glory, we should turn our attention to God, and we should well realize His nature, the nature of His virtue and power, the nature of His justice, the nature of all His glory. Then our cackling will surely be put down; for instead of our being inflated with pride and intoxicated with presumption, the consideration of God alone is sufficient so to crush us that we shall be confounded in ourselves. This, then, is why now in the person of Bildad the Holy Spirit gives us this admonition: it is, there surely must be sovereign principality in God, and we must be frightened at the thought of Him, seeing the order which He has set in heaven, and throughout all the world; and let us know that, as nothing of ours can be of worth before Him, the stars which shine are obscure to Him. Since it is so, what remains in men? Now (like all soup) they are only vermin and rottenness. And if

---

* Sermon 94 in *Calvini Opera, Corpus Reformatorum,* volume 34, pp. 405-418.

they wish to glory above the stars, what will it be? Is not their folly too great? So then, we see toward what end the propositions herein contained do tend: it is, that because men looking here below cannot humble themselves, God sets before their eyes His majesty, in order that they may know that it is no longer a matter of their being worth anything; for whoever exalts himself before God must be entirely abased.

Here Bildad, to make us feel how God ought to be feared and dreaded by us, alleges, *"He makes peace in His high places,"* that is to say, He so disposes the order of heaven that a peaceable and well-ruled government is seen there. This could refer to the Angels, as we say in our prayer, "Thy will be done in earth as in heaven;" which indicates that God is poorly obeyed here below, because of the rebellion which is in men, inasmuch as we are filled and stuffed with many evil cupidities which cannot be reconciled with His justice. So then, we ask that, as the Angels are entirely conformed to the will of God, as they seek nothing except to please Him in everything and by everything; also may it please Him to reform us, and, correcting the evil affections which are in our nature, may He cause that His kingdom and dominion should be peaceable here below. One could, then, refer this passage to what is there said of Angels; but there is no doubt that Bildad had a further consideration, namely, to the whole plan which we shall perceive in the order of heaven. So then, although the sun may be like an infinite body from our point of view, and though its movement may be rapid, though it seems that it ought to confound everything — yet no one would know how to regulate a clock at such a compass; it is impossible. We see the like in the moon, and in all the stars; for although the number of them is infinite, yet there is no confusion, but every one is as well ordered as possible.

So then, it is not without cause that Bildad here puts forward, *"God makes peace in His high places."* And we see His reign not only in His heavenly creatures; but from on high He so regulates all the order of the world that notwithstanding that things are here confused, and they stir about, and there are many changes, and troubles; nevertheless God does not cease to bring everything to such an end as He has ordained and deliberated in Himself. It is true that if we cast our glance below, we cannot see this dominion as peaceable as it is here declared to us; but if we contemplate the providence of God, it is certain that in the midst of the troubles and all the revolutions of the world we shall know that God governs everything as it seems good to Him. We see now the implication of the saying, *"God makes peace in His high places;"* that is to say, He holds in check all His creatures, in such wise that though some changes are seen, yet He does not cease to govern, and everything comes back to His will, as He conducts everything by His counsel. Since it is so, let us conclude that it is only right that there should be power, principality, and astonishment toward Him; that is to say, that we should do Him homage as to Him Who rules, and that there should be fear and dread in us, that with all reverence we should recognize Him as Master and Sovereign Lord of heaven and earth. Now at first it would almost seem that this proposition was superfluous; but when we shall have well weighed what we have already discussed, we shall surely see that it is not without cause that Bildad here points out the government and dominion which God has throughout all the world. For this word will fall from the mouth quickly, and we shall speak quickly enough of God; however, we do not conceive His majesty; we reduce Him almost to an idol. To be sure, we shall not confess this, and we would even be horrified to make such a confession; yet we do not attribute to God the power which is due Him, and which we ought to feel is in Him. For we chat about His majesty, and His Name will fall from our lips as in scorn, we speak of Him in derision most often; it is seen that men are as profane as could be, and though when the Name of God is mentioned every knee should bow and all creatures should tremble, instead we have the audacity to bring Him neither any reverence nor humility. Briefly, men do not recognize the majesty of God, and they do not apprehend His virtue in order to humble themselves before Him and to be subject to Him as they should. It is needful, then, when one speaks to us of God, that he should be qualified, that is to say, that we should experience Him as He is. And that is why Holy Scripture so often joins to Him titles, not being satisfied simply to name Him; but entitling Him, "Almighty," "All-wise," "All-righteous," "Him Who alone has immortality in Himself," then, that He has created everything, that He governs everything. To what purpose is this said, unless to awaken men who are too stupid, and who do not honor God according as He is worthy? Briefly, as often as Holy Scripture honors God, it is to reproach our ingratitude and stupidity in that we do not render to Him that which is due Him, and as much as we can we rob Him of His power and of His glory; at least we must hold Him to be as He is, adore Him, and humble ourselves before Him, and exalt and magnify Him as He deserves.

Yet let us learn when it is here said, *"God makes peace in His high places,"* and that He so governs the world that it is seen that all must take His side, and though there may be some contumacy and rebellion, that He does not fail to succeed in executing His counsel; when we hear this, we should no longer be asleep so as to play with God as we have been accustomed to doing, but we should tremble before His majesty; and above all let us return to the conclusion which is here made, namely, that there are sovereign dominion and fear toward Him; that is to say, that not only ought we to be subject to Him, but that we must tremble with all fear, that He should be so dreaded, that we may not have the foolish boldness, or rather the madness, to set ourselves against Him, and to dispute against what He does, or to murmur, as if there were something to find fault with in His works. This, then, is why here the mouth of all men is closed, in order that, being robbed of their cursed presumption, they may learn to tremble in the presence of God, and to recognize that it is to Him that they owe all homage.

And that is why Bildad adds, *"His armies cannot be numbered; and upon whom will not His light shine?"* When he says that His armies cannot be numbered, it is to indicate that men surely must be worse than fanatics when they strive so against God and wish to wage war against Him. It is true that they will not confess it; however, it is impossible to murmur against God, and to fret against His judgments, without our getting angry at what He does, without our waging war against Him. And why? For wherein consists the dominion and the principality that He has over us? It is when we recognize not only His power, but His goodness and infinite wisdom, His justice, His mercy, His judgments; when we have done this, we glorify Him. Now then, when men do not find reason in what God does, when they accuse Him of cruelty, or through impatience they get angry against Him, or they are scandalized by what He does; there is no doubt that they are trying to rob Him of His divine glory; and this cannot be done without fighting against Him. So, when we do not glorify God in His justice, in His goodness, in His power, in His infinite wisdom, it is as much as if we had toward Him an attitude of defiance, to raise ourselves against Him. Now from Whom is it that mortal man is taken? It is said here, *"The armies of God are innumerable."* There are all the Angels of paradise who are armed to maintain the honor of Him Who has formed and created them; all creatures are well disposed to avenge His majesty which is so assailed by us, who are only vermin and rottenness. Let us note well, to what purpose it is here spoken of the bands and armies of God; it is in order that we may know that however and whenever men presume to murmur against God, and to blaspheme against His justice, they must have as mortal enemies as many Angels as there are in heaven. Now we know that the number of them is infinite. They must know also that all creatures are armed to rush against them; for to what end is it that God has created all things, unless in order that His glory may shine in them? Now if men subject themselves to God of their good pleasure, and they render to Him the honor which belongs to Him; what is here said of His armies and bands will not be to frighten them, but rather that they may rejoice. In fact, when Scripture narrates to us that God has many millions of Angels all around Him, who are ready to do what He will command them — to what purpose does it lead, unless that we should recognize, when God will have received us into His

grace, although we came to be besieged from all sides, that
He is powerful enough to keep us here below in good security?
When, then, men will display all their power, they will scheme
this and that to ruin us, when even the devil will raise himself
against us, we must not be afraid. Why not? Inasmuch as
God has His heavenly armies to maintain us; as it is said,
"Angels camp all around those who fear God," in Psalm
34:7; and then, that He has ordained His angels to guide us,
so that the faithful man will not stumble. We see, then, how
the infinite multitude of Angels is to comfort us, in order that
we may be assured that God will provide for us in time of need
and that He has wherewith to do it. But although believers
lean upon God, and rank themselves with all humility under
Him, being preserved by the multitude of Angels; also it must
be that those who chafe, all the proud, all rebels should be
frightened by Him, and that they should recognize when they
strive so against God, that they have also to do with many
enemies, that all the power which is in the Angels will turn
itself against them to crush them, that all creatures as well will
be to maintain the glory of Him by virtue of Whom they exist.

So, let us remember well the word that is said, *"The armies
of God* are innumerable;" and thereupon we should recognize
that it will be in vain that men conspire against us; for when
they will have amassed all their armies, yet they will not be
the stronger; God will always win over them. Let us no longer
be deluded, then, when we shall see that we are well accompanied, that we shall have many people who resemble us.
And why not? We can all be confounded by the hand of God,
and by His power, in a moment. And then, although He alone
is sufficient either for our salvation or for our ruin, yet He
still has His armies, which are ready and equipped with an
outfit which is incomprehensible to us, which He will prepare against us when it seems good to Him. Let us fear, then,
and let us learn (as I have said) not to be puffed up when we
shall see that the world is on our side and that there will be
great power to maintain us; all that will serve us nothing,
against the power of God which is here declared to us. Now
by this it can be seen how blind the unbelief of men is; for we

have to choose, either that the Angels of paradise should keep us in their guard, and that they should watch over us, and should be ministers of salvation; or else that they should be our adversaries, and deadly enemies. Behold God Who uses toward us such a goodness and grace that He ordains His Angels for our service (as Scripture says in Psalm 91:11); He wishes that we should be warned by them, and furthermore He pronounces that they are His powers, as if He extended His hand upon us in order to be able to maintain us. What follows, then, from the fact that we are guided by the Angels, and that they secure us against all evil? We cannot choose such a good which is offered to us; it remains only to accept it. But what do we do? As much as we must receive such a gift as God gives us, we come to it defying His majesty to provoke the Angels and to arm them to our ruin and confounding. Must it not be, then, that we are entirely deprived of sense, and that the devil has as it were bewitched us, when we prefer to have the Angels for enemies than to have them for ministers of our salvation; as they are ready to help us, and to guide us, provided that we are members of our Lord Jesus Christ and that we do Him homage as to our Head? And so, let us learn whenever God is spoken of to us, not to conceive a dead thing in Him; but to think of His glory as it is here declared. And since we are too stupid, let us remember that God has His armies, and that He has an infinite number of Angels, which are ready to execute His commands, and then that all creatures obey Him, as is wholly reasonable.

When it is said consequently, *"The light of God shines upon all,"* this is expounded that God so pours out His gifts upon His creatures that some spark of goodness and wisdom is perceived everywhere; although it is especially restricted to men; for it is there also that the light of God is perceived, as it is said in the first chapter of Saint John that God not only from the beginning gave being to creatures, but that He made them alive to maintain them in their estate, indeed, by the power of His Word; but as for men, He gave them light in their life. There are, then, all creatures who are always made alive in our Lord Jesus Christ, Who is the Eternal Word of

God; but we have a life more noble, and more exquisite than
have either beasts, or trees, or the fruits of the earth. Why
so? We have intelligence and reason. So then, the light of
God shines upon men; and when we are so held and obligated
to Him, are we not all the more guilty, if we cause this light to
vanish? It is very certain; for we must remember what Saint
Paul says in Acts 17:27, that when we shall come to feel after
Him like blind men, nevertheless the glory of God will be
experienced. How so? He dwells in us, we need not seek far
for Him, it is in Him that we live and move and have power
and being. This, then, is how this passage is expounded: it is
that God, having made us partakers of His light, has so obligated us to Himself that we are worse than ingrates if we try
to annihilate His glory, and if we do not render to Him that
which is due Him. And why? Man cannot move unless he
experiences that God dwells in Him; it is from Him that we
have life, and it is also to Him that we have to render thanks
that He has made us reasonable creatures rather than brute
beasts. For why is it that we are worth more than oxen and
asses, except that it pleased God to prefer us? So then, this
light by which God enlightens us is for us such an occasion
to exalt His glory and to subject ourselves under His hand.

That is a sense which is implied from this passage which
contains a good doctrine. But when everything is properly
considered, Bildad does not wish to indicate merely that God
has poured out His light upon us in order to give us intelligence and reason; but he shows that we cannot flee His presence, that we must walk as before Him, and that He sees
everything, and that He has as it were His eye upon us. This,
then, is how the light of God is poured out upon men; it is
inasmuch as we cannot hide from His presence. And it is
following the proposition that he had already held out. For
as he had said that God has His Angels who are equipped for
His service like great armies; also now he adds, that it will
be in vain for us, that we shall not be able to flee the presence
of God. It is true that we hop like toads, and that we imagine
ourselves doing like runaway horses; yet in the end we must
submit to God. And why? For His light so shines upon us

that we cannot flee Him, as we could if we had to do with a
mortal man. Let us learn, then, to come to this conclusion
when we shall be given to such boldness that we think we can
flee the hand of God. Indeed? And where shall we go? For
we know that His power is poured out everywhere, because
His searching glance is infinite. When we shall have entered
into the depths of the earth, yet He will not cease to see us and
to mark what we do. We, then, would be worse than fools
to raise ourselves against God, knowing that it will be in vain
for us to upset and mix things up, and to plan many undertakings and conspiracies; for that will profit nothing, since we
are always observed by Him and by His watchful eye. Now
this is a doctrine common enough in Holy Scripture; but we
remember it poorly, for at least it is poorly practiced by us.
And since it is so, if this should come into our memory, that
God beholds us, and that all that we do and say is noted by
Him — I pray you, should we not walk with more fear and
carefulness than we do? But what do we do? We fear only
men; when we have not any witnesses against us here below,
we are satisfied. And this is why men release the bridle to
their wicked cupidities; namely, because the Spirit of God
does not have dominion in their lives, and it is all right to
them to have conceived of execrable things and to have actually done them themselves, provided that nobody rebukes them.
There is then very little of the light of God before their eyes.
For if they had this light in mind, it is certain that it would
repress all of their wicked desires, to purge them of all the
fancies with which they are inflated. In fact, if we are ashamed
before men, how much more ought He Who is Judge of all to
move us! For if men judge us, it is not in their authority,
nor in their own name; it is only to approve the judgment of
God, as He alone is competent for it. Now there is God who
sees us; however, we do not bear toward Him any reverence;
we do not worry about provoking His wrath against us. And
how can we do it? So then, when we shall have well learned
this lesson, that God has poured out His light upon us; it is
certain that it will be a good check to make us walk in all
purity of conscience, not only correcting the faults that we

commit outwardly toward men, but all the evil that is hidden within us, and all hypocrisy. That, then, in summary, is what we have to remember from this Word.

Now Bildad, having spoken thus, adds, *"What righteousness, then, will be attributed to man in comparison to God?"* It is word for word *"with God. And how will he who is born of woman be able to be absolved?"* This is like an authentic summons to us, to show us that we are very foolish to prize ourselves, and to make believe that we have some righteousness or power in us, something which should be worthy of praise. A robber who will be in the middle of the woods will fear neither justice nor anything whatever. It is true that he always carries a dread; as it has been seen before, God has engraved in the hearts of men such a feeling for their sins that they must judge and condemn themselves; yet thereupon robbers are so cheerful that it does not matter to them to cut the throats of as many poor passers-by as they will meet, if they can trap them. Notwithstanding, however, when they are cut short, and they see that their payment is ready; then they no longer have this boldness, they no longer have the rage in which they were brutalized. So it is with us; for as long as we do not know that we must render account before God, and we do not apprehend His infinite power, and the princippality that He has in Himself, there is such presumption in us that it costs us nothing to magnify ourselves above the clouds; and if righteousness is spoken of to us, we shall find it easily in ourselves, our vices are to us virtues. That is how men, until God has summoned them before Him, and drawn them there as by force, are so drunken with boldness that they cannot recognize themselves as they are. For if they recognized themselves, it would no longer be a matter of prizing themselves. That is why Bildad now says especially, "How shall mortal man be able to justify himself with God?" This word weighs much, as if he said, "Very well, while men are among themselves they will be well able to judge of their virtues, each one of them will say, 'Me, I am a good man,' and he will even estimate himself much more highly than others when he comes to put himself in the balance, 'And this one has some flaw in

him, he has such and such a vice.' " We know so well how
to deprecate others by putting them down that it is marvelous;
and yet we do not wish to confess our own weaknesses, we
cover ourselves as much as we can. And if there is some little
drop of virtue (at least so it seems; for all that is only smoke,
as we shall say soon), oh, we wish that God should hold us
so dear and so precious, that He should rob Himself in order
to reward us. This, then, is the arrogance of men, indeed, as
long as they consider among themselves; but when we have
come before God, and we recognize what we are, and we inquire within to examine our life, being frightened by His majesty, which does not allow us to be tangled up in our hyp-
crisy and lies — then we forget all these foolish boastings, by
which we had been for a time deluded. And so, let us learn,
following what is here declared to us, when we shall be tempted with pride, and when we shall suppose ourselves to have
some virtue wherewith to highly estimate ourselves — let us
learn, I say, to summon ourselves before God, and let us not
wait for Him to drag us there, but let each perform this office
toward himself; for here is our Lord who shows us the procedure that we have to follow. Man, then, will always imagine
himself to have I do not know what all by which he could
magnify himself; but to correct this folly and arrogance, let
him only consider, "Who art thou?" Now to know who
we are, let us come to God. For man never would recognize
himself as long as he looked only at himself, or as long as he
compared himself with his neighbors; but it is when we have
raised our eyes on high, and we reckon that we must come
before the judgment-seat of Him Who knows everyone, Who
is not like mortal men who are satisfied with bits of trash,
and before Whom we cannot commend our outward shells,
which are all those good-for-nothing things that are here
much prized. When, then, we shall have known that all that
vanishes before God, then we shall learn to put ourselves in
place, and no longer to be so elevated with such pride.

And that is why it is said, *"Man,"* indeed, *"he who is born
of woman — how shall he be able to justify himself with respect to God?"* Yet, because there is nothing more difficult

than to bring men to reason, and to cause that they should be entirely stripped of the vain confidence by which they are deluded, Bildad here adds, *"He will not shine as far as the moon, and the stars will not be pure before God; what, then, will become of man who is only vermin, of the son of man who is only rottenness?"* It is true that this word can be expounded in various ways, namely, that God will not shine as far as the moon; or else He will not extend His tabernacle, that is to say, He does not deign to approach it; and that the stars are not pure, that is to say, all creatures, in which nevertheless we see a great nobility, should be as it were removed from God; that there is too great a distance. And this is especially said, because the creatures on high are more excellent than those here below. But though that may be, there is God who is so removed from both moon and stars that there is an infinite distance. How, then, shall we approach Him? Now this sense is suitable enough; in fact, whether it is taken either as "to shine" or "to extend His tabernacle," it is all the same. In summary, Bildad wishes to indicate that, if our Lord wished to call before Him His creatures, light in the moon would no longer be found, the stars would be dark; and nevertheless they are what light the world; so everything will have to be annihilated, when the majesty of God comes forward. Men now please and glorify themselves. Where are the wings for us to ascend so high that we could take the moon in our teeth (as they say) or that we should climb above the stars? Yet when we suppose that we have nothing whatever in ourselves and God comes forward, everything must be swallowed up, and put to nothing, by His incomprehensible glory. We see now where men are when they wish to glorify themselves. Surely, I say, Satan must have entirely bewitched them; for it is as if they flew above the stars. And are they well enough equipped to do it? When man will wish to climb up only four steps, it is to break his neck, then to snap all his nerves. Now whenever we suppose ourselves to have something to glorify ourselves, we take such a jump that it is to break the necks of men and of Angels, so to speak. Must we not be, then, (as I have said) worse than mad? This is the intention of Bildad.

Besides, as for some who expound this of the Eclipses of the moon, this can in no wise be granted; but the sense is more simple: namely, creatures most noble, and which even seem to have some divinity, are nothing when compared with God; all this must be abased, and God must remain in His perfection, and we must recognize that there is neither justice, nor power, nor wisdom except in Him alone; that all the rest is only vanity. Indeed; but experience however shows that the sun is not dark, nor the stars. Yes, surely, with respect to us. And then we must note that the light which they have, they borrow from elsewhere;[1] they are like little sparks that God there shows of His glory. And so, neither sun, nor moon, nor stars can take glory as it were in their own right. Yet also if God comes opposite them, this light must be darkened with all the rest; for if the sun makes the aspect of the stars obscure to us, I pray you, what will it be from the infinite light of God? Now we have the intention of Bildad. Indeed, as far as the moon, he says, there will be no light, the stars will not be pure before God. As if he said, "It is true that we see light poured out throughout all the world. we have our eyes which receive light and rejoice in it; yet that must be nothing before God, if we came even to the body of the moon and of all the stars of heaven, all that," he says, "will be darkened and banished in comparison with the glory of God."

We come now to men. What are they? What can they do? What is their power? Of what can they boast? They are only vermin and rottenness; still will they wish to justify themselves thereupon? Now it remains to practice this doctrine and to apply it to our use. Here it is shown us that, when we shall come before God, we can bring nothing which would be worthy of praise. Men, then, are here declared void of all good, and that there is not a single drop of righteousness by which they could improve themselves; but that they must

---

1. Although we may understand the word "elsewhere" as simply meaning that all the stars borrow their light from God, it appears that Calvin's astronomy is here in error. It should be remembered, however, that in 1554, when this sermon was preached, the theories of Copernicus (1473-1543) were relatively unknown. Galileo, who popularized them, was not born until 1564, the year that Calvin died. Note also that Calvin's argument is not destroyed, but rather enhanced, by the Copernican astronomy.

accept condemnation, knowing that there is in them only all poverty and misery. Now if this doctrine were well known by men, we would not have today so many combats and disputes as we have with the Papists; for those of their side prize their free will, as if men had some power to dispose themselves toward God. It is true that they will surely confess that we are weak, and that we can do nothing without the help of God, and without being prepared by the grace of His Holy Spirit. But what of it? Meanwhile they attribute to men some preparations; and then, that they are cooperators with God to help His grace, to work in common; briefly they are His companions. And then, what a foundation they have set up! They must attribute to themselves this and that, so that it is no longer a matter of anything except magnifying men in their powers and merits. For although they always confess that we have need that God should pity us and that He should do us mercy, oh! yet they blow wind inside the bladder to inflate it; that is to say, that they get drunk on these devilish doctrines, to make believe that they have merit, and that God accepts them according as they can be worthy of His grace, and that He always has regard to their virtues. That, then, is how men are inflated with wind by the devilish fancies that reign in the Papacy. "And then," they will say, "if we fail, oh! we have our works of supererogation, we can satisfy God for our sins; and although we may have offended, and though we may know that He will pardon our faults yet we can bring Him some recompense, some satisfaction; and that is the means of reconciling ourselves with Him." Now if what is here shown us by Bildad, and what we have seen previously, were better known, all these disputes would be put down. But what happens? It is easy for the Papists to judge thus quickly of the justice of men, of their merits, of their satisfactions, and of their free will. And why? For they do not regard God, and they are asleep in the vain imagination that they have conceived, to justify men in their own powers. And yet we ought to note well this passage. Let us note, then, in conclusion, that when we shall be able to summon our consciences before God, it will be to humble us, in such a way that it will no longer be a matter of presuming anything from us; but that we shall recognize that we are only vermin and rottenness, that there is in us only every infection and stink. What remains, then? Let us learn whenever the means of our salvation are spoken of to us, to consider where it is that we ought to have all our confidence: namely, that being received by our God through His pure goodness, He purges and cleanses us through His Holy Spirit of all our spots, and washes us in the blood of our Lord Jesus Christ, which He has poured out for our purging and that He renders us so pure and clean by this means, that we can exist before His face.

Now let us bow in humble reverence before the face of our God.

SERMON 12

Does Not God Count My Steps?*

I have made a covenant with my eyes; and should I have looked upon a virgin? And what is the portion from God on high, and the inheritance from the Almighty of the heavens? Is there not curtailment of iniquity, and confounding for those who plot together (and scheme) iniquity? Does He not see my ways, and count all my steps?—JOB 31:1-4

WE HAVE already seen before how Job protested that he was not such as his friends wished to make him believe; for they had the opinion that he was reproved by God. He has, then, declared that he had lived in holiness and in perfection. He returns again to this proposition, and not without cause; for it seemed to Him a grievous temptation that he was thought to be a hypocrite, although he had walked in uprightness of heart, and in simplicity before God. And besides, he also has no regard for his reputation nor what would be thought of him; for God knew him. It is true that he should not find it strange that He was afflicted by the hand of God, although he had walked as we here see; yet it was good that he knew the end and the cause for which God had thus visited him. Now we shall see this more fully in the conclusion of the chapter. Now let us look at what is herein contained: it is that Job wishes to declare that he has served God faithfully, and now that he endures evils so grievous and so excessive, that it is not for the offenses that he had committed; but that there is some other hidden reason that God knew, and which men could neither perceive nor judge. In the first place he gives testimony of his integrity when he says that *he has made a covenant with his eyes, not to look unchastely upon a living daughter.* Now it is a sign of great perfection, and as it were

---

* Sermon 111 in *Calvini Opera, Corpus Reformatorum,* volume 34, pp. 622-635.

Angelic in a man, if he can protest that he has never invited evil; for it surely is possible for a man to have some sudden and fleeting temptation and yet not consent to it, even reject all that and hate it. In fact, it would be a great virtue when a man could have all his senses so wholesome, and exempt from all corruption, that he could never be deceived. But Job here goes further. And to better comprehend this, let us note that there are three degrees of vice in the formation of sin, I say, even though there may not be actual sin. Saint James uses the figure of a child, when he speaks of sin; for he says (1:14, 15) that concupiscence conceived, and that it gave birth to sin, and sin is completed when one comes to the act, when the thing is executed. Now I say, although there may not be an outward act, there are three degrees in a vice. The first is a fleeting imagination that a man conceives when he looks at something; it will come to him in fantasy here or there; or else, though he sees nothing, his mind is so adept at evil that he will be carried away here and there, and many fantasies will come into his brain. Now it is certain that this is vicious. But it is not imputed to us as sin. Now there is the second degree, it is that, after having conceived a fantasy, we are somehow titillated, and we feel that our will is drawn there; and though there may be neither consent nor agreement, yet there is within us some point from which to appeal to us. Now that is a bad sin, and which is, as it were, conceived. Then there is consent, when our will has ceased, and it would not stop us from doing evil if the occasion for it presented itself. Then there is the third degree, and then the sin is formed in us, although the act may not be outward. And this is very worthy to be noted; for although the thing could seem difficult to us, nevertheless there is no one, either man or woman, who would not understand what I have just said, and who would not experience it in himself every day. For example, there will come to us in fantasy, when we are afflicted, the question, "Does God think of us?" There is no one who could maintain that he does not conceive such imaginings; for our nature is so corrupt and inclined to evil, that it is impossible that we should not have such apprehensions. Now it is surely already a vice when it will come before us, though we may repulse it, though we may think, "How now? I detest this, it is a blasphemy to think that God does not pity those who call upon Him, that He does not wish to help those who seek Him; it is as much as if we wished to deny that He any longer governs the world." When, then, such things come into our brain, it is a vice, and we ought to conclude, "Alas, Lord what poor creatures and how full of vanity we are, when we can conceive such monstrous things." There is the second, it is that when evil will press us, and sorrow will be multiplied further, we come to these murmurings, "Alas! and if God thought of me would I be thus languishing? Would He have no concern to aid me? He does not do it, He hides; it seems, then, that I am abandoned by Him." When we dispute so in ourselves, and this apprehension about whether God cares for us or not; then we must understand what is declared toward us, and we must receive His promises, and be founded upon them, by saying, "No, whatever may happen, yet I shall have confidence in my God, and I shall have my refuge in Him." But although we may finally have this assurance and constancy; yet if before coming to it we are mixed up in perplexity, this is a vice which is greater than the first, and already we are guilty before God both of doubt and of unbelief, since we have power to receive such a wicked temptation. Now there is then the third degree, when we are entirely cast down, and we know how to say nothing except, "O behold, evil has conquered, and God has procrastinated too long in extending His hand to me. I see myself here, as it were, desperate." When we are so overwhelmed that we can no longer call upon God, and we do not relish His promises to bear us up, and to make us rejoice — that is the third degree of evil; as if after an infant will be formed, it only remains further to give it birth, so nothing more is here necessary except that the outward act should come.

We come now to the proposition of Job. *"I have made,"* he says, *"an agreement* or covenant *with my eyes."* We have said that is a sign of a great perfection. And why? For if a man can restrict his sight, that he may conceive nothing by looking at this and that which might draw him into evil, and if he shows that he has true chastity and honesty in himself, one must say that he is almost as pure of all corruptions as an Angel. Now Job does not protest this in vain. Let us recognize, then, that he was preserved in this world like an Angel of God. It is true that by nature he was not such; and also when he says that he has made a covenant, it is after he has profited by the fear of God in such a way that he had put under foot his evil cupidities, and gained this victory over his heart, that he is able to hold himself in check and locked in, by saying, "I shall covet no evil by desiring and wishing it. I shall have no vein in me which may tend to offend God, but I shall here be restrained both in my eyes, and in my mouth, and in my ears." That, then, is how Job had made this covenant. It is not that he should be in such perfection in his nature; he was man subject to passions like us, and no doubt he had many temptations in his life; but he walked in such a way that he was accustomed in the fear of God until he did not conceive of evil desires. He had, then, a habit, as it is called, that is to say, he was indebted to it that he no longer wandered by glancing from side to side and invited upon himself such and such a thing. In summary, we see here that Job wished to declare not only that he tried to serve God, but that he made such an effort that he had bitten and captured all the passions of his flesh in such a way that it no longer cost him anything to serve God; because he had not the struggles which we have in us because of our frailty, and even because of the corruption which is in our nature. Now let us note that this was not by his own power; he could not have acquired such a perfection by himself; but it was necessary that God should have so reformed him by His Holy Spirit that he was as it were separated from the common rank of men; for it is not without cause that David makes this request of God, "Lord, turn my eyes, in order that they may not behold vanity" (Psalm 119:37). If it had been of Job's industry that he protested, there is no doubt that David could as well acquire such a constancy, that he should have conceived no vanity, and that his eyes should not have been seduced or distracted in any manner whatever. Now it is thus that David confesses that he could not have this nor obtain it except by the pure grace of God; it follows, then, that Job could not make such a covenant by his free will,[1] by saying that reason so dominated in him that he was victorious over all his passions; but he here intends to attribute to God the praise for such a benefit. It is not, then, to boast and magnify himself, as if he had acquired such a benefit; but he recognized that God had so well governed him that he was no longer attracted by evil in his sight.

Besides, when Job speaks thus, let us note that on the contrary he intends that, if a man looks at a woman or a girl, and if he should be incited to evil, it is already sin before God. Yes, although the outward act may not be there, although the man may even not try to corrupt a girl, nor to seduce her, although there may not yet be the settled will in him to say, "I would like to," although, then, a man may not have this wish, but he resists the temptation to which he is incited, yet he does not cease to offend God. This is a point well worthy to be noted. In fact, we hear the sentence that our Lord Jesus gives us, that we must not think we shall be acquitted or absolved before God just because we have abstained from adultery in the body; but he who will have only looked at a woman, will be judged an adulterer before God, indeed, if the look is unchaste.[2] And what is more (as I have already said) when the will will not yet be fixed upon it, already we must confess the fault before God to humble ourselves. The Papists well say that if a man consents to evil, that is to say, if he so desires the evil that he is fully resolved to do evil if the occasion were there, oh! they confess that it is a sin unto condemnation; but if a man has some wicked appetite, provided that he does not entirely consent to it, the Papists say that it is not sin; there is an execrable blasphemy. It is said, "Thou shalt love thy God with all thy heart, with all thy soul, with all thy understanding,

---

1. Calvin here uses the French *franc-arbitre*, which is full of suggestion of the many errors of "free will."

2. Matthew 5:28. But I say unto you, "Whoever looks on a woman to lust after her has committed adultery with her already in his heart."

with all thy strength."[3] What is it to say, "understanding and strength"? God has not limited the love which we owe Him only to our hearts and our affections; but He says that our minds and our senses as well must be applied to it, and all our strength, that is to say, all the faculties and powers which are in our nature. Now if a man conceived some evil, although he did not entirely agree with it, and his affection was not fully given to it — I pray you, would he love God with all his understanding? Not at all. He who will have the least part of himself tending to corruption, though in the rest he strives to keep the Law — will he love God as he ought? Certainly not. For sin is nothing else than transgression of the Law of God.

Let us conclude, then, that all the wicked fantasies that we have when we are attracted to evil, are so many sins, and that we shall be indebted to God, Who not only supported us by His infinite goodness; but that He pardons His own — yet they must recognize these things as sin; and whoever flatters himself only provokes the wrath of God, and covers evil to his condemnation. For in the end hypocrisy will have to be uncovered and revealed to be punished with all the rest. Those, then, who imagine that they are not obligated, and that they do not offend God when they are attracted by evil, gain nothing; it is not to amend their walk, for this hypocrisy will have to be punished grievously. So then, let us remember (as I have already said) that although one does not consent to evil, but though we are only as it were titillated, though there is some desire and we resist it; it is already a fault and a weakness in us; when we only conceive some evil desire, it is already a sign of the corruption of our nature. And in fact if evil did not dwell in us, and we had not yet turned away from the uprightness and integrity which God had put in the first man; it is certain that our sight would be much more pure and chaste than it is; and all our senses, as hearing, speaking, touching — all these would be as it were pure and clean; there would be no infection in them. And that it may be so, let us weigh well what is said by Moses, that when Satan came to seduce Eve, and consequently her husband, after they have lent him their

3. Luke 10:27.

ears, and have been corrupted by the ambition to be like God;
it is said that they looked at the tree of knowledge of good and
evil, and saw that it was desirable in order to acquire knowledge. What, had they not looked at it? And had not Adam
and Eve already seen it? For God had said to them, "Do not
eat of the fruit which I have forbidden you; for in the hour
that you shall eat thereof I declare to you that you are separated from Me, being condemned to death." So behold Adam
and Eve, who have previously contemplated this tree. And
why, then, is it that Moses now imputes it to them for sin?
Because they have known it to be desirable, that is to say, they
had an evil and perverse appetite when they thought that it was
good to eat of it. And where does it come from? It is their
heart which was corrupted, and which tainted their eyes more
and more; as also when a man will have his sight tainted on
account of drinking through his intemperance, the evil must
be within, and there must be some burning, before the eyes are
lost; or else some accident, as when a man will become blind,
there will previously be some cataract, or some other such thing
which will take away his sight with the passing of time. So
it is with all the wicked looks which are to condemn; for if
there were not some evil appetite by which the heart is already
infected and corrupted, the eye (as I have said) would be pure
and clean of itself, so that we could contemplate the creatures
of God without being drawn to something evil. It is so now
that we would not know how to open our eyes, unless it were to
conceive some evil desire; we would not know how to say,
"That is beautiful, that is good," without immediately offending our God — is not that a great perversity? So then, let us
recognize what the sin is which reigns in us; as in fact it has
occupied its possession since Adam transgressed, in such a
way that our nature is so corrupted that we would not know
how to look at a thing which we could name beautiful and
good without our offending God, instead of being invited to
love Him as we ought, and to give Him praise for His goodness, and for so many benefits that He does for us here. Instead, then, of glorifying God and of being incited to love Him
and serve Him, we would not know how to say, "That is

beautiful, that is good," except we were titillated, indeed pushed, either into avarice, or into adultery, or into other voluptuousness. Briefly, all that which is beautiful under heaven, and that which is good, turns us away from our God, where it ought to lead us to Him. Is not God the source of all beauty and goodness? Now it is true that this wicked appetite does not have dominion, and also ought not to have dominion over the children of God; but I speak of that which is natural on the part of man until God has worked in him. It is true that believers will not be so perverted, and will not have their senses so depraved, to be always drawn to evil; yet they will always have some relic of the infection which is from the womb of the mother, that is, they will have points of contact within from which to be incited to evil, even though they may hate it and repulse it at first. In fact (as I have said) who is he who does not conceive the fantasy that God does not care for him, as soon as we shall endure some evil? And it is a blasphemy, indeed execrable, if we consent to it, and our attention is focused upon it some little while, though it may not be a settled act of the will.

So then, we see now that if man is invited to evil, though he may not consent to it, thus repulse the temptation, and fight against it, however he does not cease to offend God. And why not? For it is a transgression of the Law, as we have shown. Likewise, it must proceed from an evil source; for the eye itself will not be corrupted; it is not there that sin begins to produce itself. Where then? In the Mind[4] of man, and in his soul; for in fact evil affection must be hidden within, before the eye tends thus to evil and is invited to it. And that is why I have said that Job, in protesting that he has abstained from every evil and immodest look, shows us that those who are infected by it cannot excuse themselves before God by saying that there is no fault in them. Thereupon let us learn to be well on our guard, and not to flatter ourselves, as I have already mentioned. I say to be on our guard; for what difficulty there is, I pray you, to so hold back our eyes that they may not be tempted by any evil concupiscence or inordinate desire! When

---

4. Fr. *l'Esprit*, "spirit" or "mind," usually "mind" in Calvin.

we see the goods of the world, that we should not be touched by avarice! when we see the comforts, delicacies, and voluptuousness which are here and there, that we should not be induced to desire that God should give them to us! when we look from side to side, that there should be neither adultery, nor ambition, nor avarice, nor anything which would get under our skin! It is impossible, or else it is not without a great difficulty, and beyond all our powers; so that it is almost impossible that we should open our eyes without conceiving some offense against God. Since it is so, let us learn to keep a good watch; for we cannot so perfect ourselves that there would no longer be any fault to find, and that we would not have to have our refuge in the remission of our sins. Let us conclude, then, that we must fight valiantly, seeing that we are so corrupted that we cannot use our senses in any manner whatever, nor apply them to anything, except there would be some relic of our evil corruption displeasing to God. That, then, is what ought to invite us to diligence.

And then in the second place let us also learn to humble ourselves, seeing that the devil is trying to put us to sleep by hypocrisy, in order that we may not recognize our faults, and that this may only aggravate the evil. Let us, then, look within ourselves, and after having examined our imperfections, let us groan before God: "Alas! Lord, Thou hast done me the grace that I desire to advance myself in Thy service. I take pains, I strive, I resist all my passions, I fight against myself; yet I am not righteous before Thee; Lord, there is much to find fault with." That is how believers after having worked hard, and having exerted themselves beyond all their powers, ought always to retain this affection, in order that they may condemn themselves when there will thus be vice mixed among the good which God will give them to do, and that they may learn to pass condemnation on themselves before Him, and to humble themselves, in order to obtain grace. These are, then, the points that we have to note from this passage. Now though it may be, although we may have fantasies which enter into our brains both evening and morning, and though by that we should perceive that there is an amazing corruption in our nature; yet we must not lose courage, but let us always walk further, let us pray the good God that if He has begun to compel us, that He may continue, and that He may add the power of His Holy Spirit. So we must request it, and we should feel that we have already something worse than our evil affections; let us put the two together, and let them be so trampled down that they never could get up again. And when the devil comes to prick us to invite us to evil, let him not succeed against us, but let us always have our senses focused higher; briefly, let the Spirit of God so rule in our hearts that, though there may be wicked affections, they may be held as it were in check, indeed enchained, and that they may not raise themselves, that it may not be to toss us this way or that way, but that we may always remain firm, and may be resolved to say, "Our God must govern us, and we must follow His holy will."

This, then, is how in the midst of our wicked fantasies we must take courage to walk always honorably, knowing that the good God will support us; not that we ought to confess that they are not so many sins, but that they are pardoned for us. And this is the point on which we differ from the Papists. The Papists say that evil concupiscences are not sins, provided that one resists them; that is an execrable blasphemy. As if it were, "God must renounce Himself by upsetting all His Law." And this is not a fleeting opinion that only simple and ignorant people will have; but it is a persuasion which captures great doctors in their schools, or rather, devilish synagogues. On the contrary, we say that these are so many sins; but they are not imputed to us by God, since He erases them through His goodness and gratuitous mercy, by our Lord Jesus Christ, in Whom we believe; and having such a comfort, we ought to exert ourselves so much more, as I have already said.

Besides, Job well shows that he knew what this offense is, and that he would have been guilty if he had taken an immodest look; for he adds, *"What is the portion from God on high? What is the inheritance from the Almighty of the heavens?"* Now Job here shows that he does not speak of self-improvement before men, and of acquiring a reputation for strength and holiness (as those do who ask only to be prized here below) but he has his eyes fixed on God, and he speaks here as in His presence, and asks Him to be witness and Judge. And that is also where we must come; for (as has been discussed previously) as long as we wish our life to be approved by men, we shall be full of lies, subterfuges, and wiles; so that it will cause us to disguise the white and to change it into black, and to make vice virtue, and vice versa. That is how we shall do it, when we try to be approved by men. And so whoever will desire to walk in uprightness, and to have the integrity of which Job here speaks, oh! it is certain that he must collect himself, and that he must no longer wander here below, saying, "Who will find fault with me?" No; that must be cut off, and he must summon himself before God, saying, "Now, why am I? It is with God that I have to do; when I shall have satisfied all the men of earth, I shall have gained nothing; we must all have our mouths closed; for God is not satisfied by beautiful miens, beautiful disguises, appearances, or like things; He looks at the heart, He sounds the thought, and He discovers everything that is hidden in shadows." Since it is so, let us thereby be constrained to walk in integrity and uprightness. But on the contrary, we are distracted here and there, we are subject to inventing subterfuges, and by beautiful parades to put our best foot forward; and when we can do no better, by covering ourselves with leaves like our father Adam. For this reason let us note well the lesson which is here shown to all believers: namely, when we would wish to walk properly, we must not be as it were only before men, our eyes must not be focused only on them; but we must contemplate the heavenly Judge, and we must know that it is to Him that we have to answer, and to render account. So much for one item. Besides, (as we have already mentioned) Job here knew that God will not endure immodest looks without punishing them. And why not? For these are so many offenses.

Then he adds, *"Iniquity will be cut off."* By which he shows that he who will have his eyes given to vanity, though he may not entirely consent to it, yet is condemned as sinner and wicked before God. Let us remember what has been said of the time of Job; for although we do not know whether he lived before the Law[5] or not, yet he was before the Prophets, as we have declared that he is mentioned as an ancient man. So then, here is Job who was of the time when God had not yet given a fully ample doctrine or a light such as has come since; for the Prophets have greatly clarified what was obscure in the Law; Job lived before; so there was as it were only some little spark, if we consider the doctrine which has been since then; nevertheless, he well knew that he could not be attracted by an evil desire without being guilty before God. And now how guilty we shall be, who have the Sun of Righteousness Who shines upon us as in full midday! Behold Jesus Christ with His Gospel, Who has brought us such great light that we have no excuse. If we say, "I do not understand it, it is too high and too deep a thing" — how can we? Have we not an ample enough doctrine, when the will of God has been fully manifested to us? How, then, shall we be excused, if we do not recognize what Job recognized? And in this is seen what is the vengeance of God, namely, how horrible it is on the Papacy, when those beasts have dared to deny that man sins when he is thus tempted to evil and he has points of contact within him and evil affections which he conceives, provided that he does not entirely consent to them. And Job who had not costly doctrine (as we have already declared) nevertheless well knew this. And so let us look at ourselves closely, since God has done us the grace and privilege to make His truth much better known to us than it was at that time; let us be vigilant, and as soon as we shall open our eyes, as we shall experience in ourselves some vanity, some evil affection, let us know, "Oh, there is evil which is hidden within, we have offended our God, and already our eyes are tainted with it, when the evil appeared outside, when there are sparks — and are they made without fire?" We must, then, learn to condemn ourselves; as in fact if it were not for the mercy of God, we would be destroyed by it; for it is the portion of our inheritance which is prepared from on high. It is true that men will be able to justify us; but we must appear before God, Who will judge it entirely otherwise.

---

5. The giving of the Law by God and the recording of the Law by Moses.

And Job says especially, *"From on high, from heaven."*
This word is repeated, but it is not superfluous language. And
why not? He makes tacitly a comparison between the judgment of God, and the opinions which we could acquire, toward
men. Here, then, are men who could justify us on all accounts,
and our odors and poverty would not be recognized; we would
be, then, reputed as it were little Angels whereupon we would
suppose that there was nothing to find fault with in us. Now
what have we profited? Nothing at all; for here is Job who
calls us there on high. Very well, it is true that here below
sinners will be able to be absolved, and they will be easily approved by men; (for apparently only all virtue is seen) but on
high, for there is God Who will upset all the vain
opinions which will have reigned for a time. And so let us
learn that, as often as we are guilty, having been attracted to
evil concupiscenses, also the salary is prepared for us in heaven,
that is to say, from on high, unless the good God spares us and
uses His fatherly goodness toward us. This, then, is what
we have to remember in order to magnify the goodness of our
God, when we see that He does not punish us severely, and
also in order to be incited to ask Him to pardon all our faults
every day.

Now furthermore it is said, *"Is there not curtailment of iniquity, and affliction for those who commit crimes? And does
not God regard my ways, and does He not take account of all
my steps?"* Job here expresses more clearly the portion and
inheritance of which he had spoken; and it is in order to grieve
us more, even to the quick, with the feeling of our sins. It is
true that he does not insist upon everything of which it is
spoken in the Law, and he does not use so many words; yet
the Holy Spirit has here given us by His mouth a common
instruction. For when one speaks to us of the judgments of
God, and of the punishments which He sends upon sinners, we
are so slow that it hardly moves us. It is necessary, then, that
our Lord should wake us up, and make us more sensible of
how terrible is His wrath, that it is a horrible thing to have it
thus against us.

This, then, is why Job adds the declaration which is herein contained, *"Is there not cutting off for the iniquitous, and will not the wicked be afflicted?"* What means this "cutting off"? It is that the wicked deserve to be exterminated, that God should cast them into hell, and destroy them utterly, as the word implies more than salary or inheritance; for men (as I have said) make themselves believe that they will escape it with a very light chastisement; as when a criminal will be detained in prison, he knows that he has deserved the gallows, he makes himself believe, "Perhaps I shall escape with the whip, I shall be banished." So, I say, men do not apprehend the wrath of God such as it is; they do not recognize the punishment of which they are worthy, since they do not think of eternal death. We see, then, how Job not without cause, after having spoken of the portion which is prepared on high for all the wicked, adds that it is a cutting off, and a confounding to cast them into hell. Now by this let us recognize that the Spirit of God rebukes us for our indifference. If from the first stroke we were attentive to understanding the judgments of God, indeed to feeling our faults, we would have no need that He should thus state the proposition doubly; it would be enough to have warned us in a simple word. But the Holy Spirit, after having spoken of the portion that God prepares for all despisers of His Law, adds, "cutting off"; because we are like brutes, and when one simply declares a thing to us we do not apprehend it; we are preoccupied with such a stupidity that, if God strikes us roughly, we do not feel the blows from His hand. And how, then, shall we be grieved as it is required by the warnings which He gives us? It is certain that when He will only speak, we shall be neither touched nor cast down in ourselves, seeing that by the blows of His hand we still can not be sufficiently humbled. And so, then, let us note well that here our indifference and stupidity is rebuked. And yet let us be awakened when God invites us so carefully, and let us be better instructed to think on ourselves. It is what we have to observe in this verse.

Now in conclusion, when Job says, *"Does not God regard my ways, and does He not count all my steps?"* let us note well

that he applies to himself the doctrine which he had stated in
general. For he had said, *"What salary, or what is the portion
from God on high, what is the inheritance from God of the
heavens?"* Job had thus spoken of all; but now he applies this
doctrine to his use, and declares to what purpose he had thus
spoken. So then, whenever the judgments of God come into
our memory, whether men propose them to us or we read of
them, let us have the prudence to enter into ourselves, and let
each one look at his own person. For the judgments of God
must not remain as it were buried without ever speaking of
them; but each one must apply them to himself and to his particular use. This, then, is what we have to note when Job, after
having discussed a common doctrine, comes by and by to look
at his own person; "God," says he, "sounds and knows my
ways"; that is to say, since God is Judge of all men, no one
can escape His hand. *"God,"* says he, *"does He not know all
my ways, and does He not count all my steps?"* So much for
the first point.

As for the second, let us note also the style which Job uses,
that God looks at His ways and His steps, and that He counts
them. It is to express that God does not count them only from
afar, and only look at what will be apparent here below; but
He looks closely to note and to mark all our works; indeed,
and it is not a confused look, His sight is not misleading; but
he notes that He counts, that He numbers everything, so that
nothing escapes Him, He forgets nothing. Now (I pray you)
have we not occasion to better recognize our ways, and to count
our steps, when we see that everything is present before God?
Why is it that men scarcely recognize one one-hundredth of
their sins? Indeed, such a man will commit one fault a hundred times a day, and he will think of it scarcely once. What
is the cause of this? It is that we do not think that God watches
over us, and that we are so before His sight that nothing may
be hidden from Him, and that He forgets none of all our works
and our thoughts. And so, then, let us weigh well the words
that are here contained, that is, that God knows our ways, and
He counts our steps, that is to say, that the number of them is
set down before Him, that even to the last item all must come

to account. That is what those who by lies and flattery will have covered their evil-doing will gain; for all must come to light. What remains, then? It is that we should think on ourselves more closely than we have been accustomed to doing, and that we should always be on watch, in order not to be surprised by the ambushes from which we are assailed from all sides; and, seeing that we are subject to falling into so many vices of which our nature is filled, let us examine them well in order to be displeased by them, and to plead guilty of them before God; and that by still groaning our confessions with David (Psalm 19:12) that it is impossible that all our faults should be known to us; and yet let us pray to the good God that, when He will have beheld in us the faults and the sins that we ourselves cannot see, it may please Him to erase them by His mercy; and that by this means we may have no other assurance of our salvation except that He receives us to mercy in the Name of our Lord Jesus Christ, and that we have also the washing by which we are purged, namely, the blood which He has shed for our Redemption.

Now we shall bow in humble reverence before the face of our God.

SERMON 13

Job's Purity and Equity*

*If my heart has been seduced by some woman, that I should have kept watch on the house of my neighbor; let my wife cast herself to another, and let strangers bow down upon her. For this is laxity, and iniquity to be condemned. It is a fire which devours everything to perdition, which would even take away the root of my revenue. If I have refused judgment to my servant or to my chamber-maid, when they have striven against me; what shall I do when God rises up? and when He visits me, what shall I answer? Did not He Who made them make me in the womb? and has He not formed both of us in the matrix?—*JOB 31:9-15

WE HAVE here two protests worthy to be noted that Job makes. One is, that he has lived so chastely that before God he is pure by not having tried to seduce any woman. The second is, that he has been neither proud nor cruel against those who were subject to him; and though he had to be raised above his kindred, that he even had power over them, he has shown himself to be humane and modest toward them. Now we must remember what was discussed previously: namely, that Job does not protest to having walked uprightly before God and to having conversed with men without doing wrong to any, only in one respect; but he comprehends all the Law of God, and he deduces from the things which are contained there, as in fact we also ought to be admonished especially by them. For (as we have shown) it is not enough if we try to acquit ourselves of our duty in one article, if meanwhile we omit the rest; for God does not wish what He has joined together in His Law to be separated or dismembered. Let us remember, then, what has already been expounded on this. Now let us follow the order which is observed by Job, until the rest should be added.

---

* Sermon 113 in *Calvini Opera, Corpus Reformatorum,* volume 34, pp. 648-660.

As for what he says of adultery, the sense is that he would subject himself to suffer the shame that his wife would be exposed to adulterers, if he sought to seduce any woman. *"Let others,"* he says, *"bow down upon my wife,"* let her suffer this villainy, and also let me endure it with respect to myself; *"If my heart has been seduced, or else if I have kept watch,"* he says, *"upon the door of my neighbor,"* that is to say, "if I have spied to do evil." And then he declares why he held adultery in such great horror. *"For it is,"* he says, *"a laxity, indeed, iniquity which pertains to the judges,"* that is to say, "worthy to be condemned. *It is a fire which devours, and which would be to take away the root of my substance."* This, then, is how Job was retained in chastity, and was not given to the filthy odor of adultery: it is that he knew that it was a detestable thing, and that God could not bear it. Now as for the punishment that he puts here, it is the just payment of fornicators and adulterers,[1] namely, that as they have done to others, the like should be rendered to them; and it is not only in this passage that it is mentioned but we have the most noteworthy example of it in the person of David; for although he was a holy Prophet, and a king chosen from among all mankind, having testimony that God had found him according to His heart; nevertheless for having suddenly declined, and for having ravished the wife of another, we see the punishment which happened to Him; and the curse of God is declared to him by the Prophet Nathan, "Thou has done it in secret, and it will be rendered to thee in public; the sun," he says, "will be witness of it." David had worked by such a trick that he thought that his sin would not be known by the world and that he would be acquitted of it, since there was neither reproach nor murmur against it; but God avenged Himself of his hypocrisy, and said to him, that although he had done it in secret, his evil would nevertheless have to be published and he would have to be defamed, that the sin might be known by all. And how? It is an enormous thing, that his own son should come to cause the trumpet to sound to assemble the people, and that the wives of the king should be seen exposed to every villainy. There is

---

1. Fr. *paillards et adulteres.*

an incest contrary to nature. But God declares that this did not happen by chance.[2] "It is I," He says, "Who have caused it." As if He said, "Let no one consider the person of Absolom without going further. It is true that it ought to be held to be detestable that he has thus violated the order of nature, perverted all honor, and brought this shame to his father; yet I was at work here, and it must not be supposed that this happened by accident;[3] but it is I Who have done it," says the Lord. Since God did not spare such a Prophet, a man endowed with such excellence as we have said, and who all his life had walked in integrity, except this fall by the wife of Uriah — if, then, God was so severe against David, whom He had elected, how will He spare adulterers who make an ordinary business of seducing the wives of others, who keep watch to succeed in their wicked enterprises? Must they not feel that there is a Judge in heaven, Who will not permit that such a laxity should remain unpunished? God, then, makes a like shame to return upon their persons: only that they should recognize that they received a just payment, and such as they have deserved and that they should learn to humble themselves before God. Besides, this threat ought better to beat down the temptations in those who have some fear of God, when they hear that if they abuse the wives of others, it will also be necessary that their wives should be ravished, that they should be polluted, and that God should raise up adulterers who would be as it were to execute His justice. If a man has some drop of fear of God, and some reason, it is certain that he will be held in check, hearing such a threat by which God warned him. And that everyone may still profit from this passage, and from seeing that God cannot allow such a laxity, let us learn to so pray to Him that He may govern us in such a way that our evil affections may be tamed,[4] and that this wicked cupidity may not have dominion in us, and indeed that it may have neither access nor place there. So much for one item. However, let us note also what more is said about crime, in order that we may not

---

2. Fr. *de cas fortuit.*
3. Fr. *de cas d'aventure.*
4. Fr. *dontees,* domesticated, subdued.

find it strange that God should punish it so harshly; for because we always wish to measure sins by our scales, and we bring a false balance (as was said yesterday), we would like, if it were possible for us, to argue with God and to accuse Him of excessive severity when He punishes our faults.

And that is why I have said that we ought to observe well what Job goes on to say. *"It is a laxity,"* he says, *"too great, indeed, and an enormity to be condemned, it is a fire which burns to devour everything unto perdition."* This signifies that we must not judge adultery according to the common opinion of men who make nothing but fun of it; as we see that jokes about it fly around, and that many despisers of God and and profane people mock it. This devilish blasphemy will be heard, "And it is a venial sin, it is to be pardoned," and like things; but this did not begin today. And that is also why St. Paul, having spoken especially of adultery, says (Ephesians 5:6), "My friends, guard against being tempted through vain words; for that is why the wrath of God comes upon unbelievers." Already Satan had gotten the world so drunk on filthy jokes that adultery was not considered as detestable as it ought to have been. Saint Paul says that men will babble and flatter themselves with such taunts in vain. And why? The wrath of God will, nevertheless, have its course, as He has shown from all time that adultery was unbearable to Him. In fact we ought to note in the first place that it is to pollute our bodies which ought to be temples of the Holy Spirit. Other sins, says Saint Paul (1 Corinthians 6:18)[5] are committed in such a manner that the stain and the mark of them does not so remain in the body of the man, as with fornication; for it seems that fornicators and fornicatresses are willing as it were to disgrace themselves by bringing their filth and their shame before God. If we knew well that by fornicating one profanes the temple of God and of His Holy Spirit, that one dismembers the body of our Lord Jesus Christ, oh! it is certain

---

5. This verse says, "Flee fornication." In the modern French Bible Calvin's word *paillardise* seems to have been dropped. We read *l'adultere* in Matthew 5:28 and *l'impudicite* in 1 Corinthians 6:18. *L'impudicite* is the broader term, since it would seem to include illicit relationships among both married and unmarried.

that we would have greater horror of this sin than we do.
And then when adultery is joined with fornication,[6] it is to
pervert all human uprightness and all equity. If one robs the
goods of another, the punishment will be done, a thief will be
reproved by all, they cry after him, they strike his face; and
adultery is not simple larceny; for there one does not rob the
goods and the substance of another, one robs the honor and
everything, and not only those are robbed who are already
born, but those who are not yet formed in the womb. And
then is not marriage a sacred covenant, as our Lord calls it
in the Scripture? If one has falsified a contract on a sale, or if
one assumes some false title by bribing some false witness,
there is punishment and there ought to be. Now here is the
greatest contract that can be made in the world which is violated, it is falsified. One will make such a solemn declaration
of the faithfulness that the husband owes the wife, and the
wife the husband, one will come here into the temple as it were
in the presence of God, one will call upon Him in order that
He may be Judge whether or not each one will have kept what
he or she promises; and all that will go to destruction. So
then, if we recognize these things, it is certain that fornicators and adulterers should not be so tolerated as they are; but
everyone should hold them in horror, there should not even be
anyone who would check his feeling against them, and who
would not be his judge, and this sentence should be for law
and for regulation; and whenever there would be some so
wicked that they could not be held back by fear of God or religion, nevertheless, they should fear this threat: briefly, it is
certain that there should be a greater zeal to cut off such an
evil from the midst of us. By this, then, we see that many who
make profession of the Gospel hardly care what is remonstrated
against them; and although they think "This is God who
speaks," they are not moved by it. And why not? For Satan
has dazzled them; they are so carried away that they have
neither reason nor intelligence in them.

---

6. The sin is bad enough if neither party is married, but if one or both
parties are married, there is not only the sin in the body, but also the
sin of destroying one or both homes, as the case may be.

And yet let us remember so much better the lesson which is here contained. When, then, it is said, *"Fornication is a great laxity,"*[7] *and it is iniquity to be condemned,"* let each one summon himself before the judgment of God, and let us be advised to keep ourselves unpolluted. And since it is a virtue more than human, and it is surely necessary that God should work in us to destroy all wicked cupidities; let us pray to Him that by His Holy Spirit He may so govern us that we may detest this sin, and that we may also always have before our eyes the vengeance of which it is here spoken. And though God may not punish fornicators and adulterers in the manner which is here revealed, let us know that He has diverse means, so that we shall not be able to escape His hand. When a man will have seduced the wife of another, if God does not permit his wife to fall into such filth (as it could happen that a wicked man will have a virtuous wife, and God will pity his wife, that she will be preserved, and she will not abandon herself to evil, even though her husband may be a wicked man on his part), yet the husband must not think therefore that he is better off on account of it; for God well knows how to find another manner of punishment. Let us recognize, then, that He has enough chastisements in His coffers, as it is spoken of in the song of Moses (Deuteronomy 32:34), that He has terrible stripes which are unknown to us, and which He will be able to display whenever it seems good to Him; let us anticipate His judgment, and let Him be feared and dreaded by us, seeing that He exercises toward us the grace of warning us before His hand comes upon us.

And then if we are still so indifferent as not to feel the admonition which is here given to us, let us note well that the Holy Spirit repeats this threat, when He says, *"It is a fire which devours everyone to perdition, it is to cut off at the root his substance."* Men surely must be worse than brutes, if this does not at least wake them up; for it is not only said that "It is a laxity, it is a sin which deserves to be punished";

7. For Calvin any "laxity" or breach of godly discipline was a very great sin. Would to God that some of the Reformed Churches would wake up and realize this fact today.

but "it is a fire which consumes everything, which goes right
down to the root, it is an extreme perdition, there will remain
no substance at all which would not be scraped." When, then,
we hear that God threatens us in such a manner, in order that
His wrath may be rendered frightful to us, is it not now or
never to think to ourselves? And besides, let us practice this
doctrine in two ways: namely, let each one profit by it in his
own right; and then let us also try, as much as it will be possible for us, each one according to his station and vocation, to
correct the evil when it will be in the midst of the people, and
that we may be pure from it. As to the first, let each one look
to himself, and let him keep a good watch upon all his affections, for fear of being seduced. We have shown before, that
it would not be sufficient that a man should be prevented from
committing the act, unless he places a close guard over his eyes,
so that he may not look at anyone unchastely. For he who
will have looked at the wife of another with an evil covetousness, already is judged before God as a fornicator and adulterer; and what will happen, then, if we look at the heart?
and then if we come to spy and to keep a watch in order to
seduce women? All the more, then, ought we to be vigilant
to keep guard over our cupidities, and according as they are
rough, let each one also think to himself, and let us be held in
check under the fear of God. Also, regarding the such horrible
threat which He makes against it, let us have the zeal to correct fornicators when we see that they have dominion in our
midst; for if we shall allow them, and they should be nourished
by our indifference, we shall be held before God as mackerels
and ruffians. They must not be excused; for he who will shut
one eye or be blind, and who will permit what fornicators commit, cannot be exempt before God of being a mackerel (as I
have already said) and as much as is in us, we do only pile
up the wood of the wrath of God. If the house of a fornicator should be consumed, and the fire should devour everything there — if we are not advised on our part to extinguish
it, and to cause that fornications should not be in fashion in
our midst, and that they should not be common and allowed,
the fire will have to be lit throughout all the city, and through-

out all the country, and we shall have to experience the curse of God Who undermines us on account of it, until we should be entirely consumed. And as for what is here spoken especially of judges, those who have the charge and the office of punishing sins — they look carefully at themselves; for they will be double mackerels and double ruffians before God, if they permit that fornications pass before their eyes, and they hide them, and take no account of them, and they are even satisfied that they should always be more in fashion. This, then, is what we have to note from this passage. And besides, let us be advised not to be held back only by a forced fear from committing the act of fornication; but seeing that God has exercised the grace of choosing us to be temples of His Holy Spirit, and that He has drawn us to Himself; let us pray to Him that He may give us grace to serve Him in all purity, not only of body, but also of mind. And since we are grafted into the body of our Lord Jesus Christ, and He has even united us to Himself as His members; let us study not to cause Him the shame of bringing ourselves thus polluted in such filth.

This, then, is how believers ought to be induced to chastity, not only by a forced fear, but in recognizing the grace and the honor that God has done to them; when He was so willing to approach them; let them, then, also ask only to come to Him by means of our Lord Jesus Christ. So much for the protest which Job here made against fornication. Now let us come to the second protest that he brings forward; it is, that lest he should ravish the right of another, he even did not use pride or cruelty toward those who were subject to him. Servants and chamber-maids at that time were not as they are today; they were not kept for hire, as employed, as paid; but they were slaves as long as they lived, so that they were possessed like asses and oxen. And this is well worthy of being noted; for although according to human right a master might have power both of death and of life over his serf, yet we see how Job used them: namely, that he held himself back, and imposed law upon himself, since he knew that according to God those who have such mastery must not abuse it, they must not be tyrants, they must not tread reasonable creatures under foot.

We surely have, then, to note what was the quality and condition of serfs at that time; for it is to give better recognition to the humaneness of Job and the uprightness which he practiced, not allowing himself what would be permitted to him from man's point of view; for he saw well that it was not lawful for him according to God.

Now let us note the words which he uses: *"If I have refused,"* he says, *"judgment to my servant and to my chambermaid when they have striven against me."* For the word which he here uses means "to quarrel," "to debate," and "to have some difference" or "suit." By this Job indicates that, although he could close his mouth to his servants and chambermaids, and though he could beat them with blows when it seemed good to him, in such a way that no one would have been irritated against him; nevertheless he gave them liberty to plead their cases; as when he was angry, if there was reasonable excuse, his servants and chamber-maids could debate their case frankly, and show their right, so that he did not oppress them by force. We see, then, that there was neither pride nor cruelty in him. Now he declares more fully how he could control his passions, so that he was so humane as to support his inferiors; *"For,"* he says, *"He Who has made them has also made me, we have all been formed from One."* This could be taken that we have been formed in one womb, that is to say, we are all descended from Adam, we are all of the same nature; but it must be extended still further. Job, then, considered two things when he supported his servants and chamber-maids so humanely. The first is, that we have a common Creator, that we are all descended from God; and then, that there is a like nature, so that we must conclude that all men, although they may be of low condition and despised according to the world, nevertheless have brotherhood with us. For he who will not condescend to recognizing a man as his brother must then make himself an ox, or a lion, or a bear, or some other savage beast, and he must renounce the image of God which is imprinted in us all. These are the two reasons which Job here brings forward.

Whereupon he concludes, *"What would I do, when God should come to visit me? would He not rise up against me? Could I exist[8] before His face?* When he should call to account all my life, how could I answer, if I had not been humane toward my servants?"* This is a passage which implies great and very useful doctrine, provided that we know how to profit by it. For if we ought to be humane toward our inferiors, that, when we have the means to oppress them, we ought of ourselves to impose law and measure and rule on ourselves — what will it be toward those who are equal to us? For it seems that if someone is subject to me, it ought to be lawful for me to use such authority, that he should not speak, and that I could do everything to him; as we see that men today make themselves believe that they are much more than they are; and if God gives them some portion of authority, they will so augment it that there is neither end nor means. Yet we ought to spare those who are inferior to us, and over whom we are raised. What will it be, then, when we have to do with our equals or superiors? A master will be condemned before God if he has oppressed his servant by violence, if he has raised himself in such presumption and arrogance that he has not allowed his servant to maintain a good argument; and what will it be, if the servant is rebel against his master? What will it be if a son stands against his father, or a subject against his superior? It is certain that this is less bearable.

We see, then, here a doctrine general and common to all; it is that in the first place those who are raised into some dignity should recognize that God has not put them there to release the bridle to molest others, and to hold a foot on their throat; but they must always hold themselves back in humility and modesty. So much, then, for one item. For the authority which is among men ought to be so valued that he who will serve and be little, ought not therefore to be despised. It is certain that a man in his house will wish to have a mistress, and there is no mistress as noble as she; a man, then, only in his house will wish to be listened to and obeyed. Now we see

---

8. Fr. *consister*. An interesting study could be made of *consister, exister,* and *subsister* in Calvin. However, I have generally not taken the trouble to distinguish them here.

nevertheless that a master will not have such dominion over his servants and chamber-maids that he ought not to hear them peaceably when they will have been wronged. If, then, a man in his private house ought to use such humaneness toward those who are inferior to him, what will it be of those who have the authority of justice? For they have not dominion like masters over their servants and chamber-maids. There is an authority, and an honorable preeminence; but it is not to so dominate that others should be in servitude; on the contrary let not Kings and princes flatter themselves that it seems that the world is created for them, they are created for the multitude. Has not God established principalities and kingdoms for the common good? It was not only to raise two or three of them among the others. Not at all; but it is in order that there might be some order among mankind and some policy. So then, Kings and princes ought to consider how to live over their subjects that they may not trample them, and that they may not exercise tyranny over them; for they will be much less excusable than masters are when they will have treated cruelly their servants and chamber-maids. Now so much less will it be permitted to those who are called to administer justice, who are seated like servants of God to render the right to everyone. If they forget, if they are carried away by pride, God must surely chastise them much more harshly than masters who had done some violence or some wrong to their brothers who served them. Besides, is that the way those who have some authority over others ought to raise themselves? what, then, of those who are of equal condition? how have we to live each one with his relative and his neighbor? If a man raises himself when he ought to recognize the equality of those who accompany him, so that he comes to charge like a bull (I pray you), will it not be necessary that such pride should be subdued? And when a man having nothing but sudden boldness will wish to usurp such an authority over his neighbors, that he will only deign to look askance at them, that it seems to him that all the world ought to tremble at his look — will it not be necessary that God should put His hand upon such bravado?

So then, let us note well this passage; for it is not only to
instruct masters to modesty and humaneness, but all in general,
and for a very great reason. And while we still see that God
wishes that those who are inferior should suffer and endure
from those who have authority over them; surely each one
must consider his estate and his vocation, and we must learn to
conform ourselves to such modesty that a master may not oppress his servant, that the servant may not chafe against his
master; but that each one may acquit himself of his duty, so
that God may be served in sovereign degree. That is what we
have to note from this passage. Now in order to be more
convinced, if perhaps we were so fierce in our minds that everyone wished to usurp more than what belonged to him, let us
note that we shall be condemned not only by the mouth of God
and of His Prophets, when there will be such a fierceness in us
and we shall be cruel toward those who are subject to us; but
it will be necessary that the Pagans in the last day should be
our judges. I have already said that, according to human laws a
master had at that time power of death and of life over his servants. What have Pagans said about it? "We must use servants
as mercenaries, that is to say, as people whom we have hired,
and who would not be subject to us." These are their own
words.[9] If unbelievers who lived then had this regard for humaneness, that each one had to impose law on himself, although
he was permitted the license to do what seemed good to him
towards his servants; I pray you, what excuse will there be
for us who are enlightened by the Word of God, if we do not
at least have such consideration? And so then, let us note that
if God raises us in some authority, it is to prove our modesty;
and if He gives us servants and chambermaids who are subject to us, it is in order to exercise us in the humaneness and
uprightness spoken of here, and that we may show that if God
gives us some special grace, and holding it from Him, we are
by this means incited to use it soberly. And since He Who
has all power over us nevertheless spares us, we must voluntarily follow Him as His children, and wishing to be like Him
we must be humane toward each other. Besides, let us know

---

9. Cicero, *De Officiis*, 1, I c. 13 No. 41.

that this power is entirely perverted when a man under shadow of authority will wish to raise himself cruelly against others; it is, I say, a sign of an entirely malicious nature when a man will thus raise himself because of his credit. On the contrary those who are of a benign and lovable nature — it is certain that they will always spare their inferiors; and moreover when God gives them authority, they will be all the more held back, indeed by themselves. It is not a matter here of constraint which comes from outside, like some who will act like dogs lying down, and use every flattery, when they can do nothing; and then when they are raised, they burst forth, and show that there was no modesty in them, but that they are of a servile nature, which is considered villainous and detestable. And this ought all the more to induce us to the modesty to which the Holy Spirit commands us in this passage. But the principal thing is to observe well the two reasons that we have already mentioned: namely, (1) that we have a Creator from Whom we are all descended, and (2) that we are of a like nature.

This, then, is what we have to consider, to beat down all pride and cruelty in us, when we shall be incited to them. If, then, a man has a household, and God has given him servants and chamber-maids, and he should be tempted to raise himself too high and to use excessive severity; let him seek the remedy which is here declared to us. How? When I shall treat my servants cruelly, by plucking the bread from their mouths, that they would not dare to eat a morsel which would not be to my regret, by pressing them more than is needful, briefly, by showing myself cruel toward them; with whom do I strive? It is true that they are mine; however, has not God created and formed them? Have we not a common Master in heaven? This is what St. Paul alleges (Ephesians 6:9), when he exhorts masters to spare their servants: "My friends," he says, "although you have superiority over them, yet you have a Master in heaven; for those who are raised do not cease therefore to be subjects; for God is over them. Let them, then, consider that they will have to render account to Him Who has given them servants." Having this consideration, must we not be held back? For have we this of ourselves? By what right do we arrive at the superiority that each one has in his place? Is it not as it were a trust that God has put between our hands? Must we not, then, be advised to use it according to His will? Even the Pagans have well known how to say, when they wished to set up sovereign Dominions: "Well, it is true that Kings are made to fear and to dread; but yet they cannot flee the hand of the heavenly Judge; there is a God Who is over them." If this is said of princes who have sovereign superiority, what of those who are of the middle class, as masters and mistresses? And besides (as I have said) let us recognize, "Behold, we all have a common Creator." When we shall be able to consider that we are all descended from one God, we must conclude what is true, that we cannot oppress our neighbors without offending God. Let no one, then, raise himself in vanity; for (as Solomon says in Proverbs 14:31 and 17:5) he who mocks the blind or the poor despises his Maker. There is a poor man, I shall have despised him on account of it, I shall have caused him some shame; it is true that the injury is addressed in the first instance to a mortal man; yet God puts Himself before him, and takes the injury as done to His Person.

That, then, is what Job, or rather the Holy Spirit, wished to note in this passage, saying that He Who has created the master has created the servant. So then, when we are touched by a vain presumption, to prize ourselves more than others, and we desire such domination, that everyone should defer to our judgment, that everyone should throw himself at our feet, that we may set the fashion; let us come to this consideration, "But though I am master, God has made me servant, He has formed him as well as me." When we shall think of this, it will be to subdue the presumption which was in us, in order that all haughtiness may be reprimanded. Also we should have the second consideration spoken of here, that we are of like nature. For it is true that God has surely formed the brute beasts, the trees and other things; but He has not formed men like the beasts, He has given them intelligence, imprinting His image in them. On the other hand, I cannot contemplate a man without seeing myself there as in a mirror. Since, then, God has established such a union among us (I pray you) he who will try to break it — does he not cut himself off from mankind? Is he not worthy to be sent back to the dogs, when he does not recognize the nature that God has put in us all? But what? There are very few who think of these things; for on the contrary it will be seen that when a man will be raised only a digit, it will seem to him that he is no longer of the common rank. And all the more ought we to note well this doctrine; for if Job at that time, when there was not yet such light as there is today, knew that since all are created by one God, and that He has put us all in one rank, this ought to correct the pride of men, and all fierceness and haughtiness, I pray you, what excuse have we when God now declares Himself to be our Father? He does not say only that He is Creator of mankind, of poor as of rich, of servants as of masters, but He names Himself Father; we must, then, have brotherhood among us, unless we wish to renounce the grace of our God, and to cut ourselves off from His house, in which place we are domestic servants. We see how far Jesus Christ the Lord of Glory abased Himself, that He made Himself servant of servants; we also all have a common inheritance to which we are called, as Saint Paul says (Romans 8:17). Since this is so, then, let us learn to humble ourselves, and since we know that pride and cruelty are to shut against us the door of paradise, let us be kind and humane toward those over whom we have superiority, when our Lord owns them for His children; and let us all get along with them in such a way that God may be glorified by all, both great and small; and let us follow such an order that each one may acquit himself of his duty according to his vocation, and let us do all homage to the great Lord and Master, Who is the common Judge of all.

Now we shall bow in humble reverence before the face of our good God.

SERMON 14

Job's Humaneness*

If I have disappointed the poor of his desire, or if I have wearied the eyes of the widow; if I have eaten my morsels alone, and the orphan has not had his part thereof; (For from my youth he has been brought up with me as if I were his father, and she has been with me from the womb of my mother.) if I have seen a man perish for want of a coat, or the poor for want of a garment; if his loins have not blessed me, if he has not been warmed with the fleece of my lambs; if I have lifted up my hands against the orphan, seeing my help at the gate; let my arm fall from my shoulder, and let my arm be broken from the bones. For I have feared the punishment of God, and could not bear His burden.

—Job 31 :16-23

HERE Job shows the humaneness[1] that was in him by helping the poor and needy. He had protested heretofore that he had not done any man wrong, but here he goes still further; namely, that pitying the necessity of those who come to him for help, he relieved them with his own goods and substance, yea even without making them linger for it. Wherein he shows himself to have had a willing forwardness, that is to say, that he was no sooner requested, but he employed himself, and delayed not from day to day, as those do who love to be lugged by the ear. And this is why he says, *"If I have disappointed the poor of his desire,"* that is to say, *"If I helped not the poor when I saw him in want and needy,"* or *"If have wearied,"* says he, *"the eye of the widow."* For if we wait for any thing with a longing, our eye is always upon it, and when we look overly earnestly upon anything, our eyes faint and dazzle. We see then what Job's meaning is, that he hung not down his

---

* Sermon 114 in *Calvini Opera, Corpus Reformatorum,* volume 34, pp. 661-675.
1. Fr. *humanité,* humaneness, a characteristic virtue of Calvin himself.

groin in his bosom (as they say) when poor folks came to ask
his help, but aided them immediately. He adds that he *saw
not men who wanted raiment perish for cold, but rather* dealt
so with them that *their loins and sides blessed him*: that is to
say, they felt the favor which he showed them. *"They were
warmed with the fleece of my lambs."* To be short, he says,
*that he had not eaten his morsels alone, nor devoured by him-
self the goods that God had given him, but had given the widows and orphans part with him, whom* (says he) *"I have
brought up with me as their father."* Wherein he indicates
that he had been a father to orphans. *"From my mother's
womb* (says he) *I have had the widow with me, I have taken
unto me the poor who needed help and I have never failed
them. And if I have not been so, let my shoulders fall out of
the socket"*; that is to say, "Let me be dismembered and let
me rot and fall to pieces. *Let my arm* (says he) *be thrust out
of the joint, and let the bones of it be broken;* let the world see
God's great and horrible curse upon me and my body, (says
he) if I have done wrong to those who were feeble, and not
able to revenge themselves; as if I have lifted up my hand
against the orphan; and although I were able to do them
wrong, for any help they should have at my hand, and that
justice might uphold me in my wrong; yet notwithstanding,
if I have attempted any such thing, let me be torn in pieces,
and rot alive." And that it is so, *"I was always afraid of
God's scourge, for I was not able to bear His burden."* Herein
he declares (as he has done before) that it was not the respect
of men, or the shame of the world, or any other consideration
that kept him from doing evil; but that forasmuch as he saw
that God was his judge, therefore he walked uprightly. And
although he might have gone unpunished in the world, without
fear of being pursued by way of justice or otherwise, and
might have taken the liberty to do harm to the meaner sort,
by reason of his credit; yet notwithstanding, he always had
the consideration to say, "Verily, my God, I know that Thy
wrath would be terrible unto me. And how should I be able
to endure it?" To be short, Job shows here that his abstain-
ing from sin was not for fear of punishment (for he saw none

before his eyes), but for conscience's sake, which compelled him to obey God, and to fear His judgment to come. This is the effect of that which is contained here.

And first of all we have here one lesson to show that we are God's children: which is, that we must be pitiful to help our neighbors in their need. Almsdeeds therefore are commended to us here. It has been told you often that the word "alms" imports as much as "mercy." Now we see that among other titles, God attributes this to Himself, that He is humane and merciful. Then we cannot be His children, neither will He acknowledge us as such, unless we try to follow His example in this place. It is that we should be moved to pity when we see any poor folks in adversity, and to go about providing for them every one of us according to his ability. True it is that we may give all our substance, and yet our doing shall not be counted a virtue. For before the hand be opened to give, it behooves the heart to be touched with compassion. But if we pity those who are in adversity, it behooves us also to help them as we are able. For (as St. James, 2:16, says) if I say to a poor man, "My friend, God help you," thereby I show that I have no love in me. If I say, "It is a great pity about this man," and yet in the meanwhile labor not to help him whom I ought to relieve; it is a mockery, and I am only a hypocrite. That is to say, I see there how God shows me a pitiful case, and it is as much as if God gave me occasion to employ myself; and thereby I see that He calls me; and yet in the meanwhile I make no countenance of it at all. If there were but one drop of humaneness in me, would I not try to help such a need for my part? So then, we have to bear in mind in this text, that the Holy Spirit exhorts us to almsdeeds, and that the same consists in two points: that is to say, (1) in being pitiful toward our neighbors when we see them in adversity, and also when we have such a pitiful affection that (2) we seek the means to help them, and every man exerts himself to his ability. True it is, that we cannot supply all the needs that we see, and therefore a Christian may well mourn in his heart, without putting his hand to his purse. For it is impossible (even for those who have the best intentions) to help at all times. And therefore this pitifulness shall suffice them, and God accepts it for an almsdeed, as if the poor were nourished and fed by them; and when they have this compassion upon a poor man, it is as great a sacrifice unto God, as if he had given and dealt dole out of a full purse. Nevertheless, it behooves us always to look that we deal according to our ability, knowing that our Lord has made us stewards of His goods which He has put into our hands, not to the end that every one of us should devour them by himself alone, but that we should communicate them to such as have need of them. True it is also that no man can set any definite standard in this case; and surely when Saint Paul speaks of it, he says that God constrains us not as it were of necessity, but will have us to do it of free devotion (Romans 12:8). By the way, let us bear well in mind that if the poor do pass before us and we see their need and keep our purses shut, so that we condescend not to help them; it is a sure sign that we are as wild beasts, and that there is not one mite of pity in us, and that we ourselves shall one day feel the like cruelty if God send us any afflictions; and that although we shall be miserable, yet shall no man be moved at it, but men shall look upon us with disdain, so that we shall be rejected and left utterly destitute. For it is the measure and wages which God is accustomed to give to all who are hardhearted toward their neighbors; according as it is said, that he who is merciless shall have judgment without mercy. Yea and besides, men shall be cruel toward us according to our deserts; we must also in the end appear before God, Who will handle us with all rigor, because we have not followed the goodness which is in Him, and which He would have to be our rule and example. So much the more then behooves it us to be mindful of this doctrine which is shown us here: namely, that God thinks it is not enough that we should only abstain from evil-doing, and from hurting our neighbors, and from taking away other men's goods and substance. True it is that it is already a kind of virtue when we can justly protest that we have clean hands, and are not given to theft, deceit, and extortion; but yet for all that, let us not yet think we are acquitted. For if God had given us wherewith to help such as have need, if we do it not, we are blameworthy. And why? For we have taken away God's goods and put them to another use than He meant. If a servant is put in trust to receive his master's goods, and his master has appointed him to give thus much to such a one, and to pay such another a sum of money that he owes; or if he has given him an order telling how he will have his goods spent; if the servant plays the niggard, so that one man comes crying after him, "Pay me"; and yet he will not part with a cent, and another comes saying, "Your master wishes you to give me a certain thing," and yet he will not let anything go, and the household cries out upon him for bread, and he lets those who labor in his master's service die of hunger; I pray you is it tolerable that the servant shall answer, "Behold sir, I have not touched one mite of your goods; behold sir, I have reserved unto you all that ever I had"? For the master may say to his shame, "I have not put my goods into thy hand to that end. For thou hast put me to shame, in that thou hast not bestowed my goods where I appointed thee; and now must I bear the slander of thy niggardliness in pinching that which was not thine." Now when the master shall come with such a servant, shall he not condemn him as wicked? Likewise God gives us His goods to the intent that we should relieve our poor brothers with them. Now if on the contrary we are so straight-laced that there goes not a cent out of our purses, nor one morsel of bread from our table, what shall become of us? Is it not defrauding those whom God has ordained to have a part of our substance and robbing God in the thing that He has put into our hands? Then, as I said before, let us learn to be more merciful. And although no man can impose a definite law by saying "Thou shalt give so much"; yet nevertheless, let every man exert himself, and consider his own ability, knowing well that when we have done all that we can do, yet are we not discharged.

So then you see the particular law which every man ought to have: it is, that this charity ought to extend itself far and wide, even so far that we may still confess that we have not sufficiently discharged our duty toward the poor. And if we do all that is possible (although we come not to full perfec-

tion) so it be not with niggardliness or grudging, but of a free
heart to help those who have need; let us assure ourselves
that our Lord accepts our alms, as a sacrifice of sweet savor;
yea even though there be some saltiness in it and we do not
one-tenth of that which we are bound to do. Herewithal it
behooves us to mark the circumstance which is set down here,
that we cause not the needy to linger (for when we use such
delay, it is a token that we have not a free heart to do our
neighbors good) and we put them not off to another time, except it be upon good consideration. For it may well be that a
man may be pitiful and yet notwithstanding inquire about the
need of the party, but that is not the lingering which Job means
when he says that he disappointed not the poor man of his
desire. For here he intends to express the loatheness that is
in niggards: namely, that when a man desires any relief of
them and would fain draw a cent out of their purses, it seems
to them as if a man would pluck the guts out of their bellies; and
therefore they would always fain have some relief. They are
like an ill paymaster when men come to demand their debt; he
knows well that he must pay it, yea and that he is well able
to do it, but it does him good to brag with the money in his
purse for a day or two; or else they are like a man who is led
to the gallows; he delays as long as he can, and when he comes
to climb the ladder, he haggles at every step. Even so do these
teasers; when a man comes to demand his debt it makes them
always shrink back, and much more if a man comes to ask
them for alms. But if we were charitable, surely we would
not have this loatheness in us, we would not ask for such
respites, the poor would not languish on our account until our
ears were beaten in by their clamor; but we would try to help
at the same hour as much as in us lay.

You see then what we have to remember from this passage:
namely, that if we will do alms acceptable to God, we must
not tarry until we are importunately called and cried upon; but
when we see there is need, we must try to give properly at that
same hour; as when we ourselves endure any adversity, it
seems to us that men will never come in time to help us. And
why then deal not we likewise with others? We need to take

no other measure, but that. For it is a true natural rule that
we should do to others what we wish done to us, but we are
hasty to desire help and pitifully slow to give it. You see
then why we ought all the better to mark this saying, that Job
made not the widow linger, nor disappointed the poor of his
desire.

And now he adds, *that he had not eaten his morsels alone,*
but had given to the orphan, and the widow shared with him.
Why so? *For* (says he) *I have brought up the widow with*
me from my mother's womb, and I have fed the orphan like
a father. Here we see a wonderful example of bountifulness
and liberality. For here is no doing of some little almsdeed
for a week, three, or four; but Job declares here that he had
been a father to orphans and a protector of widows, not only
by helping them, but also by feeding them his goods and substance. When we hear this, I pray you ought we not to be
greatly ashamed that we can hardly and scarcely find in our
hearts to help one among a hundred? So that if we miss a
whole score of times, yet we think ourselves well discharged
with some light alms to some one man; not that we provide
for him what is required, but by giving him some little coin
as we pass by him, as it were, saying, "Go, buy elsewhere." Is
it not a great shame for us that Job should be given us here
for a mirror, and that in his person our Lord should show
us our duty, and yet notwithstanding, we do nothing? But
yet that which is contained here ought to serve for our learning and instruction. And contrariwise, it serves to condemn
us, insomuch that there will need to be no other record before
God to reprove us of our beastly cruelty, at least if we follow
not what is shown us here of Job. True it is, that although
we have not this perfection, yet will not God fail to accept us,
as I have said. Although our almsdeeds are not what they
ought to be, provided we have such compassion toward those
in distress that we try to do them good, and we do it with
eager courage, God accepts it. But in the meanwhile, if we
cannot match Job to the full, shall we not therefore follow him?
Shall we not at least do something to conform to his example?
Shall we not go toward the same mark? Perhaps we are not

able to bring up orphans, for even when we have the means our infirmity may hold us back from giving ourselves completely; but at least we ought to have some compassion. Let us do something, though we do not all. And then if we cannot attain the mark to which Job came, at least let us travel toward it, since God calls us to it. But is it not a great shame that we do nothing at all? Or else if we remove but one leg, we gnash our teeth about it, as these loiterers do who, when they set forward one foot, think that they drag a whole mountain behind them. And then do they raise one arm? They frown at it, and gnash their teeth, and instead of advancing they retreat. When we go to work after that fashion, is it not a sign that there is no willingness in us?

Therefore if we cannot come to such perfection as Job declares himself to have had, which thing he declares not by way of bragging, but to the intent that we should be the more moved; let us at least learn to follow his example. For God, knowing that we never become better by one easy lesson, sets before us mirrors so that we should have less excuse. If a man asks, "How then? Must we give to all men without discrimination?" the answer is that the Holy Spirit does not wish to take away discretion from almsgiving, so that men would have no regard for how their goods were used; for if we should go to it without discretion, every man would be, as it were, drawn dry, and in the end the poor would be left helpless; for the boldest (as they say) would carry away everything. And what manner of men are the boldest? Such as are least to be pitied; for they will pretend to be poor, only to rake all to themselves; their only seeking is to have double and treble, and they hardly care if other men suffer hunger and thirst. Therefore it is good that men should be prudent and look carefully to whom they give, especially considering the lewdness that is nowadays in the world; for there are so many hypocrites that it is a pity to see. Hardly will a man find one among a hundred who is worthy to be helped. For although they are poor indeed; yet no one knows how to do them good, because as soon as they get anything they fall to gluttony and drunkenness, and so God makes them waste it all away. To

be brief, we have come to the full measure of all iniquity, insomuch that we ought to use great discretion, and carefully
scrutinize when we give.   But in the meanwhile let us beware
that we seek not cover for our stinginess under the shadow of
prudence.   For God does not condemn it that men should have
regard to whom they give, so that the gift may be well bestowed; no, but it behooves us first to be fully resolved after
this manner in ourselves: "As for me I mind not to spare
according to the measure that I have; I will do good according to my ability;   I desire nothing more than to find
where I may help."   When a man has resolved this, let him
inquire whether his alms may be well bestowed on this man or
that man (for he will be able to do it freely) ; but if a man says
to himself, "Oh, good judgment is the first requirement when
it comes to the question of giving," and he always excuses himself, saying, "Oh, I find no poverty there," and it is very easy
to have some pretext for doing nothing; manifestly such a
man asks only to be exempt from helping those who need his
aid.   If, then, we wish to inquire for ourselves, good will must
precede, that is to say, we must ask only to do good, and then
we inquire for ourselves boldly: we can do it, provided that we
are rightly motivated in the first place, and that we are not
asking for cover for our stinginess.   This, then, is the attitude
to which we must come.   Meanwhile our diligence in inquiry
must not be too exacting; for in doing good it is impossible
not to be cheated, and though we may take pains to discriminate, we cannot avoid giving some alms to those who are
not worthy of them.   And this is also why St. Paul exhorts
us not to be weary in well-doing (Galatians 6:9) ; for we shall
have many hindrances in so doing.   We shall see immediately
that there will be wags who slander us, unthankfulness will follow, all of which could discourage us.   Yet we must always
have good courage and continue, whatever may be the outcome.   In summary (following what I have already said) we
cannot here lay down all kinds of special laws, but the general
rule which God gives us ought to well suffice for us: it is that
we should have a humane heart, inclined to pity and compassion, that we should desire to do good and to help those who

have need of our aid, and that we should not cause those who
wait for us to languish, but rather we should have an open
heart, in order that the hand may be open when necessity requires it. This, in summary, is what we have here to observe.

Besides, let us note well that Job said further, *that he did
not want him who needed clothes to die, he did not allow him
who had no covering to die of cold.* *"But,"* said he, *"their
sides and their reins have blessed me, and they have been
warmed by the fleeces of my sheep."* Here Job shows that
in every way he has tried to busy himself doing alms, not only
by feeding the hungry and giving drink to the thirsty, but by
clothing the naked. In fact, if we wish to be pitiful, we must
minister to the needs of our neighbors as we see them; for it
is not enough to help in only one line. It is true that everyone
cannot be like Job; for we have not thousands of beasts like
he had, so that he could be accounted among the great princes
of today with respect to his revenue; as we have seen that he
had not only oxen by pairs or by hundreds, but he had herds
enough for five or six large villages, indeed much more, for a
whole country. For we have seen that in livestock alone his
wealth and substance were like the livestock of a whole country. Everyone, then, will not come up to that; but be that as
it may, let us look at our capacity; for according to it we must
try to do good; for we know that it is said that Jesus Christ
praised the widow who had given only two mites and recognized
her above those who had thrown in large sums of money.
The reason? Because she had given all her substance, and
the others had given only a little portion, considering their
riches. So then, let each one consider himself; and in the first
place, seeing the want in which neighbors are either of drink
or of food or of clothing, at least, if we cannot help them otherwise, let us pray to God that He may have pitied them, and
that He may raise them; that we may not be held accountable
for the fact that they may not be aided. This, then, is what
we have to remember, that Job, after having spoken of his
morsels and that he had dealt a portion to those who were

hungry, adds, that he also has well clothed those who could
have died of cold without his aid.

And he even says *that their reins have blessed him*, by which
he declares that they have had occasion to be thankful to him.
However, he shows that he did not attend to men for pay,
that he did not search for what might have accrued to himself
if he did them good; but he was satisfied to know that the good
which he did was acceptable to God. This is a lesson we ought
to well remember; for although men may be unthankful, and
though those to whom we shall have done good will murmur
against us, and though they may return evil for good; yet we
have lost nothing by well-doing for them. And why? In
spite of their teeth, if we have fed them, their belly will bless
us before God; if we have helped them in another manner,
the organ must respond. It is true that sometimes they will
be so wicked that they will say, "Indeed, is this for a good
purpose? And what do I owe him?" As we shall see today
that the poorest are the proudest; those to whom we shall have
tried to do good will be the most slanderous. This is what
we shall probably see; however let us not be angered by it.
If we cannot bear such unthankfulness, let us note the word
here written down, that is, that what we shall have done will
bless us before God. Would any man be so villainous when
he is aided that he would fret and murmur? Well, the man
still has ribs; and if we have clothed him, his body must bless
us before God. It is true that the man himself may not be so
affected; but though that may be, God considers the body
which has been clothed; and this blessing will be taken into
account before Him. As I have said, the belly of a man who
has been fed speaks, and although his mouth may be so dis-
loyal, though it may convert the good into evil, and though
only poison may come out of it; yet our Lord will accept the
blessing of the almsdeed done. This, then, is what we have to
note, in order that we may be incited to help those who need
us, that we may not consider whether they are to recompense
us or return to us the good done, or even say, "Thank you."
Well, suppose they do just the opposite. Nevertheless, our

effort is not lost, since God accepts the sacrifice which has been done.

This, then, is the implication of the saying, *"The ribs or the reins bless those who may have clothed a man who was cold."* On the other hand, let us note that when the poor do not cry out vengeance against us and complain; yet their ribs will curse us when they have suffered destitution, and we have closed our eyes and have shown them no pity, saying, "I am comfortable; I do not care how others may be." If then we have been so cruel, certainly God will cause their ribs and reins to speak, when poor destitutes have died of their needs and we have not condescended to help them; although they may not open their mouths to complain of our cruelty, oh, the anguish which they may have suffered must cry out and complain before God, and vengeance must be done according to this complaint. So it will happen, though these men sound not a word, as we have said.

Now after Job spoke thus, he added, *that he had not raised his hand against the orphan even though he saw his help at the gate;* that is to say, although he could do it without being punished by men; for at that time courts were conducted at the gates of the city, which were the most popular places to visit. Job, then, says, "It is true that I might have been able to make one to tremble, another to flee, that I might have been able to be like a thunderbolt, and yet no one would have been able to sound a word against me. And why not? A man with good credit will be supported, and no one will dare to complain against him; and if someone did complain against him, the judges would not dare to do right. Although I had such a reputation that the courts would have allowed anything I had attempted; however, I did not abuse my credit; I did not even tread upon the poor; when there was an orphan, I did not try to profit by it; for we know that orphans are often exposed to prey." Job, then, shows that he was so upright[2] that when he could ravish the substance of another he never tried, he never wished to gain profit at the expense of another; indeed, although men, for their part, would have allowed it.

2. Fr. *qu'il a eu une telle droiture.*

But he adds the reason. *"For,"* he says, *"I have feared the affliction and ruin of God."* As if he said, "I do not consider only that men would not reproach me; but I have kept my eyes fixed on God, Who is my heavenly Judge." Now we see in the first place that from all time there have been great corruptions, so that men who take care to do right to everyone are not thereby acquitted. Today, then, it is no new thing if judges shake hands with the most wicked and favor them and support them in their evil deeds; it has been a common custom. All the more ought those who administer justice to consider how they are going to be acquitted before God. But what do we see? Corruption has ruled for a long time, and today it is more in evidence than ever. If someone says, "It makes no difference, since this wickedness has existed from the most ancient times; oh, he will not therefore be excused. Also, there was not then such knowledge of God; the teaching was not so familiar as it is today. Those, then, who are seated upon the throne of justice, who hold the gavel, when they allow extortions, and they see a poor man trodden down and take no account of it, seeing those of some reputation usurp more than what belongs to them; if they hide it, what excuse will there be for them, since daily they have their ears beaten with admonitions and remonstrances, and what they owe, both to God and to the people who are committed to them, is declared to them?[3] So let us note from this teaching that, if such corruption has prevailed in the world, judges have supported the wicked; when today we see a similar confusion, each one of us must console himself that it does not do us too much harm if we have neither right nor uprightness[4] from those who do us many injuries, and if we cannot see the end of such things. We must, then, be armed with patience; for we see that God from all times has thus wished to exercise His own. He surely could have established justice from the age of Job, but He wished that many poor people should sigh. If such is the case with us today, He wills by this means to teach us what it is to suffer. So much for one item.

---

3. These sermons were preached daily during 1554. Judges and magistrates were there.
4. Fr. *ne raison ne droit.*

Yet those who administer justice must well consider their part in it; for since men are inclined to this vice they will be immediately enticed from their duty, unless they continuously guard against it; as also we see too many examples of this. Now there is a second lesson which we must also record: it is, that we should not consider how much men would allow us to get away with, but after the example of Job we should have our sight fixed on God, and fear of Him should restrain us from injuring and from doing any wrong to our neighbors. And this lesson is very necessary; for today (I pray you) what is considered, except being repaid by men? It is considered sufficient, provided that anyone can succeed in it. However, what is the order of justice? Such as it was from the time of Job. Help was at the gate for those who committed extortion, who devoured widows, who molested poor people. Alas! Today we have come to such extremity, and even worse, that if a poor man is trodden down, he will have no right whatever. And why? Those who pillage the goods of another, who cheat, who strike or molest the poor, and who overflow with every iniquity are dissolute people who have conceived such boldness that it seems to them that there is no more law for them. Now the magistrates, on their part, are more timid than women, there is among them no power of the Spirit of God, or else they are content to conceal, to gratify, and even to half agree with evil-doers; and although they know that things are not going well, yet they have no zeal to remedy them; others will be still worse; for they are only asking for everything to be debauched, and that we should come to such extreme evil that there would no longer be anything but confusion, that there would no longer be any fear of God or honesty. That is where we are now.

Now then, most of them think of nothing else than how they will be able to escape when they have done evil. Some boor will spy the goods of another; or else, if there is some means to trap him, he considers, "Indeed? But, one would be brought to account. Oh, it does not matter, when I shall have corrupted such a one, immediately it is all right; when I shall have made him a present of this, I have won him; and

he will win two others; and then if I do likewise, there will
be four; and when I shall have even a half a dozen who will
be like-minded, I shall have won all." That is how those in
charge of justice will be exposed for sale like harlots, who are
no longer ashamed, and care not for their honor, nor for anything whatever; for now their tricks of pretense will be so
villainous that they are no longer plausible even to the world.
That we see. So everyone is given license to rob, to pillage,
to strike, to practice every extortion. And why? For if the
deed is brought to court, everything is corrupted. So it is a
sentence which we ought to note well when Job protests that,
notwithstanding his credit, and that he might have been so
dreaded that even judges would not have dared to do right
against him even if there had been complaints; yet of his good
pleasure he abstained from doing evil; and he did not conclude,
"I can, since men allow me"; but he had this word as a check:
namely, *he feared the affliction of God.*

Now then, let us learn to walk in openness and in good
conscience; that when we wish to undertake something, we
may take this examination, whether or not it is permitted us
by God; and when we see that a thing displeases God, that he
forbids and disapproves it, let us be satisfied with that; and
although men may applaud us, and though they may even
permit us to do what seems good to us, let us watch it. And
why? For we must come before the heavenly Judge. And
what will it profit us when we shall have escaped the hand of
men? For it will be to double His vengeance. And why?
Since in fact we shall well show that we fear men more than
God. And is it not the most villainous injury we could do
Him to prefer mortal creatures, poor carrions to His majesty? I may believe men, and yet I shall only mock God; His
majesty will be nothing to me. And then when we shall have
corrupted justice, either by hate, or by bribes, or by some other
indirect means, so that we shall have won the judges; is not
that still a second outrage which we do against God? Is it
not polluting what He had sanctified? Now justice is a sacred
thing, and we come to profane it when we turn away to evil
those who are seated on judgment-seats, and whom God had

constituted to the intent that the authority of His name ought
to reflect therein; if we come, I say, so to debauch them, is not
this a sacrilege? And for this reason I have said that we do
only double the wrath of God upon us when we have thus
escaped from the hand of men. This then is how we ought to
have our eyes fixed on God and to regard His judgment, in
order to hold us back of our free will if we can do evil, although
as far as men are concerned it would be permitted to us. Meanwhile let us also note that we must not only fear the affliction
of God when we shall experience it, but we must look ahead;
for it is too late if a man, when he has been struck by the hand
of God, feels that He is his Judge; but let us fear while God
threatens us and before His blows fall upon our heads. This
is how each one will keep himself from doing evil, when we
shall perceive from afar by the eye of faith the afflictions which
are prepared for all malefactors and those who molest their
neighbors. And God exercises great grace toward us when He
so warns us before the blow, so that we may anticipate His
vengeance. This, then, is what we have to remember.

The conclusion which Job adds is, *"How shall I bear His
burden?"* It is to show us what is also said by the Apostle
(Hebrews 10:31), "It is a horrible thing to fall between the
hands of the living God." We fear human punishments which
apply only to the body; and what will the fire of the wrath of
God which consumes all be like, indeed and yet is never extinguished, which burns in such a way that we must persist
indeed to endure it without end? Should we not consider that?
So then, let us be touched by the affliction of God, and let us
consider guarding ourselves from doing evil not only through
shame or pain before men; but let us know in our minds and
in our senses, and let us think, "How now? When men will
have schemed to put us through the most cruel torments
imaginable, yet all that is nothing compared to the price of the
vengeance of God. If a man is put upon the wheel,[5] or perhaps
he is tortured,[6] so that he is burned alive; and although these

---

5. An old instrument of torture, on which the limbs of the man were
broken with a crowbar by the executioner.
6. Fr. *tenaillé,* the flesh torn off with red-hot tongs or pinchers.

are powerfully grievous torments, yet they pass and do not last long; and then it is only bodily pain. But here is the wrath of God which consumes everything, it is a scorching fire which burns without end, it is a worm which gnaws the heart from within and eats." When the Scripture uses these comparisons, it does not yet fully express the reality; but it is only to give us some little apprehension of it. Let us note well, then, that the vengeance of God which is prepared for all evil-doers is an insupportable burden; and that by this we are incited to walk in fear and patience, knowing that if men use violence and cruelty against us, there is a heavenly Judge Who is to avenge it; and that by this we are also held back from doing evil, although it is lawful for us as far as the world goes; and let us be advised to keep our consciences clear, and that the knowledge of God should be the true rule to guide us, and that we should always have our eyes raised on high, in order to regard Him Who has placed us in this world, declaring to us that some time we must come to account before His judgment-seat.

Now we shall bow in humble reverence before the face of our God.

SERMON 15

Righteous Indignation*

*These three men¹ ceased to speak to Job, because he con-
sidered that He was righteous in himself. And Elihu the son
of Barachel the Buzite, of the family of Ram, was angry and
very indignant against Job, since Job justified himself rather
than God. He was also angry at the friends of Job, since they
had found no answer and yet had condemned Job.*—JOB 32:1-3

TO PROFIT by what is here narrated, from what we shall
see henceforth, we must remember what we have already seen:
namely, that Job having to defend a good case, has poorly conducted it; and those who had come to comfort him, having a
bad case, have had apparently good arguments and reasons,
from which one could gather useful doctrine. And while they
were at fault, since they did not build upon a good foundation;
Job was at fault, because he built poorly, having a foundation
that in itself was good. And that is why it is now said, *"Elihu
the Buzite was offended and was inflamed with anger, because
those who had not answered Job here yet had condemned him;
he was also offended against Job, because he was determined
to justify himself rather than God."* So we see that the anger
of Elihu was no more unreasonable against Job than against
his three friends who had come to comfort him. For Job had
gone too far, although he had a just and reasonable quarrel;
the others had resisted God, although they had used good reasons; for it was for a wrong purpose.

However, it is said, *"The three friends of Job ceased to dispute any longer against him, since he supposed himself to be
righteous."* We have seen that Job never supposed himself to
be so righteous that there was not much to say against him;

---

* Sermon 119 in *Calvini Opera, Corpus Reformatorum*, volume 35, pp. 1-14.

1. Eliphaz, Bildad, and Zophar.

214

on the contrary, he protested that he was a poor sinner; yet he
did not wish to be condemned according to the wishes of those
who judged evil of his affliction. The opinion and fancy of
the three friends of Job was, "Here is a man reproved by God,
since he is treated so harshly." Now it is said that we ought
to judge prudently of him whom God corrects; for we must
not conclude that each one is punished according to his of-
fences. Sometimes God spares the wicked and conceals their
iniquities; and for their more grievous condemnation, the
goodness of God will have been sold to them at a very dear
price, when He will have waited upon them in patience. So
then, since sometimes God does not seem to punish those who
have deserved it, let us not think therefore that they are better
off, and let us not justify them though God spares them. On
the contrary, when we see a man being beaten by the rods of
God, let us not estimate by that that he is more wicked than all
the rest of the world; for possibly God wishes to prove his
patience, yet He does not chastise him for his sins. Now Job
did not wish to agree with the foolish doctrine of his friends;
that is why it seemed to them that he justified himself, although that was not his thought. And so let us guard (as it
has been shown before) against taking a bad argument (for
we shall be blinded and it will seem to us that if a man does not
agree with us, that we must no longer discuss anything with
him), but before entering into a dispute let us be well assured
of the truth. There is nothing worse than to be in haste; we
know that the proverb is always said, "Haste carries us away,
and there will come out of a hasty judge only a foolish and
heedless sentence." Since it is so, let us learn to hold ourselves
as it were in suspense, until the truth may be known to us.
However, let us note that it will often happen that before men
we shall be condemned wrongly; indeed, although those who
detract against us have their mouths stopped and have no
reason to convince us, yet they will not cease to be led by such
a pride that they will defame us and will cast wicked propositions against us. By that we are admonished that, if men are
so malicious as to condemn us, having no argument, we ought
not to be too much offended; for this is not new, since it hap-

pened to Job, so excellent a servant of God; as today we see
that the Papists are satisfied to have determined that their
errors, superstitions, and false doctrines are good. For they
proceed in them with a magisterial style. Just think of it; we
need not discuss it or inquire why they act that way. For it
seems to them that they have all authority, from which they
thunder against us. However, let us know that the truth is on
our side, and let us be fully persuaded of it. Let us, then, resist
such a temptation,[2] and let it not astonish us, since it has always been true that those who had no reason on their side have
never ceased to condemn boldly and without scruple a good
case. Seeing, then, that the devil thus blinds them, let us always go our way, and let us adhere constantly to the truth
which is known to us. Also, on our part, let us be warned to
walk in greater modesty, when we shall have been a little too
hasty; as it will sometimes happen that the children of God
will foam at the mouth, that they will not sufficiently contain
themselves. So then, let us not follow such examples, and let
not obstinacy be joined with temerity. It is true that it is a
difficult thing (for he who enters a debate will most often
be obstinate), but when we shall have been mistaken, let us
not continue in a wrong opinion, but rather let us learn to
restrain ourselves. I have gone out of bounds; I well know
that I have not kept myself in such modesty as I ought. What
must I do? I must not be hardened, but I must turn the bridle,
seeing that I have taken a wrong road. That is how, then, by
the example of the friends of Job the Spirit of God warns us in
the first place to be modest, in order not to quarrel too quickly
against God; and then if we have been mistaken, even though
we have not been obstinate, let us not persevere in the wrong;
but knowing our fault let us try rather to correct it.

Concerning what is here mentioned of *Elihu*, it is not without cause that the Scripture shows us of what race he is descended; as he is named *"Buzite, of the house of Ram."* For
here we see in the first place the antiquity of that which we
have previously discussed; and it is also the principal thing
that God wished to declare to us, that there had remained some

2. Or trial.

semblance of religion among those who were surrounded with many vain fancies. Now it is a very noteworthy article; for we know how soon the world revolted, and all were turned away to corruptions and lies. I say, after the flood, although there had been a vengeance of God so horrible and worth remembering, and though the children of Noah who had escaped, having lived a long time afterwards, could instruct their children and successors how God had avenged Himself for the wickedness of the world; yet that did not prevent it that everyone had revolted and had left the true religion to turn away to lies, idolatry and every excess. By that let us see that men are as fragile as could be, and that nothing is more difficult than to retain them in the fear of God and in the good religion. It is true that with respect to evil we are so steady that we cannot be made to bend away; and when some one wishes to correct the evil in us, he does not know where to begin, he cannot find a place to begin since there is such hardness that it is a pity; indeed, but as for the good we lose it soon, it takes nothing to entice us away from it. We have a good example of this, which is shown us in that soon after the flood men are thus led astray, and have left the pure knowledge of God, although it had been shown to them.

However we see in this example of the person of Elihu that God has yet left some good seed in the midst of shadows, and that there was some good and holy doctrine. And why? In order that unbelievers might be rendered inexcusable, so that they could not allege the ignorance which reigned universally. For why was it that God was not purely served and worshipped, unless men have turned their backs upon Him? And they have not done it in ignorance, which they could honestly pretend to; rather, it was deliberate malice. Men do not like others to deceive them or make believe; but when it is a matter of serving God, they close their eyes, they extinguish every light that was shining, they ask nothing except to give themselves to every deception. That, then, is what is here declared to us. Now we ought to weigh well what was mentioned previously, that although these were not Prophets of God, yet the doctrine which came out of them had such a majesty that it was well worthy of the person of the Prophets. It is true (as we have said) that they have poorly applied it; however, there was a very ready mind in them. In fact (as we have declared) what has been deduced previously ought not to be received otherwise than from the school of the Holy Spirit. Now, although these persons were so excellent, yet they had not been instructed in the Law of Moses, they were separated from the Church of God; for if the Law was published at that time (which is uncertain), they were far away from the country of Judea, and they had no communication with it, to be partakers of the doctrine which God had designed simply for His people. We see, then, people who had had no Scripture, who had had nothing but the doctrine which Noah or his children had published after the flood; we see those to be Prophets of God, having an excellent spirit; and although they lived in different countries, yet we see how God had given them a knowledge which could be to edify all the common people. This, then, is how the world cannot be excused in its ignorance; for although idolatry had reigned from the time of Terah and Nachor, and they themselves had been idolaters (as it is said in the last chapter of the book of Joshua)[3] and those who were descended from them followed them; yet this Elihu, who was of the family of Ram, and these other three[4] have been exempt from the common corruption of that time; so that we see that the pure religion had not been abolished among them; but that there was a doctrine sufficient to lead them to God, and to convict the world of its obstinacy, and of the ignorance in which it was. This is what we have to note in the first place.

And so, when we hear that it is said that God allowed men to walk in perdition, let us note well that it is inasmuch as He has not extended to all of them the grace of giving the special doctrine which He had reserved for His people and for His Church; but this does not excuse them. God, then, has let men run wild, and they are completely plunged[5] into perdition; yet there has remained some seed in their hearts, and they have

---

3. Joshua 24:2.
4. Eliphaz the Temanite, Bildad the Shuhite, and Zophar the Naamathite.
5. Or totally lost. Fr., *se sont tous abysmes.*

been convicted, so that they cannot say, "We do not know what
God is, we have no religion whatever"; since no one can be
exempt from it; for it has remained engraven on the conscience
that the world was not formed by itself, that there was some
heavenly majesty to which we must be subject. It is true that
Saint Paul (Romans 1:20) speaks especially of the testimony
which God has imprinted upon all creatures, since the order of
the world is as it were a book which teaches us, and ought to lead
us to God; however, we must come back to what is discussed in
Romans 2:14, 15, that God has registered in our consciences
such a certainty that we cannot erase the knowledge that we
have of good and of evil. Every one will not have what we
hear in the three friends of Job; yet we shall never find a man
so crude or so barbarous that he will no longer have any remorse in himself, that he will not know that there is some God,
and that he will not have some discretion to condemn the evil
and to approve the good. There are, then, some traces which
God has left in the hearts of the most ignorant, in order that
men might not be able to cover themselves with any excuse, but
that they might be condemned by the law hidden within themselves. However, let us note that it is folly that men should
have fought against God to maintain the doctrine which had
reigned among them. For how is it possible, since the knowledge of God shone so clearly in the world (as we have seen
previously) that all could be enlightened by it, that they have
given themselves to such a stupid brutishness as worshipping
trees and stones, as worshipping the sun and the moon, that
they had made grotesque images of them, and they no longer
knew what the Living God was? How could that happen? For
it is as if a man at full noonday knowingly walked off a cliff
and drunkenness led him astray, although before his eyes he saw
the right road. We see, then, that men have not turned away
by simple lack of knowledge, but that they have despised God
through certain malice; however, let us note it well, in order
that we may no longer have recourse to the customary subterfuges, by saying, "See here, if men are so dazzled that they do
not know what God is, should it not serve them as an excuse?"
On the contrary, when anyone argues this way, let us give as our

answer what is said in Saint John (1:5), "The light has always
shone in darkness," and we see it by present example; for it
was impossible that men should have been so led astray in
stupid and enormous superstitions, unless they threw themselves into them of their own free will. There was, then, malice
and rebellion with the ignorance, when men forsook the right
way of salvation and gave themselves to their idols. That is
what we have to remember.

It is in order that we may be all the more attentive to walk,
while we have the light. I have already said that, if God exercises toward us the grace of showing us the way, we must
hurry, and it is not a matter of sleeping, and still less of closing
our eyes knowingly. Today we see as it were a great darkness
which rules over the larger part of the world; the poor Papists
have gone astray in it, and they know not what they do. And
why? For God has abandoned them, as they deserved; His
vengeance must be as it were a flood which covers them, and
which puts them in perdition, since they have deliberately forgotten the truth. On our part we have Jesus Christ Who is
the Sun of Righteousness Who shines upon us; we must not,
then, here have our eyes closed, but let us walk while we have
the day, let us follow the exhortation which is made to us, and
let us not be guilty of having knowingly erased the knowledge
which is given to us today. This, then, is what we have to remember in the first place from this passage.

Now as for the *wrath of Elihu,* let us note that he is not
here blamed for an exorbitant passion; but it is a good and
laudable indignation, inasmuch as it proceeds from the zeal
which Elihu had for the truth of God, seeing that Job wishes
to *justify himself rather than God.* The friends of Job had not
this knowledge; for they debated against him that he was a
wicked man. Job says no, and such is the truth, but (as we
have said) he goes too far, and although his case is good, he
conducts it poorly, and has chosen a bad procedure. Elihu,
then, considers that Job had gone far out of bounds, and had
sometimes murmured in impatience; and in that he wished to
justify himself rather than God. And then he is angry against
those who hastily undertake a bad case and cannot come to a

conclusion and who remain there confounded when it comes to
the extremity. Here, then, is Elihu who is inflamed with ire,
but it is not without cause. Inasmuch, then, as his zeal is good,
that is why the Holy Spirit approves the ire and the wrath
which was in him.

However, we must note the words, *"Job wished to justify
himself rather than God."* It is true that his intention was not
such, and he would have a hundred times preferred that the
earth had swallowed him or that he had never been born into
the world, than to have thought of such a blasphemy. In fact,
we have said, whenever he went too far, it was not as a settled
conclusion, but he was foaming at the mouth; as it is difficult
for men to restrain themselves so that many passions may not
often escape from them. That is how Job was; also always in
the end he excused himself; and if he was at fault, he did not
wish to excuse it. Why, then, is it said that he wished to
justify himself rather than God? Now this saying contains a
good and useful doctrine; for we are here taught that by not
thinking, we can often blaspheme against God. And in what
way? By contesting against Him. If we do not find good all
that God does, indeed, above all, when He afflicts us, it is
certain that we wish to be righteous rather than He. It is true
that we will not say it, and also we will not have such a persuasion in ourselves; but the thing shows it; that suffices for
our condemnation when we do not give glory to the righteousness of God, to justify Him. This will be better understood by
the example. Here is Job who knew that God is righteous, indeed, he frankly acknowledges it; as for himself, he confesses
that he is a poor sinner, and that there is much to find fault
with in himself, and, even if he wishes to quarrel against God,
that he will be convicted a thousand times before he has re-
sponded to a single charge. Job, then, does not wish directly
to justify himself rather than God, nor even to make himself
equal. However, what does he say? "I am amazed because
God afflicts me so, and what is there to find fault with in me?"
And then, "I am a poor creature, full of weakness; and must
God display His mighty arm against me? Oh that He might
let me die at the first stroke!" When Job thus abandons him-

self to such murmurings and defiances, there is no doubt that he justifies himself rather than God. And why? It seems to him that God has no reason to afflict him thus; and because he does not know why this was done, he asks only that God should present Himself as his adversary. And then he is angry, in the second place, in that God does not consume him at the first stroke, and that He does not send him to the pit. When, then, Job has such violent fits of passion, there is no doubt that in so doing he justifies himself rather than God. And this is what I have already said, that we shall often blaspheme in our passions without thinking of it; and that ought to render us all the more careful not to release the bridle to our passions in order not to be so miserable as to blaspheme against God without our thinking of it. This doctrine, then, is very useful for us. When the Holy Spirit pronounces that all those who are angry and murmur in their afflictions, all those who cannot subject themselves to the strong hand of God to confess that all that He does is righteous and reasonable — that all those justify themselves rather than God; and although they do not say it, but they protest a hundred times that they would never think of it, such is the case nevertheless. And here is a judge competent to pronounce the sentence; it is not proper to kick against Him, for we shall gain nothing by it. So then, what remains, unless we learn to condemn ourselves before all things, and when we come before God, that we should present our case in such a way as to acknowledge that we are poor sinners? Besides, when the judgments of God, which He will execute upon us, will seem to us too painful, may we bear them patiently, without making greater inquiries. If we find it strange that God treats us with too great strictness and we do not see the reason why He does it, if it seems to us that the evil lasts too long and that God does not spare our weakness, that He does not pity us as He ought — let us not give rein to such fancies to consent to them, but let us always remember this: God is just, whatever else He is. It is true that we shall not perceive the reason for what He does, but where else does this proceed from than from our weakness and crudeness? Must we measure the justice of

God by our senses? Where would that lead? What would be the purpose of it? So then, let us learn to glorify God in all that He does; and although His hand may be rough to us, let us never cease to confess, "Alas! Lord, if I enter into judgment with Thee, I know well that my case is lost." That is how Jeremiah (12:1) argues, and shows us the way that we have to go; for although there was such great confusion that he could be scared so as to murmur with the rest of the people, yet he uses this preface, "Lord, I know that Thou art just; it is true that I would enter into a dispute against Thee, I am concerned for my fleshly desire; and when I see that things are so confused, I might well ask myself why it is that Thou dost work in such a way. I am, then, tempted to do that; but, Lord, before giving myself the license to inquire why Thou dost so, already I protest that Thou art just, that Thou art equitable, and that nothing can come from Thee which is not worthy of praise."

This, then, is the procedure which we ought to follow whenever the incomprehensible judgments of God come before us: namely, that we know that our mind is not capable of ascending so high, and that these are depths too profound for us. And above all let us practice this in our persons; for because men are full of hypocrisy, they always suppose themselves to be pure and innocent before God; and if they are not entirely persuaded of this, nevertheless it will surely seem to them that God has no occasion to pursue them with such great strictness; each one flatters himself by minimizing his sin, although he may be convicted of it. "Very well, it is true that I am a sinner," he will say, "but I am not the worst in the world." And why do we not know the greatness of our sin? It is because we put blindfolds over our eyes. Inasmuch, then, as we are inflated with pride, we must practice this lesson, above all when God afflicts us, not to enter into a quarrel with Him, though it may seem to us that His chastisements are too severe; but let us know that there is measure in all that He does, and that it is not excessive; in order that this may teach us peaceably to conform to His will. And although God does not punish us because of our sins, let us know that it is out of grace that He exercises toward us, that it is a special privilege which He gives us; for He will always have just reason to punish us though we were the most righteous in the world. Now is it so, that we are very far from such perfection: What is it, then, that God can do with us? Even if He visits us to prove our patience, if He exercises toward us the grace of letting us suffer for His Name, still He can chastise us for our sin; let us know that He does us too great an honor, and thereupon let us humble ourselves; and let each one in his place have the modesty to say, "Very well, I would be willing that God had treated me in another fashion, and it surely seems that He has gone beyond the limit in afflicting me; but may I know that He does not do it without cause, and if it is not for my sin that He afflicts me, it is so much grace that He is showing me; for I have deserved more of it; and yet I must bow my head, submitting completely to His good will."

This, then, is how God will be glorified through us and we shall attribute to Him the righteousness which is His: namely, when we keep our mouths closed, as also Saint Paul mentions in Romans 3:19. "In order," says he, "that every mouth may be stopped, and that all the world may recognize its debt to God," and that He alone may be justified. How is it that God will be justified through us according to Saint Paul? Namely, when we shall all remain condemned, and we shall not have the boldness to reply against Him, but we shall confess freely that we are indebted to Him. If then, we come to this, then God will be justified, that is, His righteousness will be proved through us with such praise as it deserves. But on the contrary, if men rise up and do not know that they are liable to condemnation and they do not confess the debt by which they are obligated before God; although they profess to wish to justify God, that is to say, to confess that He is first, nevertheless they condemn Him. Besides, when it is said that Elihu was thus inflamed, let us note that there is a great difference between an anger which proceeds from a zeal for God and such anger as each of us will have for his goods, or for his honor, or for his self-regard. For he who is angry and provoked by a private passion has no excuse; though he

argues that his case is good; all the same he offends God by
getting angry; for we are too blind in our passions. This,
then, is one item, that we must hold the bridle tight on our
anger; indeed when we are incited to be offended against our
neighbors with regard to our own persons. But there is an
anger which is good, namely, anger which proceeds from the
feeling that we have when God is offended. When, then, we
are inflamed by a good zeal and we maintain the quarrel of
God, if we are angry, oh, may we not be guilty in that; but
let us note that this anger is here without distinction of persons.
If someone is angered by a fleshly passion or that which regards himself and he wishes to maintain himself, and then he
wishes to show that he bears favor toward his friends, and he
does more for them than for others, there is, then, distinction
of persons, inasmuch as we have regard toward ourselves.
Rather we must be angry against ourselves, if we wish that
God should approve our ire and anger. And that is what
Saint Paul says (Ephesians 4:26); for he alleges especially
what is said in Psalm 4:4, of being angry even without offending. And how is that to be done? It is when a man looks
into himself, and knowingly picks himself apart, and he is not
as much concerned to condemn others as to condemn himself,
and to fight against all his passions. This, then, is how we
must be angry, and the proper end for our anger to begin, if
we wish that it may be approved by God: namely, let each one
look to himself, and let him be angry against his own sins and
against his own vices; and let us direct our anger there, seeing
that we have provoked the wrath of God against us, seeing
that we are so full of poverty. Let us be angry and provoked
at that, that we may begin at the right place; and then let us
condemn evil wherever it will be found, both in ourselves and
in our friends; and let us not be influenced by some particular
hatred; let us not direct our rage upon someone just because
we are already preoccupied with some evil affection against
him. So, our anger will be laudable, and we shall show that
it proceeds from a true zeal for God. It is true that we shall
not always be able to restrain ourselves; for although the zeal
of God may rule in us, yet we cannot fail to go out of bounds

unless God restrains us. We must, then, have prudence and moderation in our zeal. But (as I have already said) the anger in itself will be laudable, if it springs from this source: namely, that we hate evil wherever it will be found, and especially in our own persons.

Now, then, what have we to note from this passage? In the first place, we ought not to condemn all anger; when we see a man heated up and furious, we ought not always to attribute it to vice; as we see mockers of God who will say, "O must he storm so? Must he be so angry? Don't they know how to use a peaceable manner?" They will blaspheme against God wickedly, they will provoke Him; as there are seen many who would upset all good doctrine, asking only to put such corruptions everywhere that God would no longer be known, and that His truth would be buried. Now having done that, they would like to see dissension sown, or perhaps that everything that they did was approved, and from the pulpit the preacher did nothing but tell stories, that there might be no reprimands. In this spirit they will say, "Do they not know how to preach without being angry?" And why? Is it possible that we should see only a mortal and frail creature rise up so against the majesty of God to trample under foot all good doctrine, and yet that we should bear it patiently? We would certainly show by that that we have no zeal for God; for it is said in Psalm 69:9 that the zeal of the house of God ought to eat us up. For if we had a worm which nibbled away the heart, we ought not to be so much moved as when there is some opprobrium which is done to God, as we see that His truth is changed into falsehood. So then, let us learn not to conceal vice in this manner; but let us discern between the zeal of God and the fleshly anger by which men are moved and inflamed for their own quarrels; as it is here said that Elihu was inflamed with indignation, that he was in fiery anger, and it is nevertheless considered in him a virtue; for it is the Holy Spirit Who speaks. Let us know, I say, by this that we must not at once reject all anger, but we ought to discern the cause for which a man will be inflamed; for when he is sorry that people offend God and the truth is upset, let us consider that such anger proceeds from a good source. And besides, let us learn (following what I have already said) to display our anger, when we see that the honor of God is injured, and they try to obscure His truth or disguise it, let us be moved by that, let us be inflamed, to show that we are children of God; for we cannot give better proof of it. However, let us keep things within bounds so that we do not mix up our excessive passions with the zeal of God, that we may have the prudence to discern; and after that, although we hate the vices and we detest them, yet let us try to lead the persons to salvation. Now it is true that the practice of this is difficult; but God will guide us in it provided that we allow ourselves to be led by His Holy Spirit and we give Him all authority over us. Meanwhile we ought to note well this doctrine inasmuch as today we see infinite occasions to be angry if we are children of God. On the one side are the Papists who ask only to destroy all religion. It is true that they will make a good pretense at maintaining Christianity; but though that may be, they ask only to suppress the majesty of God. We see how the truth is cut up in pieces. We hear the execrable blasphemies which are vomited up by them. I pray you, if these things do not touch us to the quick, if we are not at all cut by them as if we were given blows from a dagger; do we not show by that, that we do not know what God is, and that we are not worthy to be owned as His children? We are so delicate when our honor is wounded that we cannot endure it; however, the honor of God will be exposed to every shame and disgrace, and shall we make believe that it is nothing? And must not God reject us, and must He not show that we have no affection to maintain His honor? That is one item.

Now we need not look as far away as to the Papists, but when we see among ourselves the dogs and swine[6] who ask only to infect everything, who come to poke their snouts into the Word of God, and only try to upset everything, when we see these mockers of God, when we see these profane villains who come to change everything into laughing-stock and

---

6. Our Lord Jesus Christ Himself used these expressions, i.e., Matthew 7:6, "Give not that which is holy unto the dogs, neither cast ye your pearls before swine."

mockery, when we see how the wicked disguise things, and
that they corrupt and pervert everything by their false charges,
when we see heretics sowing their poison to ruin[7] everything;
seeing all these things, I pray you, ought we not to be touched
by them? It is said that when anyone so rises up against God,
it is just as if that person wounded Him mortally. "They will
experience," he says (Zechariah 12:10), "Him Whom they
have pierced"; God declares that someone is coming to give
Him blows of the dagger; and yet will He not apply it to us?
God declares that His Spirit is saddened and, as it were, languishing; and shall we do nothing but laugh about it? After
we hear the hateful blasphemies by which the name of our
Lord Jesus is cut into pieces; the name of God is in such scorn
and disgrace today that if we were among the Turks we would
have to be ashamed of it;[8] we see the villainies which are committed, on the one hand acts of adultery and lewdness, on the
other hand outrageous acts of violence. Briefly, people have
gone the limit in going overboard; and when we do no differently, do we declare that we are children of God and Christians? What proof do we offer of our Christianity? Surely,
then, we must be advised to have more zeal than we have had
until now; and when each one of us will be angry, let it be
because of our sins, and especially when we see that God is
grievously offended. That is how God will approve our indignation, like that of which it is here spoken, and which the
Holy Spirit praises. However, since it is easy for us to fall
back so as to release the bridle to our passions; let us pray to
God that He may so govern us by His Holy Spirit that our
zeal may be entirely pure, in order that it may be approved by
Him.

Now we shall bow in humble reverence before the face of
our God.

---

7. Fr. *perdre,* lose.
8. Calvin means that God's name is held in higher respect and esteem
among Moslems than among many groups of Christians. Alas! the observation is true.

SERMON 16

The Inspiration of the Almighty*

Elihu waited until Job had finished his statements, because they were all older than he. And when Elihu saw that those three men were all wrong, he was moved with anger. Therefore Elihu the son of Barachel the Buzite answered and said, "I am younger in age than you, and you are old; therefore I doubted and was afraid to put forward my opinion. For I thought to myself, 'The years will speak, and length of time will produce wisdom.' But it is the Spirit of God which is in men, and the inspiration of the Almighty gives understanding. Great men will not be wise therefore, neither will the aged have judgment. Therefore I say, 'Hear me, and I also will show my doctrine.'"—JOB 32:4-10

YESTERDAY we discussed the zeal of Elihu, which is here commended by the Holy Spirit, and we showed how this example ought to serve us: namely, that when we see God's truth darkened and His name blasphemed, it ought to wound our hearts. Also we showed that if we have any affection for God and His honor, then we must support His truth as far as we can. True it is, that every man will not have learning to do it, but yet according to the measure of our ability, it behooves us to show that our intention is to resist the evil and not to consent to it. However, it was declared that this zeal ought to be guided by reason, that we must not be moved by too great impetuosity, but there must be some important consideration mixed with it. And that is what we now have read: namely, that Elihu was not overly hasty, but had given ear to all the statements that had been proposed, and therein he showed his modesty. Let us note well, then, that if a man throws himself forward rashly, without considering whether or not it is needful for him to speak, it will not be accounted

---

* Sermon 120 in *Calvini Opera, Corpus Reformatorum*, volume 35, pp. 15-27.

zealousness on his part. For example, we see many who ask only to have liberty to speak, and yet it is possible that someone else will be much better able to state the case than they; but it seems to them that their time to speak will never come. This impatience can never be approved. And in proof of it, how does he who speaks to instruct others know whether or not someone else could speak much better than he? He would need to be taught, and he takes it upon himself to be a teacher. But there is still another fault; for when an ignorant man or one who is not well grounded, babbles, he stops the mouths of those who would have more graciousness and better means to edify. Let us note well, then, that where there is no modesty, zeal is rash and not governed by the Spirit of God. The Spirit of God does indeed distribute His gracious gifts, but He is never contrary to Himself. Since, then, He is named the Spirit of prudence,[1] it is fitting for us to discern when it is needful to speak and when to keep silence. It is true that a man may well put forth some good statement, although it may not be of the most becoming and others will be less so; however it behooves him to be fearful, and to show that he comes with a desire and readiness to profit, and that he would rather be a learner than a teacher. When a man proceeds thus, although he speaks before all, he will not cease to be modest and humble; but if a man draws out his sentences and makes no end to his talk, and discusses all subjects, thereby he shows that there is some vain ambition in him, and moreover, that he does not give place to the grace of God as he ought to.

So you see, then, what is shown us in the example of Elihu, when it is said that he waited till their remarks were ended; for he did not yet know where the discussion would lead. However, he adds, that he had respect for age. For he saw that both Job and those who spoke with him were old people; and since age brings experience and seriousness with it. Elihu did not thrust himself forward, knowing that when God lets a man

---

1. An interesting interpretation of Isaiah 11:2, "the Spirit of wisdom and understanding, the Spirit of counsel and might, the Spirit of knowledge and of the fear of the Lord."

live a long time in the world, He gives him grace to be able
to profit those who are younger. For he has lived longer, and
therefore he ought also to be better settled, and to have acquired some prudence. So, then, what we have to observe in
the second place is: namely, that Elihu acknowledged that
those who had spoken before him were more aged. And here
young people have a good and useful lesson, provided that
they can practice it well. For (as we have already said) if a
man has lived long, he ought to have retained what God has
shown him by experience; and that ought to serve him not only
for himself, but also to give good warnings to others who have
not like experience. Furthermore, there is also seriousness.
For young people ought to think, "Although God may have
given us some understanding, yet we have not seen much, and
it is a great defect." If a man lacks experience, surely he will
throw himself rashly into the fray; for he does not consider
the final outcome of things, nor does he know where he must
begin; and furthermore, the heat that is in young people is
entirely contrary to reason and good understanding. When
a young man is well ruled, as eventually he will have to know
how to be, yet youth always drives people, and there is such
boiling in their nature that they cannot hold themselves in
check. We see that Saint Paul exhorts Timothy that he should
not be subject to the lusts of youth (2 Timothy 2:22). And
by the lusts of youth he does not mean debauchery, playing,
adultery, drunkenness, or other dissolute actions. Timothy
was such a mirror and pattern of all holiness in himself that
Saint Paul even had to exhort him to drink wine (1 Timothy
5:23); and yet he speaks to him about the lusts of youth. And
why? For since he was young, he could still be too hasty in
some things. Now if it behooved Timothy (who passed his
elders in prudence and seriousness) to receive this warning,
how much more do the common people need it! So, let young
people look at themselves; for if they have not the honesty to
listen to their elders, and to learn from them, and to follow
their counsel, surely if they had all the virtues in the world,
that single vice would stain and defile them all. And there
is not a more common vice than this presumption. For young

people, since they have not experienced the difficulties which
are in many things, step forward boldly, for they do not count
the cost of a thing, nothing is impossible for them.   Youth,
then, always carries presumption with it, and it is a far too
common evil; and yet it' is not therefore to be defended.   For
(as we have said) if a young man has many virtues besides,
and yet he confides in himself and despises older people, and
it seems to him that he is able to lead all others; God will confound him in all his pride, and all the gifts that are in him will
be destroyed.   And furthermore those who are young and
who have not yet seen much ought to hold themselves in check.
Even today we see that the world is so far out of order that
young folks have gathered such a devilish pride that they are
past receiving any nurture or instruction at all; those who have
any fear of God ought to fight so much the more against themselves, in order that they may not be carried away after the
common manner.   We see these young clowns pretending to
be men, as soon as they are out from under the rod; however,
they are not yet worthy to be called children.   They are like
young chicks hatched only three days, and yet they wish to be
great.   Well, they ought to be kept ten more years under the
rod; but look, they are fully grown men, it seems to them.
And wherein?   In boldness; they are as shameless as a harlot,
and they no longer wish to be under any discipline or correction; that is clearly seen.   Now those to whom God has given
some grace, ought to think seriously about themselves when a
vice is so common and as it were a contagious disease, and
to guard against being entangled in it; for they would be
carried away as others are, if God did not extend to them His
strong hand.

So then, let the children of God be on their guard, and assure
themselves that when they are modest, it is much, although
there may not be so beautiful a show; and although those who
wish to advance themselves despise them, since they do not
go high-falutin,[2] let them assure themselves that they are much
more approved by God, and that He will bless their honest

---

2. Fr. *ils ne vont point le front levé,* they do not go with their foreheads
raised.

behavior and make them to profit more in two years than those who are too hasty will do in four. We see what happens to fruit. When fruit is too soon ripe and quickly gets its color, it also fades away immediately; but the fruit that comes more slowly has more endurance. So it is with those who wish to advance themselves before their time. Truly they may appear to be beautiful, and someone may taste it; but it has no firmness in it. On the contrary, those who are ashamed and honest, and not so presumptuous as to put themselves forward hastily, will surely be slow; but meanwhile our Lord gives them power which lasts longer. Here, then, is a good point to retain from this passage. It is true that modesty is a virtue suitable for all; but yet young people ought to observe what is said here, that they must honor their elders, acknowledging that they for their own part, may have excessive passions which need to be restrained by other men; for they are not sufficiently settled in their own nature, and then, they have not experience to be as prudent as is required. Besides, when a young man has behaved himself so modestly, he must at the convenient time utter the thing that God has given to him, yea even though it may be among old people. For the order of nature, when old men do not discharge their duties, does not hinder young men from performing them in their stead, and even to the shame of those who have lived long, and misspent the time that God has given them, and utterly lost it. You see, then, the middle position we have to hold: it is that the reverence which young people bear toward their elders must not hinder the continuous maintenance of the truth, that God should be honored and vices suppressed. For it can happen that the most aged will be devoid of the Spirit of God, or bad people will have in them only fraud and disloyalty, or perhaps people will be opinionated or headstrong. Then, must young people be so held under the yoke that by the authority of their elders they are turned away from God, and from His Word, and from what is good and holy? Not at all.

So then, let us note that modesty does not mean that young people should become so stupid that they neither judge nor know anything; but it is sufficient that they should not be so presumptuous that they skirmish and spit out their froth ahead of time. Let them listen, let them be docile, let them always be ready to keep silence when some good proposition is put forward; and indeed, let them guard against occupying the place of another. Have they done that? If they see that their elders do not set a good example, that they even pervert the good, turning it into evil; then (as I have already said) the Spirit of God must show where He is. As in our time, those who had been nourished in the superstitions of the papacy, the longer they had lived in the world, the less they had of doctrine. Now whereas God might have wished to be served by them, He did not care to be; I say, usually. You see, then, aged people who had long experience. But what of it? They have been plunged into shadows, there has been no knowledge of God, no purity of religion. What, then, could age do for such people except to make them so much more opinionated? For they have put their trust in errors, they have been so addicted to them that it seemed that there was no means to convert them. Now if God has willed to call young people to set forth His Word, all that is needed to check the Holy Spirit is that young people should not speak and that their elders should not be ready to hear them. It is true that God still wished to be served by the elders, as He has called them in many ways; but yet He has declared that His truth was not attached to age. So then, we see now what modesty ought generally to be in all men, and above all in the young: namely, that they become peaceable to learn as far as occasion is given to them, and that they do not desire to maintain their own importance, that they have not the foolish desire to show off; but in silence they receive what is put forward by others, and they are not so preoccupied that they do not want to be led and governed by those who have more experience. Is this done? Now, we must not be held back under the shadow of seniority from judging further, and we must not come like poor beasts, and when old people have said to us, "Thus you must do," we must not accept as an oracle all that comes out of their mouths. For discretion ought to be joined with zeal; as we have already declared, the Spirit of God contains both of these in Himself.

So then, if there is modesty in men, there must also be both zeal and discretion; and we must not necessarily be checked by the authority of those who have lived a long time; but even when it is a question of persuading the whole world, seniority ought not to bring any prejudice against what is upright and useful. How not? I have already said, that if all the old people of the Papacy had conspired against the Gospel, and they wished that people did cling to their customary habits, oh, it is not said that this closes the door to God and to His Word; that young people should be hindered from maintaining the truth, if old ones are against it, and when they have nourished evil for such a long time that they wish only that it be continued; for those to whom God has given more grace ought to be opposed to this. But we must now go further: namely, if someone says, "How so? For a hundred years our fathers and our ancestors have lived thus, for five hundred years, even for a thousand it has been observed that we are governed by an infallible law and rule." When, I say, someone argues to us the antiquity of the times, indeed, seeking to lead us back to the creation of the world, yet the truth of God must not be suppressed under this shadow. So then, we see now that we need not be poor, blind men to be modest; but we ought to observe moderation and limitation.

And this is what Elihu adds. *"I have said, 'Age will speak, and the multitude of years will announce science; but it is the Spirit of God Who dwells in men, and the inspiration of the Almighty gives intelligence.'"* You see, then, what is put first in the natural order: namely, that we ought to listen to the ancients. For when to select governors in a city or in a country they have to take foolish, flighty, and head-strong youth who do not know how to govern their own persons, who are set up to be judges and leaders; it is to pervert the order of nature, it is a shame, and it seems that they wish to defy God whenever this is done.[3] When, then, they could choose steady people, people of proper seriousness and maturity, and these are allowed to rot in their houses, and meanwhile they

---

3. Young Calvin was only 27 when he began preaching at St. Peter's cathedral in Geneva. Here we have the sober reflection of a man 45 years old.

take flat, little snails only one night old, and they are going to
seat them as judges when they do not know what it is all about,
it is as if little infants were married. They will be very glad
to come to the wedding; someone will say to them, "You will
eat roast meat and pastry"; oh, they will gladly agree to that;
but is it therefore a marriage? So, I say, it is with those who
are seated as judges when there is no more prudence or reason in them than in little infants, since no one has had the
consideration to choose those who have more seriousness and
experience. So then, in the first place, the order of nature
must be observed: that is, when we have aged people to whom
God has given grace, let them have the office of leading others,
and let young people humble themselves under them. For it
is a shame when young people wish to do great things and
will not condescend to receive doctrine from those who have
lived longer. This pride is addressed not only against mortal
men, but it is resisting God who has constituted the order of
nature and wills that it be observed. What must we do in the
office of bearing and announcing the Word of God, if there is
a man well experienced, who is prudent, who has been approved, if they do not condescend to make use of him, but
choose a flighty man? We must, then, accept the commenda-
tion of this order. But this is not by making it an infallible
rule; for it sometimes happens that God has given much more
grace to young people than to those who have lived twice as
long. Now, then, the order of which we have spoken must
not hinder the Spirit of God from being received wherever
He may show Himself and the gracious gifts as He distributes
them from being put to use. And that is why Saint Paul chose
Timothy, although there were then many older people. For
when he saw this excellent man (as he had testimony not only
of men, but also of the Holy Spirit) he preferred him to those
who were more aged. The same now does Elihu, who, after
having listened, says that he knew that *it is the Spirit of God
which is in men;* as if he said, "It is true that we ought not
(without having known the situation) to judge that old
people are in their dotage, in order not to be obliged to give
them room or place; but we ought to honor age by saying,

'Perhaps the man who has lived long is able to teach us'; but
if we know that he does not acquit himself of his duty, or that
he has squandered the time during which he has lived in the
world, then, if the Spirit of God is in a young man, he must
be advanced." Let us remember well, then, that when the
order of nature is observed, it is not on condition that when
God has given to young men some gifts of grace they should
never serve His Church, and that they should not teach not
only their kind and companions, but also older people. Consequently, older people must not be impatient on account of
their age and resist all warnings, by saying, "How so? I have
lived a long time, and a young man gives me my lesson?" But
let them acknowledge, "No, I ought to have profited in such
a way that I might be able to lead others; but I see now that
I need to be taught, that I am a young infant compared with
those who ought to be taught by me. And since God has not
given me the grace that is required to be a leader, I must be a
pupil and not a teacher." That is how old people ought to
conform when they see that God has poured out more amply
His gifts of grace upon those who ought to follow them and
not to walk ahead.

Now from what we have deduced we have a good doctrine
to practice: namely, that the Spirit of God rules over the order
of nature. Now, to still better comprehend what is herein
contained, let us note that when Elihu says, "It is the Spirit
of God Who dwells in men," he wishes here to express that
it is a special gift which God offers as a privilege when it
pleases Him that a man has more ability than others. It is
true that in general God has made us reasonable creatures, and
therein we differ from brute beasts. God, then, has surely
given to all men without exception some judgment and spirit;
but yet we see that one is slow and dull, the other agile; one
is giddy, the other is properly serious about himself. Where
does this come from? Let us acknowledge that God holds
His gifts of grace in His hand and distributes them according
to His will to whom it seems good to Him. That is what
Elihu here wished to indicate, in order that men might not
think they have an inheritance by nature which they have car-

ried from the wombs of their mothers, that they might not
think they have something which is due them and acquired by
them.   Here Elihu pronounces, "God has created all of us,
it is true that we have some reason, indeed, but it is limited;
however, if a man has the know-how,[4] if he has prudence, he
must acknowledge that God has extended His hand especially
to him, and he must acknowledge that he is all the more indebted and obliged to God."   Now when this is said to us, it
is not in order that we may be swelled up with arrogance and
not that we may suppose ourselves to be worth more when we
have intelligence and spirit; let us acknowledge that if it has
pleased God to give us this grace, we must walk in so much
greater fear; for we are so much more indebted; and meanwhile if He has willed to shower us with His gifts, it is also
in order that we may communicate them to our neighbors.
If then, we do not know how to use them to glorify our God
and to edify those who need them, it is certain that we are so
much more blameworthy.

However, we must also compare two degrees: namely, if
God gives special intelligence to men to discern things which
pertain to this decrepit life, what becomes of the doctrine of
the Gospel, of true and pure religion?   Have we that by nature?   Can we acquire it by our industry?   Alas! this is a
great mistake.   If it is a matter of a man's being a schoolmaster to teach children, being a good attorney at law or medical
doctor, being a good city merchant or a good laborer in the
fields, still the Spirit of God must work in all these things.
One man needs to be sharp in one thing, as sometimes the
mechanical arts require a more alert mind than does merchan-
dising.   Now, then, in all those things which seem to be common in themselves and of little worth, God must distribute
His Spirit to men.   Now when we come to the doctrine of
the Gospel there is a wisdom which surmounts all human sense,
indeed, which is admirable to the Angels; there are secrets of
heaven contained in the Gospel; for it pertains to acknowledging God in the Person of His Son; and although our Lord
Jesus has descended here below, yet we must comprehend His

---

4. Fr. *savoir*, science, technical learning.

divine majesty, or we cannot be grounded and rest our faith in Him. It is a matter, I say, of our acknowledging what is incomprehensible to human nature. Now, then, if God with respect to mechanical arts, with respect to human sciences which concern the transitory life, must distribute to us by His Holy Spirit, for much greater reason let us not think that by our subtlety we can understand God and the secrets of His kingdom; He must instruct us; and meanwhile we must become complete fools with respect to ourselves, as Saint Paul says (1 Corinthians 3:18) to be sharers in such wisdom. For there is the statement that he makes about it (1 Corinthians 2:14), "The sensual man can never comprehend the doctrine of God"; that is to say, while men remain in their nature they do not know the things of God, and can never taste His Word; what is worse, "It is foolish to them," says Saint Paul (1 Corinthians 1:18); for it seems that it is a doctrine without reason, and yet it is the Spirit of God alone Who gives us faith and Who enlightens us. And this ought to be carefully noted; for we are often dazzled when we see that there are so few who acknowledge the things of God, and indeed, that many aged people who have lived a long time in the world are enraged in their superstitions and fight proudly against the doctrine of the Gospel; we are astonished by that.

Indeed, but here is a passage which ought to arm us against such a scandal: *"It is the Spirit of God Who dwells in men, it is the inspiration of the Almighty Who gives intelligence."* Do we see men who are poor, blind, and so plunged into ignorance that they cannot be approached by the Gospel? Let us not be astonished by that. And why not? For it is the nature of man not to be able to judge anything about the secrets of God until he is enlightened. But on the contrary when we see a man who knows the things of God, be he young or old, when we see someone old who has been for a long time soaked in the papal follies who comes to the right religion; let us acknowledge that God has there done a miracle. If we see also young men, let us acknowledge that God must draw them to Himself in a marvelous manner, because they do not readily receive the yoke, since they are full of presumption, as we have

said. If then, God tames them and renders them docile, it is
His powerful hand which has passed by. So, we see that this
passage ought to serve us in two ways. The first is, that when
we see that with our spirits we would never know how to
climb high enough to acknowledge God or His truth, we should
be skeptical of all our senses and renounce them. And that is
what Saint Paul calls being made a fool. We must, then, be
made fools, if we wish that our Lord should fill us with His
wisdom: that is to say, on our part, we must bring nothing,
we must not suppose we have this or that; for it would be
closing the door to God. So then, if we wish that God should
continue the grace of His Holy Spirit when He has distributed
to us some portion of it, we must learn to exalt and magnify
Him as He deserves, and to acknowledge that there is not in
us a single drop of good intelligence until God puts it there.
And then, may it be to make us always persist in His obedience
and to walk in greater fear and carefulness, when we see that if
God extinguished the light which He has put in us we would
be in darkness, indeed, in such horrible darkness that we could
never find our way out of it. That is the first use of this
place. The second is that if we see the greater multitude of
the world going astray and hardly anyone is willing to conform to God, we should not find it strange that men are so
far overboard and that they act like savage beasts. And why
not? *For it is the Spirit of God Who gives intelligence.* For
that, then, should be to us, as it were, an argument to magnify
so much more the grace which we have received; and meanwhile that we should not be carried away when we see such
rebellion. And why? Men follow their natures, they follow
their heads; and meanwhile they resist God, but it is inasmuch as the doctrine of the Gospel surmounts all human sense,
and as God must work by His Holy Spirit, as He opens eyes,
or men would always remain in their bestiality.

Besides, Elihu thereupon concludes that *the great, then,
are not always wise, and that aged people sometimes have no
more intelligence,* nor knowledge,[4] nor prudence than others.
It is true that Elihu here does not wish to pervert the order
of nature (for he protests hereupon that he wished to hear his

elders and that he was all ready to subject himself to their doctrine), but he indicates what we have already discussed, that God is not bound by age or estate or qualities of men. When it pleases God to raise a man to dignity, if He wishes thereby to serve for the salvation of His people, He will give him grace to be able to acquit himself of his office; but otherwise He will dismiss him, and insofar as a man is in an eminent position, he will be considered twice as beastly. For example, if a man is chosen to proclaim the Word of God, or better, if God wishes to give grace to His Church, He will endow this man by His Spirit, He will give him intelligence of His Word, and dexterity to know how to apply it to the use of the people, and to gather good doctrine from it; He will give him zeal and other things which are required; and God thereby shows Himself so manifestly that we can say that He cares for us when He so distributes gifts of grace to men in what is required for our profit. So is it with those who are appointed judges; according as they need a double portion of the Spirit of God in them, so when God wills to be served by them He gives them a mighty power to acquit themselves of their duty. On the contrary, if God is angered against us, those who proclaim His Word will be beasts who understand nothing, they will be despised since they disguise things, so that good doctrine will be sneered at and profaned among them; briefly, they will hardly be able to be disciples, let alone that they must be good masters.

This, then, is what Elihu here wished to show, saying that *the great will not be wise, and that elders will not always be better instructed*: as if he said, "We must not here measure all alike by saying, 'This man is raised in estate and dignity; it follows, then, that he is wise'; we must not draw such a conclusion. And why not? For God can well strip the greatest so that they will be rough beasts, and since they have lived a long time, they have consumed much bread, being nourished at the expense of God; so that it would be more proper to say, 'A steer has been fed.' It would be more appropriate." So then, let us learn, since God distributes His Spirit to those who are willing to apply themselves to His service, that they

should employ them so much more carefully and in fear of
God.   If they do otherwise, those who are considered the most
wise will be seen to be entirely blinded when they do not acknowledge God, as the warning is specifically given by His
Prophet Isaiah, saying (29:14), "The elders will be no more
than a drop, the wise will grow stupid and lose all their wit."
We see, then, how God declares a more horrible vengeance
upon the great and upon the old and upon governors than upon
the common people. By that we are admonished that we must
not attribute to them an infallible authority, as if they could
never err and mislead others. Now if God so blinds the old
and the great and those who are in authority (I pray you)
when He does not give them His Holy Spirit, what more good
are they? And let us note well the cause why God makes such
a threat. It is on account of the hypocrisy of men who appeared to serve Him, but their hearts were far from Him; as
with their mouths they protested that they wished to serve
Him, and meanwhile they have given themselves to the tradi-
tions of men; that is to say, God did not rule them by His
Word alone, but they did according to the manner of men.
Now God cannot allow that His authority should be thus diminished. That is why He says that He will blind the wise, that
He will take away the Spirit and the reason of the elders. Let
us learn, then, if we wish that God should govern us, and that
He should rule in our midst, and enjoy the gifts of grace which
are necessary for our salvation, that we must let Him have
dominion and majesty over us all, and that great and small
must conform to His obedience.   Besides, let us have His
Word for our rule, and let us allow ourselves to be governed
by it; knowing that otherwise we cannot expect that the Holy
Spirit should work in us. And yet let us seek all the means
possible to be taught.   God has willed that there might be
Pastors in His Church who proclaim His Word, and that we
might receive correction and warning from them.   Is it not
done in such power as it needs to be? Let us pray to God that
it may please Him to supply such a lack.   Then, let us walk in
such humility that we may ask nothing except that God alone
may have entire preeminence over us; and let us be assured

that we could have neither reason nor intelligence, except insofar as we are enlightened by His Holy Spirit. That is how He will never allow us to be led astray; but if He has begun to lead and to teach us, He will cause us to be more and more confirmed in all wisdom; as Saint Paul says in the first chapter of the first letter to the Corinthians,[5] that since God has once begun in us, He will not permit that anything should be lacking in us at the last day, when we shall have full revelation of things which now we know in part.

Now we shall bow in humble reverence before the face of our God.

---

5. 1 Corinthians 1:8, "Who shall also confirm you unto the end." Cf. Philippians 1:6, "He Who has begun a good work in you will perform it until the day of Jesus Christ."

SERMON 17

The Authority and Reverence We Owe to God's Word*

(This sermon is upon the last three verses of the preceding chapter and upon the text that follows.)

"Therefore, Job, hear my speeches and listen to all my words. Behold, I have opened my mouth; my tongue shall speak in my palate. My words are the uprightness of my heart, and my lips shall utter pure doctrine. The Spirit of God has created me, and the Breath of the Almighty has given me life. If thou canst, answer me, and address thyself against me, and debate thy case valiantly. Behold I am toward God as thou sayest; I am also formed out of the clay. Fear of me shall not make thee afraid; neither shall the pressure of me be a heavy burden to thee."—Job 33:1-7

I BEGAN to explain Elihu's affirmation that he spoke uprightly without regard to mortal men; and a man who wishes to speak uprightly according to God must have his eyes closed to pleasing individuals. For if we are led either by hatred or by favor, there will be no good principle in us, there will be nothing but trouble. Above all when it is a matter of teaching in God's name, we must be well advised to turn away from all fleshly affection. And Elihu especially said that God might root him out if he had respect for men's greatness. Now it might seem hard at first sight that God would destroy one for no more than magnifying some man's greatness. But let us note first of all, that when God grants us the grace to speak in His name, it behooves us to give authority to His word and to commend it. If we are so distracted by looking at creatures that we do not speak as freely as we ought to, do we not dishonor God? If a man is sent from some earthly prince,

---

* Sermon 122 in *Calvini Opera, Corpus Reformatorum*, volume 35, pp. 40-52.

and lets other men scorn him and ducks his duty and dares not deliver the message that is committed to him, is it not unpardonable cowardice? God receives us to His service, even us who are only dust before Him, who are altogether unprofitable; He gives us an honorable commission to carry His word, and He wishes to have it be delivered with all authority and reverence. Then some man makes us tremble so that we disguise God's truth by turning it into a lie, or else we bear it in such a way that it will no longer have its natural right. I pray you, is not that as great a reproach as can be heaped upon God? So then, if God's word is not borne so openly and freely that men may honor it, it is no wonder that punishment is prepared such as Eliphaz describes. So we have a double lesson to gather from this passage.

(1) The one is for those who preach God's word, who are in office to teach as pastors. These must be so firmly resolved that they bend for nothing whatever, as it is said in Jeremiah that he must be as bold as brass in the fight;[1] because the world will never be without great stubbornness, and those who are raised to some dignity or honorable estate cannot be captive to God's obedience, but do always raise their horns against Him. When men so forget themselves that they cannot subject themselves to Him Who has created and fashioned them, it behooves us to have an invincible constancy, and to reckon that we shall have enmity and displeasure when we do our duty; yet nevertheless let us go through it without bending. You see what we who are ordained as pastors to preach the word of God have to remember.

(2) It also behooves all people to receive a general instruction. Therefore when we come to hear a sermon, let us not bring here such haughtiness that we chafe against God when we are reproved for our sins. Let us not bring any bitterness so as to be angry when our itching backs are scraped; let us not be so foolish and presumptuous as to think that God ought to hold His peace for us; let us not ask to be spared under the pretext that there is some good quality in us. Even if we

---

1. Fr. *qu'il faut qu'il prenne un front d'airain pour batailler.* Jeremiah 15:20. "I will make thee unto this people a fortified brazen wall."

were kings and princes, it would behoove us to bow down our necks to receive God's yoke; for all haughtiness must be cast down, as St. Paul says.[2] For the gospel is preached in order that both great and small should submit themselves to God and allow themselves to be governed by Him. It cannot be done unless we put down our haughtiness (as St. Paul says in that place) which exalts itself against the majesty of our Lord Jesus Christ. We must not wait until we are forced or compelled to obey God, but every man must do it willingly. Let those who are of high estate know that, even if they were more than kings, they ought to humble themselves at the preaching of God's truth. And why? For they must be aware of this. From what Lord or master is he sent who preaches? Even from Him Who has sovereign dominion over all mankind and unto Whom all men ought to be in subjection. If we are of low estate, I pray you, is it not foolish rage to desire that men should support us and hide and cover our faults, indeed, that the word of God should be falsified in our favor? Can God be transfigured? No! He wills that His word should be His live image. Now if we seek to be flattered it is as if we required God to change His nature and disown Himself in order to please us. And is not that too devilish a rashness? Then let us learn to come to hear God's word with all humility and modesty, knowing that our obedience must be tested in this respect, and that no one should be spared, but faults exposed with straightforward liberty, as is proper.

We come now to what Elihu adds. *"Job,"* he says, *"listen to me. It is true that I speak with my tongue, and that I utter my words from my palate; yet my sayings are the uprightness of my heart, and thou shalt not hear anything but truth and uprightness from my mouth."* See the plea that Elihu makes to be heard: namely, that he will not speak feignedly and as a double-minded man, but will set down things purely, according as he knew them to be, and as they had been revealed to him. That is the first point. Secondly, he adds, *"Behold I am with respect to God as thou art,"* or "according to thy mouth." The word he uses properly means "mouth," but it is sometimes

---

2. 2 Corinthians 10:5.

taken for "measure." Now we have seen previously that Job asked that God should come to him without bringing him any such terror as he felt. "If God were like me," Job says, "I could answer Him; and although He might have complete authority over me, yet I could maintain my case." See how Job spoke. So this sentence might be expounded: *"Behold I am according to thine own mouth,"* that is to say, "according as thou hast asked," or else: *"Behold I am according to thy measure,"* that is to say, "I am like thee," with respect to God. However, the thought will always remain the same; therefore we must not insist too much upon this word. Let us always consider where Elihu intends to come: namely, that he is not God Who could frighten Job, but he is made of clay like Job: that is to say, that he is a mortal and frail creature which has no strength in itself. For *"It is,"* he says, *"the Spirit of God which has formed me, and the Breath of the Almighty has given me life."* In summary, we see that Elihu tells Job here that he will speak against him with such reason that he will be convinced by it. "Thou shalt no longer allege," he says, "that God makes thee afraid, that His glory is terrible to thee, and that thou canst have no right at His hand; thou shalt not be able to say that. For who am I? Behold, I am a poor lump of earth and mud. It is true that I have breath and life, but I have them from God; yet I am as full of frailty as thou. So, only reason will prevail between us two, and thou must remain confounded." We see in summary the two points that are contained here. The first is that Elihu declares that *his words are the uprightness of his heart,* and that he will not speak anything but what he has thought of or conceived in himself. This is well worthy to be noted; for thereupon we may gather how he who bears the word of God ought to be disposed: namely, that he must not babble from the end of his tongue, or make remarks unadvisedly, or even farce; but according as he has been taught by God he ought to communicate to those who are committed to his charge what is imprinted within him. So then, do we wish to serve God purely in our office? We must above all hold our tongues, that they speak nothing except what is printed within our hearts. In fact we hear

what is said by David and quoted by St. Paul (who applies it
to all the ministers of God's word), "I have believed, and
therefore I shall speak."[3] It is true that this is common to all
Christians and children of God; but above all it ought to be
observed by those whom God has ordained as instruments of
His Holy Spirit. Whenever we speak God wills to be heard
in our persons. Since He has done us so great an honor, at
least we should have His doctrine printed in us, and it should
take root there, and then our mouth should bear witness that
we know it. Briefly, it behooves us to have been taught by
God, before we can be masters or teachers. Especially when
we preach, let it be not only for others; but let us include ourselves in the number and company. That, I say, is what we
have to observe.

In fact, when a man speaks God's word without feeling the
power of it in himself, what else is he doing but farce? And
what a sacrilege that is! What a pollution of God's word!
So then let us think diligently about ourselves; and as often
as we go into the pulpit, let us meditate well upon the lesson
that is given us here: namely, that the uprightness of our
heart should show itself in our tongue. Therefore when we
see that a doctrine is upright, and that the man who speaks is
trying to edify us; let us know that we are unthankful and
utterly rebellious against God, if we do not hear with all
humility what he proposes to us. Now when Elihu makes this
preface, he does not speak humanly, but he shows how God
intends to hold us to Himself. By what means is that?
"Behold me," he says, *"listen to me; for there is nothing but
uprightness in my statements."* It is as if he set down a rule
in God's name, that if a doctrine which is set forth is holy and
we are convinced that it is so; then if we do not yield with all
reverence to conform to it, we shall not be guilty of having
resisted the man who spoke to us, but it is just as if we
provoked the living God. So then, let each one be attentive
when God's word is preached; and since He is so gracious to
us as to raise up men by whom He declares His will to us as
individuals, let us not be toward Him as savages, but let us

---

3. Psalm 116:10; 2 Corinthians 4:13.

yield ourselves teachable in the things that we know proceed from Him. And since the Law, the Prophets, and the Gospel have been conveyed to us by men whose uprightness is well enough known and witnessed, let us observe that whoever does not subject himself to this doctrine needs no other trial for his condemnation. In summary, let us observe that our Lord has authorized His Prophets and Apostles in order that the doctrine which they have given us should no longer be in doubt, but that we should accept it as an irrevocable decision. So much for one point. At the same time we are warned that the faithful must not deliberately be so stupid as to receive whatever is told them, but must examine whether or not the doctrine is of God. And that is why we are told to test the spirits. And this must be well observed. For we see that the poor Papists let themselves be led without any discretion, and the faith which they have is nothing but pure stupidity, that they must stop their eyes and have no reason at all in them. On the contrary, God wills that we should have mind and prudence in order not to be deluded and seduced by the false doctrines that men will bring us. How will this be done? It is true that we must not presume to judge God's truth according to our judgment and fancy, but rather our reason and understanding must be captive to Him, as the Scripture shows us. Nevertheless, we have to pray to God that he may give us prudence to discern whether or not what is proposed to us is good and upright. Furthermore, let us with all humility ask nothing except to be governed by Him, and to be under His hand, being certain that by this means we shall be able to know whether or not there is uprightness in the statements that are put before us.

It is also what our Lord Jesus alleges, when He wishes us to receive His sayings. "I seek not my own glory," He says, "but the glory of Him Who sent me."[4] We must always inquire then, into the intention of the man who speaks to us. For if we see that the end toward which he aspires is that God should be glorified and have dominion over all men, there must be no more disputing against him, but we must be fully satis-

---

4. John 8:50.

fied with that. But on the contrary if his doctrine tends to obscure God's glory, to turn us away from His service, to advance ambition and vanity, so that it does not edify us to be true temples of God, if by it we are not established so as to submit ourselves wholly to God and to call upon Him purely, to confide and to rest ourselves upon His grace and upon His fatherly goodness; then we surely see that there is no uprightness in it. True it is, that if God had not in the first place shown us what uprightness is we would be seriously handicapped here, but if we have the principles that He has given us it is our mistake if we fail. Behold God tells us that He wills to be exalted and to have men acknowledge that all goodness comes from Him; again, He wills also to have all lordship and to rule over our life, and therein so hold us in check that we may be governed by Him and according to His good will; He wills to have men be utterly abased and void of confidence in their own righteousness, wisdom, and strength; He wills that we come to draw water in our Lord Jesus Christ, as in the fountain of all goodness; He wills to have us call upon him purely; He wills that the Sacraments which He has ordained should be received as testimonies of His grace, and as means and helps to invite us to serve Him with so much the more free and earnest heart. These are things wherein there can be no gloss, nor any obscurity or difficulty. So then, let us always have this touchstone when we come to test any doctrine. Then we shall know whether it is upright or crooked, true or false, pure or corrupted and mixed, according to the true uprightness which God has shown us. I say, we need not be wrapped any more in doubts on this matter; only let us open our eyes, and then pray to God that He may guide us by His Holy Spirit; for without that we shall always wander, and not be able to discern so much as little children, according as St. Paul says, "God's Spirit must be as a lamp which gives us light,"[5] or else we shall never comprehend God's secrets. They are spiritual, and we of our nature are fleshly and earthly, and we always bend downward. But if God enlightens us by His Holy Spirit, then we judge the

---

5. Ephesians 1:18.

doctrine and so discern that we cannot be deceived by all Satan's temptations. And although he sends us seducers and raises up many mischief-makers who try to turn all things upside down, yet this cannot win against us, provided God's Spirit is our light. Furthermore, although God does sometimes speak by the mouths of the wicked (as it is said that the kingdom of our Lord Jesus Christ will sometimes be advanced accidentally, that hypocrites or people who have no fear of God but are led by vainglory and other vanities will be able to serve for a time, and God will commend their doctrine to the salvation of His elect, although it be to the great condemnation of themselves) although, then, this may sometimes happen, yet it is not the ordinary means. For when God wills that we should be edified in Him, immediately He raises up men who speak heartily and zealously, and indeed He gives such a mark to the word that comes out of their mouths that men may know the power of the Holy Spirit, as also Saint Paul says. And this is why those who are in office to preach God's word ought so much the better to practice what I have said: namely, to be taught before putting anything forward, so that their heart may speak before their mouth. To do this, let them pray to God that He may so touch them to the quick that they may have His word well rooted in their souls, that they may be able to serve their neighbors and to perceive that they do not thrust themselves forward unadvisedly, but that they are compelled by the Holy Spirit. You see then what we have to remember from this passage.

Now in the second place Elihu affirms that he is a transitory and frail man so that *he cannot make Job afraid,* but he does not wish to win the argument except by reason and truth. Before we come to the main point, we have to observe in passing the manner of speech which us uses: that *the Spirit of God has created him, and* that *the Breath of the Almighty has given him life; and further,* that *he is only mud and dirt.* This is worthy to be noted by all men. For if we could properly bear in mind what is shown here, undoubtedly all pride would be buried in us. For why do men glorify themselves, and why are they so presumptuous, unless in the first place they cannot acknowledge their origin, and secondly they do not know how to be fully aware that what they have they hold from God and that it is not an inheritance but that they have both life and everything pertaining thereto because it pleases God to preserve them? If then, men could first remember whence they have come, and secondly that all the good that is in them they hold merely by God's grace, it is certain that they would be truly humbled. Therefore it is said that we are made of dirt and mud. Now we may boast and commend ourselves as much as we wish, but we cannot change our nature. Therefore, when a man finds himself tempted by pride and wishes to raise himself too high, let him examine himself and consider: "Whence came I? Whence did God take me?" If only our feet are muddy it seems to us that we are worth less. If the dirt only touches our shoes it seems to us that we are soiled. Yet we are made of mud. Therefore we ought never to forget our pedigree: namely, "Thou art only earth and dust." It is true that this saying is common enough and every man confesses it, but meanwhile no one acknowledges it. Such an acknowledgment would purge us of all pride. What is the impertinent presumption that is in men except wind, because they are puffed up with ignorance, and have forgotten themselves? So much the more, then, ought we to weigh well this speech in which it is said, "We are created of mud and dirt." It is true that there would be some dignity and excellence in our nature worthy to be commended if we were whole, but it would not be lawful for us to be proud of it. Since we are as corrupted in Adam as we are, it is certain that we ought to be doubly ashamed. And why? We were created after the Image of God. And what manner of Image is it now? It is disfigured; we are so perverted that the mark which God had put into us to be glorified thereby is turned to His shame; and all the gracious gifts that were bestowed upon us are so many witnesses to render us guilty before God, because we defile them; and as long as we continue in our nature, we only abuse the benefits that we have received and apply them to all evil. So you see our confusion always increases by all the gifts which God has communicated to us. But let us suppose that we were as uncorrupted as our father Adam was at first. Should we therefore presume of ourselves on the pretext that God had so ennobled us? We hold all things from Him. What separates us from the brute beasts and makes us more excellent? Have we this through our own industry? Have we acquired it by our own strength? Have we it by inheritance from our ancestors? Not at all! We have it because God has given it to us by His own free goodness. So then, what is to be done except to humble ourselves?

You see in general what we have to remember from this passage, where Elihu confesses that he was made of dirt, and that he owes it to God that he has life and breath, because they are communicated to him merely of His goodness. However, those whom God wills to serve Him in honorable estate ought to remember this lesson all the more. For, when God extends to men His hand and puts them in some degree of honor, it is not in order that they should exalt themselves, but rather that they should acknowledge how much they are bound to Him, that they should be so much the more incited to honor Him, and that they should sharpen and apply all their wits and affections to so do that God may be honored by them; as it is said, that a candle must not be hidden, but set upon a table or a buffet in order that it may give light through all the house. Those, then, to whom God has shown the favor to exalt them to some higher or more worthy calling ought to be all the more inflamed to enlighten their neighbors and to give them such an example that the grace which they have received may not be as it were choked. This is what we have to observe here in the second place. Hereupon let us observe in general that men cannot attribute to God the glory that is due Him unless they completely strip themselves. For as long as we pretend to reserve ever so little to ourselves, the glory of God is to that extent diminished. What must be done, then? When we have well analyzed the good that is in us, let us count the items we have received and acknowledge that we have nothing of our own which we did not receive. This is how men will not rob God of His praise: it is when they study to know themselves and that there does not remain a single drop of goodness in them, but every bit of it must be put into an inventory of that for which they are accountable before God. Besides, when our selves are thus annihilated, we lose nothing; for we shall not fail to be clothed again; indeed, if we are truly joined to God and attribute to Him the praise which is due Him, we shall be much richer than those who are so full of presumption, supposing themselves to have I know not what kind of an inheritance. So then, let us not fear to be diminished when we are thus stripped of all glory; for our Lord does not will that we should be deprived of any goodness; yet we must be thus confounded. However, when we know that we can do nothing except what is given to us from above, let us be advised to apply everything that God puts into us to such use as He commands. For our Lord has not endowed us with the powers of His Holy Spirit except that He wills that they should be applied to good use; they must not remain unused. Therefore, let us be advised that what we have received should be presented and offered to God as it were in sacrifice and, since He wills that the salvation of our neighbors should be promoted by them, let us above all have a regard to edify one another. You see what we have to bear in mind here.

Now let us come to the propositions that Elihu holds here and to the substance of them. He has said, *"The Spirit of God has created me, and His Breath has given me life. So then,"* he says, *"there is no terror in me to make thee afraid,"* but reason alone shall prevail. Here Elihu shows what the duty of a good teacher is: it is, that he should properly look at himself and view and contemplate himself before he opens his mouth. And why? For those who have not known their own frailty will have no compassion toward their neighbors, and when they wish to rebuke those who have failed they go at it with such violence that they make the wretched wanderers stray further rather than bring them back to the right way. When it comes to comforting, they have no skill to do it; if they come to teach, they do it with disdain. Therefore, if we wish to teach God's word as we ought to, let us begin by knowing our own infirmities. And when we have known them, it will lead us to such a modesty and gentleness that we shall have a good-natured spirit to utter the word of God. It is true that, since there are many who are full of pride and rebellion, the word of God must be to them as a hammer to bruise and break their hardness; yet we ought first of all to teach those who render themselves teachable. And how can we do it, unless we have known that we need to bear with them? But bear with them we cannot, except we feel how frail we ourselves are. For he who knows not his own lacks has no compassion to share the sorrows of others and to respond to them. So then, do we wish to teach the ignorant faithfully? We must understand that there is nothing but ignorance in ourselves and that it would have been worse with us than with all other men if God has not given us what we have received from Him. Again, do we wish to comfort the wretched and afflicted? Let us first understand what it is to be afflicted, let us have passed that way ourselves, and let us be touched with affliction and sadness, that we may comfort ourselves with those who are in sorrow and know how to bear with them. Furthermore if we wish to rebuke those who have failed, let us not do it with too great violence, but rather let us pity their destruction. It is true that sometimes vehemence surely must be joined with it immediately; for when we see wretched souls perish, it is no time to wheedle them; if men are obstinate in their rebellion, we must not only sting them, but also wound them to the quick. Indeed, yet we must previously have done this: namely, we must have known our own infirmities, and it must grieve us to deal rigorously; as, although a father beats his children and uses much more rough words to them than he would to strangers, yet his heart bleeds when he must so transform himself. Then let us observe that a man will never be fit to be a teacher unless he has put on a fatherly affection and first of all known his own infirmity in order that he may frame himself to such a compassion that he may pity all with whom he has to deal. This is what is shown us here by Elihu.

Furthermore, let all who are placed in authority well consider that they must not abuse their power unto tyranny by oppressing those who are inferior to them. For they shall have a double account to render before God if on the pretext of their authority they wish to have men fear them and stand in awe of them and do not seek principally the honor of God and the salvation of those who are committed to them. See how Ezekiel speaks of evil shepherds who have mistreated God's people through tyranny.[6] He says that they ruled over them in power and with all authority. Indeed, on the contrary it is shown us here that all who wish to acquit themselves loyally toward God and their neighbors when they are set in higher degree must not therefore exalt themselves, but rather know that, if they intend to carry terror with them to put poor people in fear, God must show them that His intention was not to set wild beasts here to scare His flock or goats to push at them with their horns and to trouble their water, as He speaks in this passage from Ezekiel.[7] God, then, wishes to show that those to whom He has given the sword and judgment-seat and those whom He has put into the pulpit to teach His word are not set there to be goats to tread down and oppress the poor sheep. You see what we have to note in this passage. Hereupon Elihu shows how we ought to receive doctrine: it is, that if we know that it is true and upright we must approve it without contradicting, although we are neither forced nor compelled.

You see, then, what we have to remember pertaining to the circumstance of the place and the proposition: namely, when a doctrine is proposed to us, very well, he is only a mortal man who speaks, but do we see that it is right and true? Let us know that in replying against him we fight not only against God but also against our own conscience, which is a sufficient judge to condemn us. From this we have a very profitable warning to gather: it is that whenever we come to be taught in the name of God, if we see that the doctrine which is presented to us is upright, there must be no more replying. For we shall win nothing by pleading; if it is right, we must submit to it. Furthermore, this ought not to hinder us from setting God's majesty before our eyes. For we must not judge

---

6. Ezekiel 34:4.
7. Ezekiel 34:18.

the doctrine that is proposed to us according to our own wit and fancy. Therefore two things need to be combined. One is, that we fully determine that we are ready to obey God, concluding in ourselves, "Our Creator must have entire mastery, and we should be subject to Him." This is the preparation that must be made. Then we must enter into judgment, that is to say, we must examine the doctrine, indeed not with pride, nor with an opinion that we are wise enough of ourselves, but praying to God that He may govern us by His Holy Spirit, that we may follow the doctrine which He has shown us. You see, then, the two things that ought to be combined. And this combination brings no confusion. For he who is prepared to obey God, will not therefore cease to open his eyes and to consider how he ought to distinguish falsehood from truth. However, let us learn not to be so frightened that we do not consider the man who speaks; but let us acknowledge that God does us a great favor in that it pleases Him to use his creatures and to so lower Himself to us in order that we may have more leisure to consider His word. For if He came to us in His majesty, we would be lost; but when He presents Himself to us through men, he accommodates Himself to our infirmity in order that we can more conveniently know His truth which He proposes to us. You see, then, in summary, what we have to remember from this passage, and the rest will be reserved until tomorrow.

Now we shall bow in humble reverence before the face of our God.

SERMON 18

God's Power Is Just*

The eye of God is upon every man's ways, and He sees all the steps of man. There is no darkness or dimness so thick where those who work iniquity can hide themselves. God puts nothing further upon men, so that he walks with God in judgment. He breaks the mighty without asking questions, and puts others in their place. He brings their works to light, and turns the night to break them. He smites them as wicked in the sight of others. —Job 34:21-26

WE SAW yesterday that if God wishes to punish men He needs not make any great preparation, or arm men, or borrow strength elsewhere; for He could destroy all things by His look alone. Therefore, He needs not serve Himself by man's hand, as by necessity. It is true that He often does so; but it is to show how everything is subject to Him, and that there is no creature which is not amenable to His service, indeed to execute the punishments which He wills to have done. Yet He does not need to prepare Himself beforehand to punish us. Hereby we are warned to humble ourselves under His mighty hand, knowing that we have no way in this world to be armed when He is against us, but He can execute upon us all that He has determined in His own counsel. So, in vain do men exalt themselves in pride; for in the end they will feel that it is not in them to resist God.

Now, following the statement which we have already discussed, Elihu adds that God does these things not by an absolute power, but because *He knows men's ways, and He considers all their steps.* So then, if these great chastisements happen so that a mighty people are overthrown in battle and a kingdom is conquered, let us know that God does not dis-

---

*Sermon 132 in *Calvini Opera, Corpus Reformatorum*, volume 35, pp. 168-179.

play such power without cause, but He does it through His justice. And though we may not perceive the reasons why God uses such severity, let us refer the knowledge of everything to Him as it belongs to Him, and let us be satisfied to know what is shown us here: namely, that *the ways of men are known to Him.* Why is it that often we enter into dispute with respect to God's judgments and they seem strange to us? It is because we see not so clearly as He does. However, since it is His office to judge men's ways, let us agree with Him, and although we do not see why it is, let us know that His case will always be found good and just, since He ought to chastise not only individual persons, but also whole peoples and nations. The saying that *God knows men's steps* is taken two ways in Scripture. For sometimes it is referred to His providence, because He is careful to govern us. But in this text (as also in many others) it is said that *God beholds our steps,* because nothing is unknown to Him, but all our life must come to account before Him.

So, let us learn to walk as before His eyes; for it will be in vain for us to hide ourselves, as also Elihu adds that *there is neither darkness nor mist so thick that the wicked can hide themselves in it.* Not without cause is this added. We see that, although every man confesses that God beholds all our works and He must be our Judge, nevertheless men wink at it and do not consider that God perceives them. In fact it is not in vain that it is said in the Psalm that the wicked make believe that God does not see their craftiness and malice at all.[1] Also they are upbraided by the Prophet Isaiah that they dig themselves caves under the earth to hide themselves from God.[2] Since, then, hypocrisy does so blind men, it is needful to note this sentence: that *there is no darkness so thick that the wicked can hide from God's sight.* And to better understand this we must first remember what I have discussed: it is, that men, although they are convinced that they must one day come before the judgment-seat of God, nevertheless do not cease to seek subterfuges, and thereupon they oversleep in their hiding

1. Psalms 10:11.
2. Isaiah 2:19.

places, as if they could deceive God. See what our hypocrisy
is. Hereupon let us observe that men are mistaken in standing
so aloof from God; when they no longer remember Him it
seems to them that He also has turned His back and does not
think of their misdeeds. Let us not be trapped by such imaginings. For although He may disguise things for a time, in
the end He will show that He has not forgotten His office,
which is to be judge of all the world; and not only to bring
every man's works to light, but all their deepest thoughts, according as it is His own right to search men's hearts, and it is
not in vain that He claims this title.

There are, then, two points which we have to deduce from
this passage. (1) One is that we should consider the vice
which is so deeply rooted in us: namely, that we should not
presume that we shall escape God's hand by our subterfuges;
and according as we are drunken in our sins, it also seems to
us that God has His eyes closed or blindfolded, or that He
has a curtain drawn before Him, so that He cannot perceive
what we are hiding. (2) However, on the other hand, and
for the second point, let us note that it is said that all our
darkness will be exposed before Him when it pleases Him;
and thereupon let us also be warned not to consider that we
have made a better bargain merely because men have not
known our iniquities; for the very cause that sends many to
destruction is that they pass for good men, or at least they can
stop the mouths of those who might know their villainy; for
then they triumph and they dare to provoke God Himself. Let
us know that we have gained nothing by our deceiving the
world; for no matter how beautiful a show we may put on, in
the end we must come before the Heavenly Judge, Who will
open the books that were previously closed, Who will bring
to pass His great day in order to bring all the darkness to light
which now keeps things confused. This is why the Holy Scripture so often speaks of it. It is not in one place or only at one
time that it is said that there is no darkness before God. But
why is this sentence so often repeated? It is because we cannot be persuaded of it. For when we have avoided shame
before men it seems to us that God ought not to stir our filthi-

ness or even discover it; but let us know that He will cause
the knowledge of it to come even into heaven. Since, then,
we cannot be persuaded of it, it is not superfluous that the
Holy Spirit so often pronounces that God will judge in another
manner than mortal men do today. That is why it is purposely said here that sinners will not be hidden; as if Elihu
said that it happens every day that men's eyes are so dazzled
that they take their vices for virtues; indeed, that they are so
malicious that it is very easy for them to be flattered; as we
see that when evil is in fashion vices are no longer condemned
but everyone approves of them. So, then, it may happen (as
is seen by experience) that vices will prevail, and that there
will be such a flood of iniquity that all things will be confused
among men, and there will no longer be ability to judge or
discriminate; yet this circumstance must be changed before
God. So then, let us learn to raise our eyes above the world
and to contemplate by faith God's judgment, which today is
hidden from us, knowing that there all things must be exposed,
as it is said in Daniel[3] that the books will be opened, that is to
say, the records will then be laid before us. What kind of
records? Not of paper or parchment, but conscience must answer so that each one will bring his own arraignment, not
written, but engraven so deeply that there will no longer be
possibility of disguising anything. Then God will be there
in the person of His Son with such a light that all things will
be known, even what are now under deep dungeons. All these
things must then be seen both by the Angels of paradise and
by all creatures. Let us remember this, in order to walk in
another manner of fear than we do, in order to free ourselves
from all hypocrisy; since we cannot increase our worth by
flattering ourselves. Finally, let us learn not to make our
reckoning without our host,[4] but whenever it is a matter of
examining our life let each one summon himself before God's
face, and thereupon acknowledge what is said here, that since
it is His office to search men's hearts and even their deepest
thoughts; it is to no purpose that today we are absolved by

---

3. Daniel 7:10.
4. Or landlord.

the world, since by this means we shall not escape from His hand.

Let us learn, then, to examine ourselves in this way; further-more let us allow our darkness to be enlightened by God's word, seeing that this office is also properly attributed to it. It is said in this passage that *there is neither darkness of death nor any mist so thick that can hide those who work iniquity.* Therefore the Apostle to the Hebrews testifies that as God knows men's hearts so He wills that His word should be as a sharp sword to cut asunder our thoughts and affections, in-deed, to enter into the marrow to expose what is hidden in us.[5] And Saint Paul says[6] that when God's word is preached we must be reproved, as though all the charges were written against us and our whole life were laid before us; we must be convicted and utterly cast down, in order to glorify God, ac-knowledging how guilty we are before Him. Therefore, let us not only summon ourselves before God's judgment-seat in order to correct all pretense, but whenever His word rubs our sores and rebukes our vices let us take it patiently and not pre-sume to be wilful. For what shall we gain by it? We see many men today who chafe and fret when their vices are mentioned to them; for they wish to be spared. It is as if they wished that God should no longer have any authority over them and that He should no longer be their Judge. If they properly considered what is said here they would not be so stupid as they are seen to be when they always ask, "What?" If a man shows them anything that is commonly known they are as scornful as can be. And why? Because they never felt the worth of the doctrine that there is no darkness in God's sight, but they defile themselves, throwing their snouts on the ground like hogs, and they are so sleepy that it seems to them that all their sins are nothing, although there are so many that it seems that they are pickled in them. But their rottenness does not stink to them because they are infected with it. There-fore it would behoove them to think a little about this doctrine; then they would be more quiet than they are when men show

---

5. Hebrews 4:12.
6. Romans 10:15, 16; 1 Thessalonians 2:13.

them their vices. And it is astonishing that, although many men's wickedness is notorious to everyone and even little children can be judges of it, yet they raise themselves against God and despise Him and cannot stand being rebuked. And what a shame it is! I do not speak of unknown things; here it is not a matter of examining men's thoughts or of seeking under the earth what is unknown by men, but the evil which so overflows that it is pitiful is apparent. The very air stinks with it; and yet these good Catholics who would be taken for good Christians and who always have the Gospel in their mouths (indeed, to bite it like mastive dogs that are mad) wish that men would still disguise it; and they think that men do them great wrong to expose their lewdness, which (to say the truth) is not exposed by us, but only spoken of because all men know it. Yet nevertheless those who today cannot stand it that God should expose their corruption, in order that they might be ashamed of it, and repent it, shall feel in the end that they must come before His judgment-seat, where there will be no more darkness or mist.

So then, let us know that it is greatly for our profit that God today sends us His word to enlighten us in order that we may properly think about our sins. Indeed, if for a time they have been unknown to us, they come into our memory, and we practice what I have alleged from Saint Paul: which is, to cast ourselves down and to be ashamed before God and to condemn ourselves by feeling the wickedness that is too deeply rooted in us. Behold, I say, how God procures our salvation; it is when we feel such a power and effectiveness in His word that we take pains to examine our whole life thoroughly, in order to be displeased with ourselves. But those who are stubborn and despise God and come like crazy men to strike against Him and cannot stand any warning, He must send like unreasonable people to the day of which Elihu speaks here in which there will be no darkness or hiding place so obscure that everything will not be exposed, indeed, before all creatures. They cannot endure that God should make them ashamed, in order to bury their sins forever; but in spite of their teeth both Angels, men, and devils must know their wickedness, and they

must be defamed everywhere by the power of this light which
will expose all secrets. This is how we ought to apply this
passage to our instruction. For surely our Lord's threatening
men with the great day is in order that they should prepare
for it; and so the remedy is ready for us. God does not wait
until we appear before Him to indict us, but he executes His
jurisdiction daily by the Gospel, as also our Lord Jesus Christ
says, "The Spirit when He comes will judge the world."[7]
Therefore when the Gospel is preached God executes sovereign
jurisdiction not only upon men's bodies as they are today but
upon their souls, and He wills that we should be condemned
thereby in order for our salvation. So then, since God so often
warns us that we must come to this great light in the end, let
us not shut our eyes knowingly today or willingly be blinded
when He sends us His word to expose our filthiness and to
make us feel that we cannot hide ourselves from His sight.
So, let us profit by the means which are given to us today. But
if we wish to play we are wild beasts and always seek foxholes,
yet in the end we shall feel, knowing we are accursed, that it
is not said in vain that there is no darkness before God. For
He will cause us to behold those things in His countenance
and glorious majesty which we were not willing to see here in
the mirror of His word.

Elihu adds immediately that *He will not put more upon men
than that they should come into judgment with Him.*
This passage is variously expounded. Some take it as if God
would not impose more burden upon a man than He ought
and than a man could bear. But when the main theme of the
text is properly considered, we find that because it is a matter
of God's judgments Elihu maintains that God does not afflict
in such a way that we may have occasion to dispute against
Him. We must always consider the intention of a proposition.
If a man wishes to know what is meant by a sentence, let him
consider with what something deals, the subject being treated,
and what it all implies. Then, if everything is considered,
the general theme of this passage is that men can surely murmur against God, but in the end they will find themselves

---

7.. John 16:8.

confounded. And why? For although God seems today to handle us with too great a severity, yet when things are fully known our mouths will be stopped and God will be glorified, as it is said in Psalm 51.[8] Let us note well, then, that it is shown us here that, though we may be able to plead much against God, our case shall be lost in the end. And why? For it will be found that God has not handled us unjustly or laid too heavy a burden upon us, that is to say, He has not afflicted us unreasonably. For although He sometimes strikes men with heavier blows than they are able to bear, yet it is never more than right or more than they have deserved. Hereby we are warned of the pride, or rather of the rage, that is in us, which drives us to murmur against God. For how do we plead with Him? It seems to us that we have some judge or umpire by whom He should be judged. If God had to render an account, would we not be more bold to provoke Him when He treats us not to our own liking and things do not come to pass as we would have them?

Let us learn, then, that men are here condemned for the devilish pride which incites them to plead against God. Howbeit, we must consider well that God will not stoop so far as to answer us when we summon Him to the law; He will not in this case appear as our counterpart. He will doubtless come there. But for what purpose? To express what is told us here: namely, that even if we had the power to summon God, and He had to answer, so that He would be accountable for all His doings, and we could have our mouths open to speak against Him; yet it would be no advantage to us; for in the end when everything is added and balanced it will be found that God has not burdened us too heavily or beyond reason. And why? Because our sins are known to Him, and so known that He can tell the measure of chastisement we deserve. But our pride comes because we wish to be our own judges in order to justify ourselves. And who has given us such great authority? Behold, judgment is given to our Lord Jesus Christ; therefore we must come before Him with all humility and reverence to hear and receive what He pro-

---

8. See also Psalm 63:1, 2, 11.

nounces about us without any contradicting. But each one
of us wishes to be believed in his own case; therefore we do
not grant so much to the living God as to mortal men. For in
worldly justice he who is seated upon the judgment-seat must
not be both judge and party, and yet he will often judge unjustly, for men are corruptible. But yet for all that, men do
not change in that respect concerning the outward order which
God has established. And what, then, shall we do when we
come before His glorious majesty? So then, we see how men
are carried beyond all reason when they murmur so against
God; and we see also that the cause from which this evil proceeds is what I have discussed: namely, that we esteem our
works according to our own fancy. Nevertheless you see here
that God reserves judgment to Himself. "It belongs to Me,"
He says, "to consider your steps. I observe you and search
you even inside. It is not for you to meddle with that matter.
For whoever takes upon himself to wish to judge usurps what
is not due to him." What is to be done, then? When our
Lord afflicts us, let us refer our case to Him, knowing that
He observes many vices in us which are hidden from ourselves. "Behold, Lord, it is true that I do not perceive even
one one-hundredth of my faults. Why is that? Because I
am blind, because I am steeped in evil and the devil has as it
were bewitched me. So, Lord, may I be able in the first place
to perceive better the iniquities I have committed before Thee,
and surrender myself as guilty; then, since I am not a competent judge to acknowledge my own faults, yet, Lord, since
Thou hast done me the honor of constituting Thyself my just
judge, I put my case into Thy hands, knowing that Thou seest
what is unknown to me." This is why it is expressly said in
this passage that although we went to law with God, yet He
would not be found indebted to us. Let us guard, then, against
presuming to plead against Him. For however beautiful show
and pretense we may have before men, we shall be confounded
in all that we pretend when we come before God. Thus, you
see in summary what Elihu wished to say in this passage.

Hereupon he adds that *God will break the mighty, indeed,
without questioning them and put others in their place.* And

why? *For He will bring their works to light and turn the night in order to break them.* When he says that *God will break the mighty without questioning them* it is in order to make us feel better the authority which we despise so boldly, because we are too stupid. It is true that some expound the word *questioning* as *number*; as if it were said, "Although the mighty were infinite in number, yet God would not fail to break them. But word by word it is thus: *He will break the powers or multitude of men;* for the word implies both; and then, *there will be no questioning.* Since the word "questioning" is there and it signifies properly "to search" or "to make inquiry," no doubt Elihu meant to say that God does not need to make any inquiries as earthly judges do. Since they are creatures, there is ignorance in them; therefore they must help themselves by this means. For they cannot prophesy things. Since all things are open to God, He will judge men without any procedure such as we see by police in this world. But yet there is more to it: which is, that Elihu wished to indicate that God will not always let us know why He executes His judgments, but we shall be blind in that respect. This questioning, then, of which he speaks, is properly referred to God's chastising men; as if it were said, when judges pronounce a sentence it will be spoken of and the form and style of it will be observed, so that men will know the items; and then the sentence will be published in order that men may know the crimes of the offender and how he was convicted. But we must not measure God's power and authority by these laws of men. And why? For *He will break without questioning,* that is to say, without showing us why. He will not always publish His sentence; men's crimes will not always be recited there in order to decipher why He punishes us; that will be hidden from us; but yet in the meanwhile He will not fail to put His judgments into execution. Now we see the natural sense of this passage.

But yet he adds that this is not done unjustly; *"For God,"* he says, *"will bring their works forward."* Although, then, God punishes without questioning (that is to say without observing such formality as is required in human policy,) yet

He does all things with reason and uprightness. And if this is not perceived the first day, let us wait until all things are discovered, and until He brings to light what is now confused and confounded. Here we have to exhort ourselves not to flatter ourselves as we have been accustomed to doing. For behold the cause why we always follow our own way when God seems to spare us and we think we have liberty to do evil because we are unpunished. It is because when God begins to chastise us in the common manner we do not perceive it but are preoccupied with stupidity and carnal assurance. And afterward when He comes in great roughness we are so frightened that we do not know where we are as soon as He thunders suddenly, which thing He does when it seems good to Him. For after He has hidden a long time, He needs only to lift up His hand and men must perish in a minute, as it is said here. Therefore, in order that every one of us may be solicitous both evening and morning, let us remember this passage, in which it is said that God will not conduct a long trial in order to punish us or be bound by any laws. Let us consider that we must always be ready and prepared; and let us not wait until He strikes us, but rather let us carefully anticipate His judgment, as it is said, "Happy is the man who has a careful heart."[9] Besides let us also remember the horrible threat, "When the wicked shall say, 'Peace, all is well,' destruction will fall upon their heads."[10] So then, let the faithful understand that when it pleases God to punish them He does not need to begin at a certain point and follow through and then delay, as mortal men do, by reason of the hindrances which they have. And why? He will condemn and execute His sentence all at once; He does not need to trouble Himself to conduct a long trial against us; we shall have no leisure to breathe or to languish in distress until we are entirely ruined by His hand; but we shall be confounded quickly, as if heaven fell upon our heads. If, then, we do not wish to be overwhelmed by God's horrible vengeance, let us feel our own

---

9. Proverbs 28:14. "Happy is the man who is always afraid (of God); but he who hardens his heart will fall into mischief."
10. Jeremiah 6:14; 8:11.

faults. Besides, when we feel them, let us know that we have
also wherewith to comfort ourselves in Him, provided we are
sorry for our faults and do not seek to hide evil but expose it
before our God, and groan in order to be received in mercy.
For it is said that He absolves those who condemn themselves,
and buries the sins of those who have them before their own
eyes, and who ask only to confess them.[11]   Therefore, let us
not doubt that God will wipe out all our faults if He sees that
we confess them freely.   Indeed, but yet we must pass this way
also: namely, to bear in mind the saying, "God punishes without questioning"; in order that every one of us may do his
duty of entering into himself to examine his life thoroughly,
that we may be ashamed and humble ourselves.

Now it is said that *God having so broken the great and
mighty men puts others in their places.*   And again on the
other hand it is said that *He punishes them in open sight and,
indeed,* that *He punishes them as offenders.*   I have said already that when it is said that God discovers their works and
punishes them in such manner, it is in order that we should
always fear God's justice and not come to imagine that He
uses any tyranny or cruelty.   Therefore let us keep from thinking of such a power in God as He might display without
reason.   It is true that the reason which He holds is unknown
to us, and we must be contented with His only and simple will
as with the only rule of uprightness; and whatever comes to
pass, let us not wickedly imagine that God goes crookedly or
obliquely or that He judges otherwise than with reason; on
the contrary let us be fully persuaded that, although His judgments seem strange to us, yet they are ordered according to
the best rule that can be: namely, according to His will which
surpasses all justice.   This is what Elihu declares in this passage.   The same ought to serve chiefly for us.   Then, if any
man is afflicted in his own person, he ought always to consider
that God is just, in order that he may repent of his faults; for
we shall never have true repentance, unless we know that God
afflicts us uprightly; neither can we glorify God, and confess
that He is just, unless we have first condemned ourselves.

11. 1 John 1:9.

You see, then, how we must apply to ourselves the doctrine that God exposes men's works and brings them to light when He punishes them. Indeed, although we may not examine word for word the sins and offenses that we have committed, yet the chastisement which God sends us ought to profit us in that condition.

That is why it is said that *God punishes them instead of the wicked,* that is to say, in such a way as to indicate that they can gain nothing by their replies, that they cannot allege that they are righteous, when they do not appear so even before men. So much for one point. The other is that he says that *He puts others in their place.* That is in order that we may know the cause of the changes which often happen in the world, as also it is said in Psalm 107, which is for us a correct exposition of this sentence. We are carried away in astonishment when we see a plague depopulate a country or if famines happen or if the land which has been very fertile becomes barren, as if salt had been sown upon it, or else if all things are so troubled with wars that a country is laid waste or the princes thereof are changed. When we see any of these things we are astonished. And why? For we do not know God's providence, which reigns over all worldly means; neither do we think upon men. For if we considered how men governed themselves, we would not find it strange that God makes changes and alterations.

Thus you see why it is expressly said that *God puts others in their places*: namely, in order that when we see things change in the world we should not think it any novelty. And why? For therein God shows Himself to be Judge. Let us not attribute it to fortune; but let us know that our Lord displays here His arm, because men can not maintain themselves in possession of the benefits which He bestowed upon them. Thereupon let us consider how unthankful we are, in order to correct it. For as soon as our Lord has made us fat and done us good, we turn to kicking against Him like horses which are too well treated. Is it any wonder that God lays His hand upon us, when we are so proud and unthankful? Let us observe what the modesty of men is nowadays. When God

does them any good, do they govern themselves so that they
may possess it long? No; on the contrary, they spite God,
in order that He should despoil them of it immediately. Seeing then that pride and unthankfulness are so villainous, we
must not murmur at the change of things or at the great number of revolutions. And why? For we provoke God to it.
Howbeit, it is not enough to know that God takes away one
people and puts another in their place and sets new inhabitants
in a country and removes men in that way. It is not enough
to know these things, indeed, and that He does them justly;
but also even when we are in our best state, let us pray to Him
to grant us the grace to enjoy His benefits in such a way that
we may still possess them and be led by them into the eternal
heritage which is prepared for us in heaven. Thus you see
how we ought to put this sentence to use; and as for the rest,
it will be reserved until tomorrow.

Now we shall bow in humble reverence before the face of
our God.

SERMON 19

The Right Use of Affliction*

He does not enliven the wicked, but gives judgment to the afflicted. He will not turn His eyes away from the righteous. He will set kings on their thrones and they will be exalted forever. If they are in the stocks and bound with the cords of affliction, He will show them their faults, and make them feel their sins, and they will be touched with them. He will open their ear in order to amend them; He will speak to them and make them depart from iniquity. If they hear and obey, they will pass their days in prosperity and their years in glory. If they do not hear, they will pass away by the sword and be consumed without knowledge. The hypocrites of heart lay up wrath; they do not cry even when they are bound. Therefore, their soul will die in youth, and their life among the whoremongers. —Job 36:6-14.

AFTER Elihu has said that in general God does not turn His eyes from the righteous but cares for him, and that on the contrary He does not enliven the wicked; he adds particularly to better prove God's providence that *He gives judgment to the afflicted.* For if a poor man who is utterly destitute of help and an outcast in the world is nevertheless delivered from affliction and persecution, the same must proceed from God. Indeed, it must be attributed to God. For if we have no support from the world and yet have strong and powerful enemies, what is to be said except that we are lost and that there is no longer hope for our life? If, then, we are restored, it is manifest that God has been at work. So, it is not without cause that Elihu does purposely set down this saying to prove that God governs all things here below.

Also he sets down a second example of God's providence: namely, the *government by princes* and by men who sit in the

---

*Sermon 140 in *Calvini Opera, Corpus Reformatorum*, volume 35, pp. 266-278.

seat of justice, in which we perceive that God is just and that
He does not will to have things be out of order. Although
there is not permanent equality, yet when we see that there
is some order in the world therein we can see as in a mirror
that God has not so let loose the reigns to all confusion that
He does not still show us some sign and token of His justice.
In fact, if a man considers on one side what the nature of
man is, and on the other side how governors and magistrates
and those who have the sword of justice in their hands discharge themselves; he will see and easily discern that it is a
miracle of God that there is any common weal among us, and
indeed we must know it and perceive it. I say that the nature
of men is such that every man would be lord and master over
his neighbors and no man is willing to be a subject. When,
then, our Lord does not permit the strong to prevail, but there
is some fear and obedience toward those who are in preeminence; therein it is to be seen that God not only bridles but
also chains men's nature in order that this pride may not raise
itself so high that public government should not be above it.
Then we see that all men are given to evil and their lusts are
so boiling that every man wishes to have complete license and
that no man should be under correction. Therefore it is to
be concluded that the order of justice comes from God, and
that therein He shows that He has created men in order that
they should govern themselves honestly and modestly. For
the second point, we see how kings and princes and those who
are of lower estate behave themselves when God has armed
them with the sword of justice and how they turn all things
upside down, so that it seems that they wished to defy God and
to destroy what He had ordained. Now if those who ought
to maintain peaceably the order constituted by God force themselves to overthrow it and deliberately fight to put things in
confusion, and yet for all that government continues in the
world, and things are not so utterly confounded that there do
not still abide some marks of what God has established; is it
not to be seen thereby that God is doubly just?

Therefore it is not without cause that Elihu, after he has
spoken of the relieving of the afflicted, immediately adds an

example in that *God establishes kings,* and not for only a day but in order that the same order should be continually in the world. It is true that many changes will be made from one side to the other and that there will be great revolutions among principalities and lordships, but therein God shows also that it is His office to pull down the proud. Yet even in spite of men and all their rage, some order will yet remain here below, even with respect to tyrants. If a king reigns unjustly so that he is a despiser of God, and full of cruelty, violence, and insatiable covetousness; yet notwithstanding he must keep some shadow and appearance of justice, and he cannot go beyond it. Whence comes this, except that God thereby declares Himself? Therefore let us learn to profit in such a manner by what is seen in this world that God may be glorified in His creatures as He deserves; and above all when we see that He delivers the poor oppressed who can do no more and who neither have nor expect any help from men, let us there perceive His power and His goodness, and let us be disposed to render to Him His due praise. This is what we have to observe. However, in order to prove that we are God's children, let us also be advised to lend our helping hand to those who are unjustly persecuted, according to the means which God gives us to help those who are trodden under foot and who have no means whereby to avenge or support themselves. We must busy ourselves and consciously exert ourselves in this work. Secondly, when we see that men who govern are so perverse and wicked and yet God does not let them go entirely overboard, let us humble ourselves to honor His providence, and let us know that if He did not restrain their wickedness, we would be overwhelmed with a horrible flood, and everything would be immediately swallowed up and drowned. Therefore God must be magnified in that we see that some residue of justice and good order remains, although those who rule and hold the sword in their hands are utterly wicked and given to all evil. So, let us know this, and let us as much as is in us support the order of justice, seeing that it is a sovereign benefit that God bestows upon mankind, and that therein also He wills to have His providence to be known. And when we see that princes and magistrates and all officers of justice are so perverse, let us be sorry to see the order so profaned which God had dedicated to the salvation of men; and let us not only detest those who are enemies of God, and who resist the order of government which He had set over them, but let us know that they are the fruits of our sins, in order that we may impute to ourselves the blame and the cause of all the evil. Thus you see what we have to remember from this passage.

Now let us come to what Elihu adds. He says that if the *good men* or else the great men of whom he had spoken, whom God had exalted to high estate and dignity above the rest of the world, are sometimes *set in the stocks*; if they are sometimes brought down even in shame so that men put them in prison and in stocks and they are tied with ropes to their confounding; God does not forsake them in such necessity, but He makes them feel their sins, He tells them the faults that they have committed in order that having known them they may amend themselves and return to the right road; He opens their ears in order that they may think more correctly about themselves and know themselves. Elihu, then, shows here that when it seems to us that God shuts His eyes and that He no longer regards the governing of men, He has just reason to do so; and although we find it strange, we must acknowledge that He is just and equitable in all that He does and we have occasion to glorify Him. It is true that what we discussed before must always be borne in mind: namely, that things are not governed in this world in a uniform manner and that God reserves a great part of the judgments He intends to execute to the latter day, in order that we should always be in suspense, waiting for the coming of our Lord Jesus Christ. It ought to be sufficient for us to have some signs by which to perceive what is told us here. Now, the intention of Elihu is to anticipate the stumblingblock that men might conceive, when good and just people are trampled under foot and God exposes them to the tyranny of the wicked and they are tormented without cause, so that although they have not done wrong to anyone, yet they do not cease to be molested. For when we see this, it seems to us that God does not think about the world, that His view does not extend to us, and that He lets fortune rule. See how our eyesight is immediately confused by our seeing things out of order, and there is nothing more easy for us than to stumble at this. For this cause Elihu shows here, that, although good men are persecuted, or else those who were advanced to power are overthrown as if God confused earth with heaven, we must not therefore be too frightened in our minds. And why? For God has just reason which we are not able to see at first glance, but let us wait in patience, and we shall know that God will make such afflictions to do us good and that they tend to a good end. And why?

"For then," he says, "*God announces to those who are so tormented their sins,* and makes them feel what they are; it is in order to lead them to proper correction." Here we see in the first place that we must not estimate things according to outward appearance but search deeper and seek the cause that moves God to do what we find strange at first sight. It seems quite contrary to all reason that a good man should be so persecuted and that everyone should overrun him; but God knows why He does it. Therefore we must look toward the outcome, and not be too hasty to pronounce our verdict, like those who judge heedlessly. What is the purpose of our afflictions? It is to make us feel our sins; and it is a very noteworthy point from which we can gather a mighty useful doctrine. It is true that we often hear it spoken of; yet we cannot hear it too much; for we know that afflictions are so irksome to us that every one of us frets as soon as he feels the glow of the rod at God's hand, and we cannot comfort ourselves or hold ourselves in patience. Therefore so much the more it behooves us to note well the doctrine that when God permits us to be tormented even unjustly with respect to men, even then He is procuring our salvation in that He wills to make us feel our sins and to show us what we are. For in time of prosperity we are blind; in fact we shall not know rightly what is contained here, unless God brings us to it by His chastisements. Are we at our ease and in delights? Every one of us falls asleep, and flatters himself in his sins, so that our prosperity is like drunkenness putting our souls to sleep. And, what is worse, when God lets us alone in peace, although we have offended Him a thousand ways; yet we do not cease to applaud ourselves, and it seems to us that God is propitious toward us and that He loves us because He does not persecute us. You see, then, that men cannot feel their sins if they are not driven by force to know themselves. Therefore, seeing that prosperity makes us so drunken after that manner, and that when we are at rest every man flatters himself in his sins; we must suffer patiently that God should afflict us. For affliction is the true schoolmistress to bring men to repentance in order that they may condemn themselves before God and being condemned may learn to hate their faults in which they previously bathed. Therefore, when we have known the fruit of the chastisements that God sends us, we shall bear them in greater mildness and more peaceful courage than we do. But it is pitiful how indifferent we are, because we do not know that God procures our salvation when He so afflicts us. Besides, let us note well that we need not look at the visible hand of God to feel our faults. For it may come to pass that God will unbridle men so that we shall be persecuted by them, even unjustly, when we shall not have done them any wrong. Yet even in that case we must learn that God calls us to His school. For when He refrains from striking us with His hand but puts us into the hands of the wicked, it is to tame us and humble us better; and then He puts us to greater shame. Then, if the wicked are in control so that they have the means to torment us and they do to us the worst that they can, it is as if God declared to us that we are not worthy to be beaten by His own hand, and that He wills thereby to make us ashamed.

All the more ought we to be incited to think about our faults and to be sorry for them and therewithal to observe what Elihu adds, that *God then opens our ears.* This saying means two things in the Scripture. For sometimes it signifies simply to *speak to us;* and sometimes it signifies *to touch our hearts* in such a manner that we hear what is said to us. God therefore opens our ears when He sends us His word and causes

it to be proposed to us; and then He opens our ears or He
uncovers them (for the Hebrew word properly means this)
when He does not permit us to be deaf to His doctrine, but
He gives it entrance in order that we may receive it and be
moved by it, and that its power may be demonstrated. See the
two ways of opening our ears which we daily perceive that
God employs toward us. Also He opens the ears of those
whom He afflicts in that He gives them some sign of His
wrath in order to teach them to think more correctly about
themselves than they have done. If a man asks, "What then?
does not God speak to us when we are in prosperity?" Yes,
surely He does; but His voice cannot come to us; for we are
already preoccupied with our own delights and worldly affections. In fact we see that, when men have their fill to eat, and
can have a good time, and live in health and peace, they are
overjoyed. Then they are so joyful that God can no longer
be heard. But afflictions are messages which He sends of
His wrath; then we are touched with having offended Him,
in order that we may come to our senses again. So, afflictions
in general ought to serve for instruction to those who receive
them, so that they may draw near to God, from Whom they
had previously been estranged. So much for one point. Yet,
however, men do not let themselves be governed by God until
He has softened their hearts by His Holy Spirit and opened
the passage for the warnings that He gives and pierced men's
ears in order that they may dedicate themselves to His service
and obedience, as it is said in the Psalm.[1] This is what we
have to observe. Therefore when we are afflicted, first let
us remember that it is as if Gòd addressed Himself to us and
showed us our sins and indicted us in order to draw us to
repentance. But, since we are hard to prick and, what is more,
we are utterly stubborn and deaf to all the warnings that He
gives us, we must pray to Him that He may pierce our ears
and make us so open to His instructions that they may be
profitable to us, and that He may not merely permit the air to
be beaten without touching our hearts but that we may be
moved to come and return to Him. Otherwise let us know

---

1. Psalm 40:6.

that we shall do nothing but provoke Him and reject His corrections, as experience shows in most men that those who are beaten with God's rods do not improve thereby but rather grow worse. Then, since we see such examples, let us learn that nothing is done until God opens our ears, that is to say, until by His Holy Spirit He makes us listen to Him speak to us, and having listened also to obey Him. You see what we have to note from this passage.

He adds immediately that *if they hear and obey they will spend their days in wealth and their years in glory, but if they do not listen to Him they will pass by the sword and die without knowledge.* Here Elihu shows us still better the profit that we have by being in affliction. It is undoubtedly a great benefit and one which cannot be sufficiently valued when we are drawn to repentance and that instead of our traveling into perdition our Lord is bringing us back to Himself. This is what ought to sweeten all our sorrows in our afflictions. But there is much more: namely, that our Lord shows us a proof of how profitable it is for us in order that we may be delivered from our adversities and aided by Him and that He may show that He favors us by this means. When, then, all this is known by experience, have we not cause to be glad when God has thus delivered us? For if He let us be drunken in the pleasures of the world, in the end we would become incorrigible; therefore He must remedy it at the right time. And if He does it by means of afflicting us and thereupon delivering us in order that we may perceive His hand, is it not a singular proof of His grace and of our faith? If God let us wallow in our own filthiness and in our dregs (as the Prophets term it)[2] we would rot away; and besides, we would not prize His grace toward us as it is shown to be when He draws us out of the affliction into which we had fallen. Behold here is a double benefit which comes back to men when God corrects them in that manner. For in the first place they are led back to Him; and secondly they perceive His fatherly goodness when they are delivered by His grace. You see, then, what we have to observe in this passage. Now a man could ask, "Indeed, is

2. Jeremiah 48:11, Zephaniah 1:12.

that so? How do you know that God wills to draw us to repentance when He afflicts us or when He permits us to be tormented by men? How do we know whether or not this is His purpose or His will?" To which we answer: When we see that afflictions are temporary and God delivers us from them, let us know that He does not will to make us utterly perish but He is contented that we are beaten down and humbled under His hand. But when we resist Him with our brass necks and will not bow for the corrections which He sends us, we do nothing but continually double His strokes. On the contrary, then, if we feel our sins so that we ask pardon for them and He knows that we are rightly touched by them, then He makes our afflictions to turn into a wholesome medicine for us, and thereupon He delivers us from them. We see all this even with our eyes.

So then, let us not murmur any longer when we see that God sends such troubles into the world, neither let us be offended at it as if He had His eyes closed. For He well knows what He is doing and He has an infinite wisdom which does not appear to us at first sight; but in the end we surely see that He has disposed things in good order and measure. Also let us learn meanwhile not to be too much grieved when we are so afflicted, knowing that God does by this means further our salvation. Besides, do we wish to be healed when we are so in torment and pain? Do we wish to have a good and desirable result from them? Let us follow the way that is here shown us: namely, to hear and obey. How hear? By being taught when God holds us as it were in His school so that our afflictions may be as many warnings to draw near to Him. Then let us hear these things, and let not things go in one ear and out the other; but let us obey, that is to say, let us yield such obedience to God as we ought to do, and let us not seek anything else than to frame ourselves wholly to Him. This is how we may be delivered from our adversities. What follows? We must not be astonished if men languish in pain, indeed if they are plunged daily deeper and deeper in their miseries. For which of them listens to God when He speaks? It is apparent that in that so many are afflicted and tormented God's rods are busy everywhere today. But how many think about them? You will see a whole people oppressed with wars until they can stand no more; yet you will find hardly a dozen men among a hundred thousand who listen to God speak. Behold, the snapping of His whips do sound and echo in the air; there is horrible weeping and wailing everywhere; men cry, "Alas!" but meanwhile they do not look at the hand which strikes them, as the Prophet[3] upbraids the obstinate that though they feel the strokes they do not acknowledge God's hand. We see the same thing in times of pestilence and famine. So then, is it any wonder if God sends incurable wounds and does what is said by the Prophet Isaiah:[4] namely, that from the sole of the foot to the crown of the head there is not a drop of soundness in this people, but there is a leprosy, so that they are all rotten and infected and their sores are incurable? Is this to be wondered at, seeing that today men are so unthankful to God that they shut the door against Him and are not willing to hear Him in order to obey Him?

So then, whenever we are beaten by God's hand let us learn to come quickly to Him and to listen to the warnings that He gives us in order that we may feel our sins and be displeased with them. Having done that, let us be touched to the quick in order that it may please Him to have pity upon us. If we proceed to it this way, God will not forget His office of instructing us and delivering us from all our adversities. But do we wish to play we are restive horses? He will surely snub us, then, as it is said here, *"We shall pass by the sword and be consumed without knowledge,"* that is to say, in our foolishness. When it is said, *"We shall pass by the sword,"* the meaning is that the wounds will be utterly incurable, that we must no longer hope for healing, there will no longer be any remedy for us. If we are not obstinate when God warns us of our faults, He will show Himself a good physician toward us in purging us of them, at least if we are not incorrigible. But if there is no reason or amendment in us so

---

3. Isaiah 9:12.
4. Isaiah 1:6.

that we chew upon the bridle without feeling our sins in order
to be sorry for them, let us know that all the afflictions of the
world will be deadly to us. Unless we learn to return to God
when He calls us and gives us opportunity to repent, that is to
say, unless we come at the right time and enter when the
door is open to us: unless we do so, all the chastisements that
were given us for our profit must turn to our greater condemnation and they must be so many warnings God will give,
indeed, the heaping up of all misery upon us must be accomp-
lished. All the more ought we to think about ourselves, that
we may not knowingly provoke such vengeance of God upon
us. For is it a small matter that it is said that the obstinate
must be wounded by God's hand, indeed, since men as much as
is possible provoke Him and are not willing to surrender themselves to Him when He has done them the favor of warning
them and gives them entrance to Himself? In fact when men
chafe so, is it not open defiance of God? Is it not trampling
His grace under foot? God cannot stand such spitefulness;
for He swears by his majesty[5] that when men make merry
and say "Let us eat and drink" while God calls them to repentance, it is a sin that will never be erased. Behold God is
so irritated with that sin that He swears that it will be registered forever before Him. All the more, then, ought it to incite us to humble ourselves when God gives us some warning,
knowing that He procures our salvation at this point, in order
that we may not reject His yoke when He wills to put it upon
us, and that we may not repulse the strokes of His rods which
He gives us, as if He struck an anvil.

It is said specifically that *those who do not listen to God
will die without knowledge,* that is to say, their own foolishness will consume them. This is said in order that men may
be left without excuse. It is true that we surely shield ourselves with ignorance when we wish to minimize our faults
or else to wipe them out completely. We say, "I did not
think of it; I was not advised about it." But let us learn
that when any mention is made of men's ignorance it is to
condemn them all the more because they played beasts and

had no reason at all in them. Even so does the Prophet Isaiah
speak of it.[6] "The very reason," says the Lord, "why hell
is open and why the grave swallows up everything and why all
my people are consumed is that they had no knowledge." God
complains there that sinners wilfully cast themselves into destruction; however, He says that it came because they had no
knowledge; indeed, but immediately He upbraids the Jews that
they had become brutish. For the Lord on His part sufficiently warns us, so that it is our own fault if we are not
well taught. How come? God is a good schoolmaster, but we
are poor scholars; God speaks, and we are deaf, or else we
stop up our ears in order not to hear Him. So then, the
ignorance of which Elihu here speaks is voluntary, because
men cannot allow God to show them their lesson or teach them
to come to Him, but they would rather follow continually their
ordinary path and therefore shut their eyes and stop up their
ears. Thus you see an ignorance that is full of malice and
rebellion. Now it is true that for a time the wicked please
themselves when they do not feel God's hand, but so much the
worse for them, as we see examples of it every day. If a man
speaks to these debauchees who are given to all evil and threatens them with God's vengeance, they only shake their heads
and mock it and it seems to them that it is only a joke. Again,
they take sermons in mockery and turn all the Holy Scripture
into ridicule in order that it may no longer have reverence or
authority. We see this before our eyes. They always worsen
their condition, since this saying will not be frustrated: namely,
that whoever is not willing to hear God in affliction must
perish without knowledge; that is to say, the ignorance in
which he is besotted must cause a greater ruin and plunge him
deeper into God's curse. Now since we see this, let us learn
to be teachable, and as soon as God speaks let us give ear to
Him and be ready to subject ourselves to His word, and let
nothing hinder us from returning to Him. This is what we
are taught in this passage. In fact it is certain that otherwise
our own nature would always induce us to chafe against Him,
as it is said here. Besides, men's foolishness is seen in that,

6. Isaiah 5:13, 14.

although they do not wish to be considered fools and unadvised, yet they labor to excuse themselves by folly and ignorance when it comes to rendering their account before God. But all this will profit them nothing. All the more must we try to humble ourselves in good time and to come to the comfort which God gives us when He says that He teaches us by double means. For on the one side He causes His word to be preached to us; and on the other side He beats us with His rods in order that each one of us in his own behalf should be induced to return to the right road. Therefore, let us have our ears open to receive the doctrine that is set before us in the name of God in order that He may not speak to deaf people or tree trunks. Meanwhile also let us be patient in order to endure the afflictions which He sends us; and when something does not happen as we would like it, let us not therefore ever cease to magnify God and His grace, knowing that by that means He makes us feel our sins in order that we may not be so confident in them that we perish. You see, then, that unless we wish to provoke God wilfully after we have heard His word, we must also understand what He intends when He chastises us and sends us some afflictions from whatever side they may come upon us; for there shall never happen to us anything except from His hand.

Elihu immediately adds that *the hypocrites of heart lay up wrath, and they do not cry even when they are bound; their soul will die in youth, and they will perish with the whoremongers.* He says "hypocrites of heart." Why does he name them so? He means those who confide in wickedness and have a shop in the rear to hide from God, and can not be drawn to any soundness. For we see many poor people who sin through oversight because they are fickle so that they are easily debauched and yet there is no malicious or rooted obstinacy in them. But there are others who are "hypocrites of heart," that is to say, who have in them the root of contempt and of all rebellion so that they mock God and have no reverence for His word but the devil has so bewitched them that they condemn the good and follow the evil or at least approve it and they wish to delight in it and to feed upon it. Therefore, let

us note well that when Elihu speaks here of hypocrites of heart
he means those who are so wholly abandoned to Satan that
they sin not only through oversight but are so wholly framed
to evil that they are fully bent on doing evil and mocking God;
and of such men too many examples are seen. For if a man
includes those who are fickle and who offend through weakness
with the wicked and the despisers of God, the number of the
wicked will be far greater. So let us note that it is not without
cause that Elihu calls them hypocrites of heart, or perverse of
heart, that is to say, utterly given to extreme maliciousness, so
that in their afflictions they are not willing in any manner to
subject themselves to God but rather they heap up wrath. And
let us note well the phrase *heaping up wrath;* for it is like
kindling the fire still more and more, and throwing on wood
to augment it. In fact, what are the perverse doing when they
strive and fret so against God? Do they improve their case
or condition? Alas! They only heap up more wood, and the
wrath of God must burn hotter. So then, let us note well that
if we resist God's chastisements, thinking to repulse them by
our malice and obstinacy, we shall only increase wrath, and
God's curse will be augmented more and more until we are
utterly consumed by it. Now when we hear this, what have
we to do except to pray to God that in the first place He may
so purge us that we may not have this rebellion rooted in us
and this malice hidden; but, although we have failed through
infirmity, yet there may always be some root of the fear of
God in us so that we may not become utterly incorrigible.
Also let us be advised always to conduct ourselves in sobriety
and singleness of heart in order that we may not be so wrapped
in our sins that we like them and feed upon them. Morever,
let us note well that if we wish to work wiles and tricks upon
God it will not improve our status but rather we shall increase
His wrath against us.

You see, then, that men ought to properly correct their evil
doings, seeing that God's curse will be so increased upon them.
And here is express mention made of the increasing of God's
wrath because men suppose they have escaped when God has
delivered them from some ill; it seems to them that the worst

is past. But we do not think about the means which are hidden from us: namely, that God will afterwards display new rods, that He will draw new swords, and that He will suddenly thunder upon us when we do not expect it. Since, then, we are not sufficiently afraid of God's wrath, therefore it is purposely said that it increases and that we heap it up more and more upon us, insomuch that a hunndred thousand deaths must be waiting for us when we have despised the message which God sent to bring us back and to lead us into life. Therefore, when we have so despised God's warnings we must feel His horrible vengeance upon us, whereas otherwise He affirms that He is always ready to comfort those who submit themselves willingly to His good will.

Now we shall bow in humble reverence before the face of our God.

SERMON 20

The Lord Answers Job*

The Lord, answering Job from a whirlwind, said, "Who is this who obscures counsel by words without knowledge? Gird thy loins like a valiant man, and show me that which I shall ask thee. Where wast thou when I founded the earth? Declare it, if thou hast understanding."—Job 38:1-4

WE HAVE seen previously that Elihu, wishing to rebuke Job, protested that he, Elihu, was also a mortal man, in order that Job might not complain of being treated by too high a power. He showed then, that God wished him to proceed by reason, and with sweetness; as He also uses it toward us; for He spares us, causing His Word to be preached to us by men like us, so that we can come with greater familiarity to what He proposes to us; the doctrine is chewed for us.[1] We see, then, that God has pitied us, when He ordains men who are ministers of His Word, and who teach us in His Name and by His authority; for He knows what we can bear, and that since we are feeble, we would soon be swallowed up by His majesty, we would be cast down by His glory. And that is why He condescends to our littleness, when He instructs us by means of men. However, it is also needful that we be touched, in order to bear toward Him the reverence which He deserves; for without this we would abuse His goodness, and when He draws near to us, finally we would as it were make companionship with Him.[2] This is what is now narrated to us: that God, seeing that Job was not sufficiently subdued by the propositions and reasons which Elihu had brought forward, causes

---

* Sermon 147 in *Calvini Opera, Corpus Reformatorum,* vol. 35. pp. 351-362.

1. It is the work of the preacher to present the doctrine of God in such a form that the hearers can digest it.

2. In modern slang, "We would come to treat God like any other good pal."

287

him to experience his grandeur *from a whirlwind;* in order that, being thus frightened, he might reform by recognizing his fault, and that he might obey entirely what is set before him. Thus we see how God in every way accommodates Himself to us, in order to win us. For on the one hand He abases Himself. And why? Seeing that we are too crude and gross to ascend to Him. However, because there is too great a pride in our brains, we must experience Him as He is; in order that we may learn to fear Him, and to hear His Word in all humility and solicitude. This is a point that we have to observe well; for by this we see the love which He has for our salvation. For He surely must be concerned about us, when He is thus transfigured, so to speak, that He is not satisfied to speak on equal terms; but when He sees that it is good and proper for us, He begs with us; and then, seeing that this goodness cannot turn us from scorn, He rises and magnifies Himself as is proper to Him; in order that we might know our condition so as to subject ourselves entirely to Him. And all the more ought we to desire to be taught by His Word, seeing that it is conformed to the measure of our understanding, and that God has forgotten nothing of that which was required and useful for our salvation. Seeing, then, that our God was so willing to come down to our level; and that, however, He ascends to reform us to obey Him; may we take all the more courage to listen to Him when He speaks. And let us not use the frivolous excuse that the Word of God is too high and obscure for us, or perhaps that it is too terrifying, or perhaps that it is too simple. For when we shall have taken account of and reduced everything, it is certain that our Lord proposes to us a majesty in His Word, which is to make all creatures tremble; there is also a simplicity, in order to make it be received by the most ignorant and foolish; there is such a great clearness that we can eat away at it without having been to school, if we are teachable; for it is not without cause that He is called "Master" by the humble and little ones.

This is what we have to note in the first place from this passage: namely, that when God speaks to us through the mouth of men, it is in order that we may draw near to Him

more freely, that we may receive what He proposes to us on
His part with greater leisure, and that we may not be astonished beyond measure; but since we are hardened beyond
hope, and we do not bear toward Him the honor which he
deserves, He makes us to experience Him as He is, and He
rises in His majesty, in order that it may induce us to do Him
homage.

Now it is especially said that *"the Lord spoke to Job from
a whirlwind";* that it was not enough that He gave him some
sign of His presence, but that He was there like a storm. We
shall find very often in the Scripture, that God moved thus by
claps of thunder, when He wished to speak to His believers:
but especially here we have to weigh the circumstance of the
place, that inasmuch as Job was not yet completely check-
mated,[3] God had to show him a terrible force. For this cause,
then, He thundered, and moved this whirlwind, in order that
Job might know with what master he had to do. In general
it is well said that God dwells as it were in an obscure cloud,
or perhaps that He is surrounded by clearness; and yet we
cannot comprehend this, that if we wish to contemplate God
our senses are dazzled, that there is a very special obscurity.
It is, then, thus well said of the glory of God in general, in
order that we may not presume to inquire too much into His
incomprehensible counsels; but that we may thereby relish
what it pleases Him to reveal to us, and meanwhile that we
know that all our senses are worthless, unless it pleases Him
to draw near to us, or perhaps to raise us to Himself; but for
still another consideration: namely, because of our rebellion
God must show Himself in terror. It is true that He may ask
only to draw us to Himself in sweetness; and we see that He
uses a loving manner, when men are well disposed to submit
to Him, that He invites us with as much humaneness as
possible; but when He perceives some hardness of heart, He
must cast us down at the beginning. For otherwise what will
it profit that He speaks to us? His Word will be despised by
us, or perhaps it will not enter into our hearts at all. And that

---

3. I am almost certain that Calvin is using this metaphor from the
chessboard.

is why in publishing His Law He moved the thunderbolts, that the trumpets might sound in the air, that everyone might tremble, in such a way that the people might be frightened by it, so as to say, "Let the Lord not speak to us, or we are all dead, we are then cast down." Why is it that God thus moved all the earth, and that His voice rang out with such a fright? Did He wish to chase the people so far away that He would not be heard at all? On the contrary, it is said, "He did not give His Law in vain"; but He wished to give a certain instruction to the people, namely, the way of life.

So, then, it was not to frighten when He moved the thunderbolts and the tempests in the air; that was not, I say, His intention; but this served as a preparation in order to bring down[4] the haughtiness of the people; who never would have obeyed God or His Word, who never would have known even the authority of Him Who spake, without these marks which were added to it. So let us note well that it is not a superfluous thing that God thus spoke to Job from a whirlwind. And if such a holy man who had applied all his study to honoring God needed to be thus checked, what about us? Let us compare ourselves with Job. Here is a mirror of angelic holiness. We have seen the protestations that he made here below; and although he was afflicted to the limit, though he murmured, and although there escaped from him extravagant statements; yet he always retained the principle of worshipping God, and of humbling himself under His majesty; he kept this in general, although he fell down in part. Now we are as carnal as could be, and our vanities so carry us away that we are as it were drunk; we hardly judge that there is a God in heaven; and when His Word is proposed to us, we are even more crude than asses. Is there not need, then, that our Lord shall cause us to experience His majesty, and that we should be consciously affected by it? Now it is true that God will not stir up tempests and whirlwinds in order that we may know that it is He Who speaks; but He must by other means dispose us to come to Him, as we also see that He does. When, then, one will have some scruples, and some troubles in his conscience,

---

4. Or "checkmate."

another will be afflicted by illnesses, another will have other
adversities, let us know that it is God Who calls us to Himself
seeing that we do not come to these things of our own free
will, seeing that we do not draw near to hear His word; He
checks such hardness of heart, as is required in order that our
spirits may be beaten down into right obedience. Does God,
then, see such a rebellion in us: He must use these manners
and means that I have already spoken of to draw us and win
us to Himself; in order that we may hear it, He must speak
to us as it were from a whirlwind, not that it should be in all;
for we see some who kick against the spur, and they act like
restless horses, and although God cares for them, they gain
nothing by it. How many are seen of these ill-starred fellows
whom God will have chastised in so many ways, whom He will
have struck on the head with great blows of the hammer, so
that no matter how hard they are they should have softened?
However, they never cease to gnash their teeth. It is seen that
they cannot move without showing that they are full of pride
and rebellion against God, and they despise Him as much as is
possible.

So then, it is very necessary that those whom God chastises
should be disposed to come to Him; for such is His intention.
So let us be advised not to frustrate our God; always and
whenever He sends us some adversity, let us learn to run to
Him, as if He spoke with thunder, and as if it had to happen
to us in order to make us hear. Let us know this, and let us
know it in such a way that our spirits may be truly checked
under Him, and that we may seek nothing but to humble ourselves fully in His obedience. That is what we have to remember in this passage. Besides, let us note that, although today
God does not thunder from heaven, yet all the signs which
have been given in ancient times to prove His Word ought
to serve us today. When the Law of God is preached to us,
we must join to it what is narrated in the nineteenth chapter
of Exodus; that is, that the Law has been duly ratified, and
that our Lord has given it full authority, when he sent thunderbolts and flashes of lightning from heaven, which He did
to call to mind the appearance of trumpets; that all this was

in order that His Law might be received until the end of the world in all reverence. So is it in this passage. For when it is said that *"God appeared from a whirlwind,"* we must know that He wished to ratify what is contained in this book; and not only that; but we must extend this authority through all His Word. There is still this consideration, that if God began by an amiable manner to call us to Himself and He showed Himself rough and bitter in the end, we should not find that at all strange; but rather let us examine our lives to know if we have obeyed Him; and in that let us know His goodness is all of one piece; and then we know that it is very necessary that He should use this second means to win us, when He sees that He has profited nothing by His grace which He had shown us. Example: God may be kind toward us sometimes when He wishes to have us for His own and of His band; without sending us any affliction, He will propose His Word. Or perhaps, we see that it is His will and we acquiesce in it. However, we do not profit by it, by being made sure as we should of His goodness, by renouncing our wicked desires, by forgetting the world, and by giving ourselves entirely to Him. He supports us for a time; but in the end when He sees that we are so indifferent, He begins to strike. By this we surely ought to experience that not without cause He speaks as from a whirlwind, because we have not heard Him when He wished to teach us graciously, and in a humane and fatherly manner. It is needful, then, that God speaks to us with such a vehemence, since He sees that we would never draw near to Him until He had thus prepared us. It is true that He will win some by the simple Word; but when He sees that others are peevish. He sends them some trouble, some affliction. In fact there are many who might never have come to the Gospel, who might never have been rightly touched in their hearts to obey God, unless He had released to them some sign that He wished to chastise them. Upon that, when they have experienced by afflictions that there are only miseries in this world, they have been constrained to be displeased with themselves, and to curtail their delicacies, in which they were previously plunged.

That, then, is how God in various ways draws men to Himself. But let us always profit by the means He uses with us; besides, when He does not speak in a whirlwind, let us on our part become familiar with Him, and let us allow ourselves to be governed by Him like sheep and lambs; for if He sees some hardness in us, He must check us perhaps with a curse; and if for a time He lets us run like escaped horses; yet in the end we shall experience His terrible majesty to be frightened by it; indeed, if it pleases Him to give us grace; for it is a special benefit that God gives us, when He thus awakens us, and He thunders with His voice, in order that it may enter into our hearts, and that we may be deeply grieved[5] by it. That, I say is a privilege which He does not give to everyone. Besides, when He thunders against unbelievers it is too late; for there is no longer any hope that they may return to Him. He summons them to hear the condemnation. Furthermore, we ought to receive peaceably this help which God gives us, when to check all the rebellions of our flesh He stirs up some whirlwind; that is to say, He causes us to experience His majesty. This, in summary, is what we have to remember from this passage.

Now we come to the saying, *"Who is this who obscures counsel by words without knowledge? Gird thy loins like a valiant man, and answer all my questions."* God here, in the first place, mocks Job, inasmuch as he was rebellious, and it seemed to him that by arguments he could win his case. That is why He says, *"And who art thou?"* Now when the Scripture shows us who we are, it is to empty us of all pride. It is true that men will prize themselves too much, making themselves believe that there is some great dignity in them. Now they can well prize themselves; however, God knows in them only odor and stink, He rejects them; indeed, He holds them to be detestable. And so, although we may be so foolish, and though we may be so presumptuous as to glorify ourselves in our own imaginations to have power and wisdom in ourselves; yet God to empty us and render us confounded uses only the word, "And who are you? Thou man." When this

---

5. Or wounded.

is pronounced, it is as it were to completely despoil us of all occasion to glory. For we know that there is not a single drop of good in us; and then we no longer have any occasion whatever to commend ourselves.

And that is why God also adds, *"Gird thy loins like a valiant man,"* that is to say, "Dress thyself as thou pleasest, make thyself believe that thou art as it were a giant, mayest thou be well equipped, mayest thou be armed from head to foot. Very well, what wilt thou gain thereby in the end? When I shall oppose thee, poor creature, wilt thou think of a way to subsist? What hast thou?" Here, then, we see the intention of God. For (as I have already said) this folly of prizing ourselves and of presuming that we are worth something is so deeply rooted in us that it is very difficult to lead us to a right knowledge of our poverty, so that we may be void of all pride and presumption. Furthermore, then, we must note well the passages of the Scripture, in which it shows us that there is in us no worth whatever. And let us weigh that well; for it is spoken of not only part of the world, but of mankind in general.

May great and small, then, learn to be ashamed of themselves; since God includes everything as it were in a sheaf, when He says that the wisdom of man is only foolishness and vanity, that instead of power there is only weakness, that instead of righteousness there is only filthiness and dirt. For when God speaks in these terms, it is not for two or three people, but for everyone in general. Let us learn, then, from the greatest to the least, to humble ourselves, knowing that all our glories are only confusion and shame before God. May we think thus on the word, *"Who is he?"* Let us not take it as referring only to the person of Job, but let us take it as referring to all mortal creatures; as if our Lord said, "Why? Is there, then, such an audacity in a man who is only a fragile earthen pot? in a man who is only a vessel full of all filth and villainy, and in a man who is less than nothing? that there should be the audacity to dispute against Me, and to wish to inquire so far? and where is this to stop? Who art thou, man?" As we see also that Saint Paul rebukes us by this

word (Romans 9:20), "And man, who art thou who repliest
to God, and who pleadest against him?" When he has set
down the objections which men suppose to have some plausibility for disputing against God by saying, "And why will
God lose those whom He has created? And without having
reason, that He may come to discern one from another; that
one may be called to salvation, and that He may reject another;
why is this done?" When, then, Saint Paul has said this, although men please themselves with such objections, he says,
"O man, who art thou, that thou addressest thyself thus to
God?" This is what we have to note from the word, "Who
is he?" May each one, then, always and whenever he will
be tempted with pride, think to himself, "Alas! who art thou?"
It is not here a matter of entering into combat against our
fellow-creatures, and against those who are like us; but if we
wish to be so bold as to inquire into the secrets of God; if we
release the bridle to our fancies and to our tongues to imagine
useless things, or to speak against God and His honor; we
must think, "Alas! and who am I?" When each one will have
looked inside himself, that he will have regarded his weakness, when he will have known in summary that he is nothing
at all; we shall be sufficiently rebuked, all these cacklings[6] will
be put down, that we may have conceived previously; even all
our fancies will be bridled and held captive, as will afterwards
be yet more fully declared.

Now it is especially said, *"Gird thy loins like a valiant man"*
to signify that when all the world will have amassed its forces,
and will have displayed them, it is nothing at all. That, then,
is why God here defies Job by saying, "Let him be equipped,
and let him come armoured and armed as a giant, or as the
most agile man that could be found." By this He expresses
still better what we have said: namely, that if men are condemned in the Scripture, this is not intended simply for the
vulgar, for those who are contemptible, who have neither
credit nor dignity; but it is extended to the greatest, to those
who suppose they touch the clouds. And so, then, although
men think they have in themselves some appearance of being

----
6. Fr., *caquees.*

honored.; may they know that this is nothing with respect to
God. As for example: Those who are excellent when they
compare themselves with their neighbors, it is true that they
will conceive some opinion of their own persons, and they will
be content with themselves; when a man will be reputed wise,
of good mind, of good grace — well, he will be prized in the
eyes of those who have not the same qualities; a man will be
rich, a man will be endowed with great and praiseworthy virtues — as men go. That, then, could well enable us to feel
very big-hearted (as they say) to commend ourselves, when
we shall thus have special virtues; but when we shall draw
near to God, all must be emptied. There is then, none so
gallant nor so robust that he may have a single drop of
strength; there is here no longer any holiness, there is no
longer any wisdom, there is nothing whatever. So, then, may
all the world know that its equipment will profit nothing
before God; but we must be completely emptied, God must
void us, that He may not leave a single drop of virtue[7] in us,
unless that which we shall take from Him, as though borrow-
ing, knowing that all proceeds from His pure goodness. We
see, now, what the word *"valiant man"* implies; it is to signify
that, though we may have some special virtues, it ought not
to give us occasion to pride ourselves before God.

Besides it is also said that *"Job wrapped counsel (or obscured it) in propositions without knowledge."* By that God
declares that, having treated His secrets, we surely ought to
think of ourselves, in order to proceed here soberly and in all
fear; for under the word "counsel" God wished to signify the
high things of which Job had spoken. We can well dispute
about much minor rubbish, and dispute it willingly — well,
our propositions will be vain and frivolous — but yet there
will not be blasphemies, and the Name of God will not be at
all profaned. But when we enter into the doctrine of salvation, that we enter into the works of God, and that we dispute
about His providence, and about His will; then it is not proper
to come thus heedlessly; for we wrap, or entangle counsel in
propositions without knowledge. We see, then, for what it

---

7. Or power.

is that God rebukes Job: namely, in that he had too hastily spoken of that which was beyond his grasp; for although he had excellent gifts, yet he ought always to have humbled himself, knowing his infirmity; and he ought also to hold himself in check when he was as it were at the end of his senses, that he had only to think of the judgments of God; and finding himself thus confounded, he ought to have regarded the feebleness of his spirit; and knowing himself as a mortal man he ought to have said, "Alas! there is only ignorance and silliness in me." Meanwhile he ought also to have regarded the inestimable majesty of God and His incomprehensible counsel; that ought to have rendered him humble. He did neither the one nor the other. So, then, although he was not led astray from the right road but he always aspired to the true end, yet we see that he is here rebuked by the mouth of God.

Now this passage ought to warn us of the reverence which God wishes us to bear toward His high mysteries, and to that which concerns His heavenly kingdom. If we dispute about our affairs — very well — we need not proceed with such extreme caution; for these are things which pass; but always and whenever it is a matter of speaking of God, of His works, of His truth, of that which is contained in His Word; may we come to it with fear and solicitude, may we not have our mouths open, to cough up everything which will come to us in fancy; may we not even have our minds too open to inquire into what does not pertain to us, and is not lawful for us; but let us hold back our minds, let us bridle our tongues. And why? For it is the counsel of God, that is to say, these things are too obscure for us, and too high; we must not, then, presume to come to them, unless God will wish to instruct us in them through His pure goodness. And may it please God that these things might be well practiced, and that we did not have the combats which are throughout all the world. But why are they? It is seen that very few are affected by the majesty of God; when one discusses His Word, and the doctrine of our salvation, and of all the Holy Scripture, each one will go his own way; if anyone chats about it under the shadow of a lamp, each one will beg his leave of it. These are things that

surpass all human understanding; however it is seen that we
shall be more bold to discuss such high mysteries of God —
which ought to carry us away in astonishment, and which we
ought to adore with all solicitude — we shall be, I say, more
bold to babble of them, than if one discussed a transaction involving five cents, and I do not know what. And what is the
cause of this, unless that men have not considered that God
hides from us and obscures His counsel and that in the Scripture He has displayed to us His will to which we must be subject? We see on the one hand the Papists who blaspheme
against God, and who turn upside down, falsify, deprave, and
corrupt all the Holy Scripture, so that it costs them nothing
to mock God and all His Word. And why? For they have
never tasted the meaning of the word *"counsel."* Among us
are seen drunkards, who also would subject God to their fancy.
When they will be the most agile in the world, most experienced in the Holy Scripture; still they must come to this:
The counsel of God is above us. But they are stupid and entirely brutish; there is neither sense nor reason, wine rules
them like pigs; and they will wish nevertheless to be theologians, and to upset things in such a way that, if we believed
them today, we would have to build and forge[8] an entirely new
Gospel. Yet let us remember what is here shown us: When
we speak of God, we must not take license to chat and babble
what seems good to us; but let us know that He has revealed
His counsel in the Holy Scripture, that both great and small
may submit to adore it. And this is what is said about *"propositions without knowledge."* Now then, God here shows,
that always and whenever we speak of Him, and of His works,
it is a doctrine of counsel, a high doctrine. And on the contrary that which we shall be able to put forward, and which
we shall be able to conceive in our minds, what is it? Propositions without knowledge. Let men put themselves in the
balance, and they will be found to be lighter than vanity, as
it is said in the Psalm.[9] Furthermore, then, we must well
note this doctrine, that there will be in us no knowledge, there

8. Referring to a blacksmith, not to falsification in writing.
9. Psalm 62:9.

will be no grace to know how to discuss the works of God, unless He will have instructed us. That is how we shall be wise, being governed by the Spirit of God and by His Word. However, when we shall not find in the Word of God what we wish to know; let us know that we must remain ignorant; and then after that we must keep our mouths closed; for as soon as we may wish to say a word, there will be no knowledge; there will be only deception in us. This, then, is the accusation which God here makes against Job.

Upon that He says, *"Answer all My questions; indeed, if thou hast understanding, mayest thou also give Mĕ to understand that which I wish to know of thee."* Here God persists in mocking the foolish presumption of men, when they think they have so much subtlety in them that they can dispute and plead against Him. He says then, "Very well, it is true that you are very ingenious, it seems to you, when you speak, and that I release the rein from you; but I must have my turn, and I must speak a little to you, and you must reply to Me, and you will surely see your default." What is the cause, then, that men are so rash as to advance themselves so foolishly against God? It is because they give themselves license to speak, and they occupy the place, and it seems to them that God has no reply. Now here is the remedy that God gives us to put down the foolish temerity that is in us: it is, that we think of that which He will be able to ask of us. If God begins to interrogate us, what shall we answer? If this came into our memory, oh! it is certain that we would be entirely held back; and although we had very frisky minds, and though it seemed that we could move all the world, we would be, as it were, put in our place by following in simplicity that which our Lord shows us; provided, I say, that we could think, "Alas! and if we come before God, has He not His mouth open, and has He not the authority and mastery to interrogate us? And what shall we answer Him?" This, then, is where we must come. It is what we have to remember from this passage, to have right instruction from it. Then, may we not be too hasty to speak, that is to say, that we have the vice by nature of meddling in more than what pertains to us;

let us learn to keep our mouths shut. For why is it that we immediately open our mouths to vomit up what is unknown to us? It is that we do not think that it is our office rather to respond to God than to advance ourselves to speak. For is it not to pervert the order of nature, that mortal man who is nothing anticipates his Creator, and makes Him give audience, and that God meanwhile keeps silence? How far does this go? It is, nevertheless, what we do, always and whenever we shall murmur against God when we shall tear His Word in pieces, as we frame propositions at will, saying, "This is how it seems to me." What is the cause of this, unless we wish that God keep silence before us, and that we be heard above Him? Is this not a pure rage? So then, to correct this arrogance that is in us, let us learn not to presume to answer our God; knowing that when we shall come before Him, He will have the authority to examine us; indeed, according to His will, and not according to our appetite for it; and at our station; and that when He will have closed our mouth, and He will have commenced to speak, we shall be more than confounded; let us learn to humble ourselves, so that we may be taught by Him; and when we shall have been taught, may He make us contemplate His brightness in the midst of the shadows of the world. Meanwhile, let us also learn to serve Him and to adore Him in everything and by everything. For this is also how we shall have well profited in the school of God; it will be when we shall have learned to magnify Him, and to attribute to Him such a glory that we may find good, everything that proceeds from Him. Meanwhile, may we also be advised to be displeased with ourselves, in order to run to Him to find there the good that is lacking in us. And beyond that may it please Him to so govern us by His Holy Spirit that, being filled with His glory, we may have wherewith to glorify ourselves, not in us, but in Him alone.

Now we shall bow in humble reverence before the face of our God.